A
TRAVELLER
IN
ROMANCE

UNCOLLECTED WRITINGS

1901–1964

W. SOMERSET MAUGHAM

EDITED BY JOHN WHITEHEAD

In every work regard the writer's end,
Since none can compass more than they intend.
                                        Pope

Clarkson N. Potter, Inc./Publishers
DISTRIBUTED BY CROWN PUBLISHERS, INC., NEW YORK

Frontispiece: *W. Somerset Maugham.*
painted by Sir Gerald Kelly R.A. 1913.

Published in the United States of America by Clarkson N. Potter, Inc., One
Park Avenue, New York, New York 10016, and simultaneously in Canada by
General Publishing Company Limited.

First published in Great Britain in 1984 by Anthony Blond, an imprint of
Muller, Blond & White Limited, 55/57 Great Ormond Street, London WC1N
3HZ, England.

Manufactured in Great Britain
Typeset by DP Press, Sevenoaks, Kent

Library of Congress Cataloging in Publication Data

Maugham, W. Somerset (William Somerset), 1874–1965.
    A traveller in romance

    I. Whitehead, John 1924–   II.   Title
PR 6025.A86A6 1984   823'.912   84-17926
ISBN 0-517-55618-9
10 9 8 7 6 5 4 3 2 1
First American Edition

Contents

INTRODUCTION

Twenty years after his death in 1965 at the age of ninety-one there is still no consensus among scholars as to the correct placing of W. Somerset Maugham in the pecking-order of English authors. Meanwhile he continues to occupy the attention of critics and biographers, and – more important – to win new readers. It may be timely, therefore, to resurrect his occasional writings from the files of old newspapers and magazines and less obvious places, where they have been inaccessible to all who would find them interesting, and to make a collection of them

My purpose in this volume has been to assemble all Maugham's writings (except letters and translations) which, having appeared in print in Britain or America, were not subsequently reprinted in any of his books. It therefore excludes the large quantity of material that exists only in manuscript or typescript; but in the case of one of the addresses, of which only a condensed version was printed in a newspaper, the full text taken from a typescript has been given. The sixty-six pieces spanning his entire career which fall within these criteria furnish examples of most of the kinds of writing – plays, fiction, essays, journalism, prefaces, tributes to friends, addresses – in which Maugham at one time or another engaged. Their subject matter – ranging from literature, the theatre and painting to travel, his friends, and the game of bridge in which he delighted – reflect most of his principal interests. The articles published in American magazines during World War II, designed to influence opinion, are also represented.

In organizing this variety of material I have been influenced by the method adopted by Geoffrey Keynes in his selection of Hazlitt's essays in the Nonesuch Press edition, a model of which I like to think Maugham, a great admirer of Hazlitt, would have approved. The pieces have been subdivided into ten subject groups, in each of which they are printed in chronological order; and the sequence in which the groups themselves have been arranged is the result of an attempt to give a coherent and satisfying shape to this mass of heterogeneous writing. Source and date are given in a footnote on the first page of each piece, and in Appendix III all the pieces are listed in chronological order with particulars of the publications in which they first appeared.

Textual editing has been confined to the silent correction of obvious printers' errors and the occasional insertion or correction of punctuation when orthography or the sense of a passage seemed to demand it. Where in a few places a corruption in the text or an authorial slip has been corrected – as when in the short story 'The Buried Talent' Mr Convers is first said to have been married for fifteen years and a few pages later for nineteen – my own insertions are enclosed within square brackets. A few passages in the two articles 'On Playing Bridge' have been deleted solely in order to avoid verbatim repetition, and each deletion has been noted by means of three dots. As a consequence of such light editing there will be found to be minor inconsistencies in the system of punctuation and occasionally in the spelling (for example, 'Burmah' and 'Burma') adopted in different pieces, but I felt that in presenting work extending over more than sixty years the advantages of leaving it in its original state far outweighed considerations of verbal consistency. Since a number of them were written as untitled prefaces, introductions, addresses and the like, I have where necessary supplied my own titles; and once or twice original titles have been amplified by the addition of the name of the person the piece is about.

As I have mentioned, one of the criteria for inclusion in this collection is that the work should not previously have appeared in any of Maugham's books. In some cases the decision as to whether or not this criterion has been met has involved the exercise of judgment. My aim being to make the collection as complete as present knowledge permits, I have in cases where the pros and cons are finely balanced inclined rather towards inclusion than omission. This problem arose principally in four areas. First, the spoof exchange of correspondence in 'Novelist or Bond Salesman' reappeared in shortened form in *The Writer's Point of View* (1951), a pamphlet containing an address Maugham gave to the National Book League in London. Secondly, 'My South Sea Island' and 'The Terrorist: Boris Savinkov' are reworkings of raw material to be found in *A Writer's Notebook* (1949). (Conversely, because Maugham's foreword to *The Little Fellow* (1951), a book on Charlie Chaplin by Peter Cotes and Thelma Niklaus, is taken verbatim from the notebook, it has been omitted.) Thirdly, the six magazine articles which deal with incidents, often in identical language, described in *France at War* (1940) or *Strictly Personal* (1941) have been omitted from the 'Wartime Articles in America' section. Fourthly, I have excluded the original versions of two short stories, 'The Point of Honour' (1904) and 'The Mother' (1909), because they were reprinted, in revised form, in Maugham's last collection *Creatures of Circumstance* (1947).

At this point it is relevant to refer to *Seventeen Lost Stories*, a book of Maugham's early short stories published in New York in 1969, which has never been published in England. It contains, besides the six stories which made up the content of Maugham's first collection *Orientations* (1899), eleven magazine stories. Three of these he revised and reprinted in later books, one of them 'The Happy Couple' in *Creatures of Circumstance*. Thus, with the two referred to above, there are three stories in that volume which are revised versions of early magazine stories; which being so, Maugham's statement in the preface that 'some of these were written long ago, but I have left them as they were' is oddly misleading.

In conformity with my criteria this collection contains none of the stories in *Seventeen Lost Stories* and none of the essays in *Selected Prefaces and Introductions* (1964).

Since my object has been to present a text uncluttered by editorial matter, I have generally resisted the temptation to annotate; but for the reader's convenience I have occasionally provided a footnote when a reference, because the piece has been removed from its original context, requires elucidation. And it may not be out of place in this introduction to draw attention to a few of the pieces included here which possess features of special interest. The short story 'The Making of a Millionaire' anticipates one strand of the plot of Maugham's play *The Tenth Man* (first produced at the Globe Theatre in London in 1909), the other strand being taken from the story 'Pro Patria' included in *Seventeen Lost Stories*. Regarding the brief homily "'Above All, Love . . .'", it seemed appropriate to place it as the tail-piece to the American articles, even though it was written some years after the war was over. The newspaper article 'My South Sea Island' has, surprisingly, twice been the subject of a separate pirate printing by a press in Chicago, in 1936 and 1965, and copies of these scarce pamphlets have fetched high prices at auction. Perhaps by making it available in this collection book-collectors will no longer be induced to spend money on what Maugham's bibliographer has described as having 'every mark of a bibliographical fraud without finally altogether being one'.

'On His Ninetieth Birthday' with which this collection ends needs a more extended explanation, because it was not written by Maugham himself. Mr Ewan MacNaughton has kindly given me an account of how the article was put together. Some three weeks before Maugham's ninetieth birthday, 25 January 1964, MacNaughton twice interviewed him at the Villa Mauresque in the presence of Alan Searle, Maugham's secretary, for the purpose of obtaining a statement from him for newspaper publication in order to mark the occasion. He found Maugham feeble and slow to remember, 'just this side of dotage', and had to guide his thoughts towards likely topics, even to the extent of producing for his reconsideration quotations from the preface and postscript of *A Writer's Notebook*. The transcript, a patchwork of his guided thoughts and quotations from his work, was approved by Maugham before appearing in the *Sunday Express* on the day following his birthday. It forms a poignant coda to this collection.

Although my aim has been completeness within the criteria, it seems certain that there are further pieces in old newspapers, magazines or more fugitive publications such as theatre programmes which remain undetected. For example, in the essay on Francis de Croisset (1929) Maugham wrote:

> I have reviewed but three books in my life. For the first (it is true my review took up three columns of a now defunct Sunday paper) I was paid two pound ten; for the second I was paid twenty-five shillings; and for the third twelve and six.

The first two were presumably 'The Ionian Sea' and 'Growing Up' included here, so – unless, as is quite possible, Maugham for the sake of effect converted two reviews into three, in order to underline the point he was making that reviewers are underpaid – there may be another book review written before 1929 waiting to be traced. Two other omissions have been deliberate. Maugham's memoir 'Looking Back', extracts from which appeared in the *Sunday Express* and the American magazine *Show* in 1962, will no doubt one day be published entire in a separate volume. The other deliberate omisson is the long article entitled 'The Wisdom of W.S. Maugham' printed in the January 1966 issue of *Playboy*, only a month after Maugham's death. It is written in the first person singular and is introduced wîth the words:

> In a revelatory summing up, one of the world's great storytellers synthesises his thoughts on writers and writing, women and love, life and death;

but the 'Playbill' section of that issue of the magazine states ambiguously that the summing up had been 'gleaned from him by California's nonprofit Wisdom Foundation'. In the absence of a statement from the Foundation as to the provenance of the article its authenticity remains in doubt; and its style and content are so uncharacteristic of Maugham that I have assumed it was written by another hand and omitted it from this collection.

The epitaph from Pope on the title page is one Maugham himself prefixed to his novel written for an American wartime audience, *The Hour Before the Dawn* (New York, 1942), which has never been published in England. It is repeated here, not in order to sound a defensive or apologetic note, but as a reminder of the importance, when reading this rag-bag of his miscellaneous writings, of keeping in mind the purpose for which, and the context in which, each was written. Besides plays and stories which have long been lost sight of, the collection contains occasional pieces in which Maugham discourses in his characteristic voice on a number of topics of interest to him. They are full of good humour and common sense. And out of this rich harvest of minor work emerges a sympathetic portrait of the artist which may be nearer a true likeness of Maugham than any biographer has so far achieved.

JOHN WHITEHEAD

Acknowledgements

The starting-point for this collection was the late Raymond Toole Stott's *Bibliography of the Works of W. Somerset Maugham*, to which I am greatly indebted, though a number of the pieces included here have come to light since the revised and extended edition was published in 1973. For information about these newly traced items, for help in the task of ascertaining which libraries in England or America hold the publications in which the sixty-six pieces included were originally published and in obtaining copies of them for me, and for other assistance connected with the assembling of this collection – even when the results of their searches were negative – I am most grateful to the following persons and institutions. It is a pleasure to record that to each and every request for help I made there was an immediate and constructive response.

B.C. Bloomfield; British Film Institute (Pat Perilli); British Library, Bloomsbury and Colindale; British Theatre Association (Enid M. Foster); Dr Robert L. Calder, University of Saskatchewan; Grenville Cook; Anthony Curtis; Professor John O. Hayden, University of California, Davis; Humanities Research Center, University of Texas (Cathy Henderson and Mark E. Cain); Bill Jacob; Library of Congress, Washington (Anthony J. Kostreba); Ewan MacNaughton; the late Raymond Mander and Colin Mabberley of The Raymond Mander and Joe Mitchenson Theatre Collection; Professor Edward Mendelson of Columbia University, New York; Anthony Rota of Bertram Rota Ltd.; Sevenoaks Public Library; David H. Stam, Director, New York Public Library, and Ruth Carr and Rodney Phillips of that Library; University of California, Santa Barbara, Department of Special Collections (Christian F. Brun); University of Kent (S. Gerrard).

For permission to reproduce as the frontispiece to this volume Gerald Kelly's 1913 portrait of Maugham I am grateful to Mr N.V.S. Paravicini, Maugham's grandson, who owns the picture, and to the executors of the late Lady Kelly.

Acknowledgements are due to the institutions, publishers and magazines named in the footnotes on the first pages of the pieces included here, in whose publications they originally appeared.

Finally, I must record my gratitude for the immense and enthusiastic help throughout the preparation of this book I have received from my wife Ella, which went so far beyond preparing an immaculate typescript from often barely legible photocopies that, but for her reticence, her name would have appeared on the title page as my co-editor.

J.W.

CURTAIN-RAISERS

MARRIAGES ARE MADE IN HEAVEN

A Play in One Act

CHARACTERS
Jack Rayner
Mrs Vivyan
Herbert Paton
A maidservant

SCENE: *A drawing-room in Mrs Vivyan's house.*

JACK *and* MRS VIVYAN *are having tea.* LOTTIE *is a rather elaborately dressed woman of eight-and-twenty, handsome and self-possessed. She has an easy manner which suggests that she has consorted with men rather than with women.* JACK RAYNER *is thirty-two; there is about him a certain weariness as if he had lived hard and found life difficult. His face is sunburnt, somewhat lined and worn.*

JACK: I say, Lottie, has it occurred to you that this is our last day of single blessedness?

LOTTIE: Of course it has. I've been thinking of nothing else for a week.

JACK: Are you glad?

LOTTIE: I think I'm anxious. I want to have it over safely. I'm so afraid that something will happen.

JACK: (*with a laugh*): What nonsense! The fates can't help being friendly at last.

LOTTIE: I've gone through so much. I've lost all confidence in my luck.

JACK: And you're solemnly going to swear that you will love, honour and obey me. By Jove, I'm a nice object to honour.

LOTTIE: I think I can, Jack; and love and obey you too.

JACK: That's very good of you, old girl. I doubt whether either of us has many illusions; but we'll do our best.

LOTTIE: A breath of country air and they'll all come back again.

JACK: I hope to goodness they don't. Illusions are like umbrellas, you no sooner get them than you lose them; and the loss always leaves a little painful wound. But don't let us be sentimental. . . . How shall we celebrate the last of our liberty?

LOTTIE: Do you want to do anything? You're so energetic.

JACK: Shall we dine out and go to the Empire, and then on to the Covent Garden?

THE VENTURE, 1903. A German version *Schiffbrüchig* [Shipwrecked] was produced by Max Reinhardt at Schall und Rauch, Berlin in 1902.

LOTTIE (*with sudden passion*): Oh no, I couldn't stand it. I'm sick of the Empire, sick to death. I want never to go to a music-hall again. I want to live in the country, and bathe my hands in the long grass, and gather buttercups and daisies.

JACK (*smiling*): As it was in the beginning.

LOTTIE: Oh, I shall be so glad to get back to it after these sultry years of London. I often think of myself in a large sun-bonnet, milking the cows as I did when I was a girl.

JACK: But cows are milked by machinery now, aren't they? And it's sure to rain when you want to put on your sun-bonnet.

LOTTIE: Oh, Jack dear, don't be cynical or bitter. Let us try to be simple. We won't say smart things to one another; but just dodder along stupidly and peacefully.

JACK: When I was in Africa and the sun beat down pitilessly, I used to think of the green lanes and the silver mists of England. . . . But don't you think you'll be awfully bored?

LOTTIE: Jack, have you no faith in me?

JACK (*going to her and taking her hands*): I've got more faith in you than in anyone else in this blessed world; but I'm afraid I haven't much in anybody. Ah, Lottie, you must teach me to have faith – faith in my fellows.

LOTTIE: I want to teach you to have faith in yourself.

JACK: I'm afraid it's too late for that. But for goodness sake, don't let us sentimentalise. It hurts too much.
(*He walks away and then, regaining his composure, turns round.*)

JACK: Did I tell you that I've asked Herbert Paton to tea, so that I might introduce him to you?

LOTTIE: It's odd that I should never have met him. Did you know him before you went to the Cape?

JACK: Yes, rather! We were at school together. I'm sure you'll like him. He's the very worthiest chap I know.

LOTTIE: That sounds a little dull.

JACK: Oh, but we're going to cultivate respectability ourselves.

SERVANT (*enters and announces*): Mr Paton.
(*Herbert comes in. He is a grave, youngish man – soberly dressed, a little heavy, and without any great sense of humour.*)

JACK (*going towards him*): We were just talking of you. Allow me to introduce you: Mr Paton, Mrs Vivyan.
(*Herbert bows and Lottie smiles cordially, holding out her hand. He hesitates a moment and then takes it.*)

LOTTIE (*shaking hands*): It's so good of you to come. I was most anxious to make your acquaintance.

HERBERT (*gravely*): It was very kind of you to ask me.

JACK: I want you to be great friends. I always insist that the people I like shall like one another.

LOTTIE (*pouring it out*): You'll have some tea, won't you?

HERBERT: Thanks.
(*She gives him a cup.*)

LOTTIE: Jack has told me a great deal about you.

3

HERBERT: I hope nothing to my discredit.

LOTTIE: On the contrary, he's so full of your praise that I'm almost jealous.

JACK: You know, Lottie, I've asked Herbert to be best man.

LOTTIE: And has he accepted?

JACK: Certainly! He accepted straight off, before even he knew your name.

LOTTIE: You're a very confiding man, Mr Paton. I might have been dreadfully disreputable.

HERBERT: And have you finally decided to be married tomorrow? Your preparations have been very rapid.

LOTTIE: There were none to make. Everything is going to be quite private, you know. There'll only be one person beside yourself.

HERBERT: And aren't you even going to have a bridesmaid, Mrs Vivyan?

LOTTIE (*looking at him quickly*): Er – No! I believe it's not usual.
(*The Servant comes in and brings a letter to Jack.*)

SERVANT: The man's waiting for an answer, sir.

JACK (*opening the letter*): Oh – I'll just go and write a line, Lottie. I'll be back in two minutes.
(*The Servant goes out.*)

LOTTIE: Very well! Mr Paton and I will say unkind things of you while you're gone; so don't be long.

JACK (*laughing*): All right!
(*He goes out.*)

LOTTIE (*making room on the sofa upon which she is sitting*): Now, come and sit by me and we'll talk, Mr Paton. It was so good of you to come and see me.

HERBERT (*sitting not beside her, but on a chair near the sofa*): I was most anxious to make your acquaintance.

LOTTIE: One always is curious to see what the people are like whom one's friends are going to marry.

HERBERT: It was not for that reason that I wished to see you.

LOTTIE (*slightly surprised*): Oh!

HERBERT: I'm glad Jack has left us alone; I wanted to have a little talk with you.

LOTTIE: I'm sure I shall be delighted.

HERBERT: You know, Jack is my best and oldest friend?

LOTTIE: Yes, he told me so; that's why I want you to like me too.

HERBERT: We were at school together, and afterwards at the 'Varsity; and then we shared diggings in London.
(*He pauses for a moment.*)

LOTTIE (*smiling*): Well?

HERBERT: I tell you all this in justification of myself.

LOTTIE: How very mysterious you are! Jack didn't mention that in the catalogue of your virtues.
(*Herbert gets up and walks up and down.*)

HERBERT: You can't imagine how delighted I was when Jack told me he was going to be married. He's had rather a rough time of late, and I thought it was the best thing possible that he should settle down.

I asked him what on earth he was going to marry on and he said you had twelve hundred a year.

LOTTIE (*with a laugh*): Fortunately! Because poor Jack lets money slip through his fingers like water; and I'm sure he'll never be able to earn a cent.

HERBERT: And I asked him who you were.

LOTTIE: What did he tell you?

HERBERT: Nothing! He seemed astonishingly ignorant about you. He knew your name, and that's nearly all.

LOTTIE: He's a wise man who asks no questions.

HERBERT: Perhaps! But I did; I made enquiries.

LOTTIE: D'you think that was very nice of you? How did you do it? Did you employ a private detective?

HERBERT: Unfortunately there was no need for that. The information I sought was all over London. Jack must be the only person in town who has not heard it.

LOTTIE (*laughing icily*): I always look upon myself as safe from the scandalmongers. You see, they can never say anything about me half so bad as the truth.

HERBERT (*looking at her steadily*): I found out, Mrs Vivyan, how you obtained the money upon which you and Jack are proposing to live.

LOTTIE: You must be quite a Sherlock Holmes. How clever you are!

HERBERT: I want you to pardon me for what I am going to do, Mrs Vivyan.

LOTTIE (*very coldly*): Pray don't apologise!

HERBERT: I know it's a beastly thing, it makes me feel an utter cad; but I must do it for Jack's sake. It's my duty to him.

LOTTIE: Doubtless it is very praiseworthy to do one's duty. I notice people are always more inclined to do it when they will inflict pain upon others.

HERBERT: For God's sake don't sneer, Mrs Vivyan.

LOTTIE (*bursting out violently*): You do a shameful thing, and you expect me to pat you on the back.

HERBERT: I don't want to hurt you. I haven't the least animosity towards you. That's why I came here today.

LOTTIE: But really I don't understand you.

HERBERT: I should have thought it plain enough. Isn't it clear that Jack can't marry you?

LOTTIE (*with scornful surprise*): Good gracious me! Why not?

HERBERT: Do you wish me to tell you to your face what I learnt about you?

LOTTIE: In the course of your – discreditable enquiries? Well, what is it?

HERBERT: I wished to spare you this.

LOTTIE (*scornfully*): Oh no, I'm sure you wished to spare me nothing. Far be it from the virtuous to refrain from trampling on the wicked.

HERBERT: If you insist then, I know that this money was settled on you by Lord Feaverham when he married.

LOTTIE: Well?

HERBERT: Do you deny it?

LOTTIE: Why should I when you probably have proof that it is true?

5

HERBERT: I also know that Lord Feaverham had good reason to do this. . . . Oh, you hate me and think me a cad and brute; but what can I do? If you knew what agony it has caused me! I believe Jack loves you, and I daresay you love him. For all I know he may hate me for what I'm doing now. I wish with all my heart there were some other way out of it.

LOTTIE: Do you wish me to sympathise with you?

HERBERT: Oh, you're stone-cold. I only come to you because I want to be your friend. And even if you'd married Jack he must have found out sooner or later, and then it would have been a thousand times worse.

LOTTIE (*angrily*): What d'you want me to do?

HERBERT: Break off the marriage of your own accord. Don't let him know the reason. Let us try to save him from the humiliation and the pain. Write to him and say you don't love him enough. It's so easy.

LOTTIE: But I haven't the faintest wish to break off my marriage with Jack.

HERBERT: It's not a matter of wish; it's a matter of necessity. The marriage is utterly impossible – for his sake, for the sake of his people. It means absolute social ruin to him.

LOTTIE: What you say sounds to me excessively impertinent, Mr Paton.

HERBERT: I'm sorry, I have no wish to be so.

LOTTIE: And you want me to go to Jack and say I won't marry him?

HERBERT: It's the only thing you can do. Otherwise he must find out. It's the only thing you can do if you want to save your honour in his estimation.

LOTTIE (*scornfully*): I should be as it were defeated, but not disgraced.

HERBERT: It's for your own sake.

LOTTIE: Then let me tell you that I haven't the least intention of giving Jack up.

HERBERT: But you must.

LOTTIE: Why?

HERBERT (*violently*): He can't marry you. It would dishonour him.

LOTTIE: How dare you say such things to me! You come to my house and I try to be friends with you, and you insult me. You dishonour yourself.

HERBERT: I came here to give you a chance of retiring from the engagement without the real reasons being known.

LOTTIE (*passionately*): What business is it of yours? Why do you come here and interfere with us? D'you think we're fools and simpletons? Why don't you leave us alone? Who are you that you should preach and moralise? You're ridiculous, you're simply absurd.

HERBERT: I've tried to do my best for you, Mrs Vivyan.

LOTTIE: You've behaved like a perfect gentleman.

HERBERT: You can say or think of me what you choose, Mrs Vivyan. I've shielded you as much as I could. But my business is to stop this marriage, and by God, I mean to do it.

LOTTIE: You don't think of me!

6

HERBERT: It can make no difference to you.

LOTTIE *(about to break out passionately, but with an effort restraining herself)*: Oh, what a fool I am to let myself be disturbed by what you say! It's all nonsense. And how, pray, are you going to prevent me from marrying Jack?

HERBERT: I have only one way left; and you've driven me to it. I shall tell him everything I know.

LOTTIE *(bursting into a shriek of ironical laughter)*: Very well. You shall tell him now – immediately.

(She touches the bell and the Servant comes in.)

LOTTIE: Ask Mr Rayner to come here.

SERVANT: Yes'm.

(Servant goes out.)

LOTTIE *(smiling scornfully)*: I warn you that you're going to make an absolute fool of yourself, Mr Paton. *(Herbert bows.)* But perhaps that experience will not be entirely new.

(Jack comes in.)

LOTTIE: What a time you've been, Jack. If it weren't for the high character that Mr Paton has been giving you, I should fear that you had been writing love-letters. Mr Paton wishes to speak to you on matters of importance.

JACK: That sounds rather formidable. What does he want to talk about?

LOTTIE: About me.

JACK *(laughing)*: That is indeed a matter of importance.

LOTTIE: Shall I leave you alone? Mr Paton would much rather say ill-natured things of me behind my back.

HERBERT: On the contrary, I should like you to stay, Mrs Vivyan. I am quite willing to say before your face all I have to say.

LOTTIE *(sitting down)*: Very well. To me it's a matter of perfect indifference.

JACK: Good Heavens, you've not been quarrelling already?

LOTTIE: No, of course not! Go on, Mr Paton.

HERBERT *(after a momentary pause)*: I was rather surprised to hear of your engagement, Jack.

JACK: To tell you the truth I was rather surprised myself. The thing was a bit sudden.

LOTTIE: The idea had never entered Jack's head till I indelicately proposed to him.

JACK: But I accepted with great alacrity.

HERBERT: Have you known one another long?

JACK: Ages.

HERBERT: And who was Mr Vivyan?

JACK: My dear Herbert, what are you talking about?

LOTTIE: Answer his question, Jack. It's better.

JACK: But I can't. I haven't the least idea who the lamented Mr Vivyan was.

HERBERT: Have you never spoken to your fiancée on the subject?

JACK: Well, you know, in such a case as this, one doesn't very much care to talk about one's predecessor. I believe he was a merchant.

LOTTIE (*smiling quietly*): Something in the city.

JACK: Of course! How stupid of me to forget. I remember now quite well.

HERBERT: And on his death he left his widow a fortune.

LOTTIE: Twelve hundred a year.

HERBERT (*to Jack*): You must consider yourself a very lucky chap.

JACK: I do, I can tell you.

HERBERT: I wonder if you would have married Mrs Vivyan if she had been penniless.

LOTTIE: If I had been I should never have felt justified in asking him.

JACK: What on earth are you trying to get at, Herbert?

LOTTIE: He wants to know whether we are passionately in love with one another. . . . I don't think we are, Mr Paton. We've both gone through a good deal and we're rather tired of love. It makes one too unhappy. The man a woman loves seems always to treat her badly. We're content to be very good friends.

HERBERT: That makes it easier for me.

JACK: What the Devil d'you mean?

HERBERT: D'you know how Mrs Vivyan got this money?

(*Jack looks at Herbert without speaking. Paton leans towards him earnestly.*)

HERBERT: Are you quite sure there has ever been a Mr Vivyan?

JACK: Look here, Herbert, I can hear nothing to Mrs Vivyan's discredit.

HERBERT: You must! It affects your honour.

JACK: I don't care. I don't want to know anything.

LOTTIE: Let him go on, Jack. It was bound to come out sooner or later.

HERBERT: I'm awfully sorry for you, old man. I know what a horrible shock and grief it must be to you. When you told me you were going to marry Mrs Vivyan I asked people who she was. I found out – things which made me enquire more particularly.

JACK: Why the Devil didn't you mind your own business?

HERBERT: It was for your sake, Jack. I couldn't let you be entrapped in a scandalous marriage.

(*A pause.*)

LOTTIE: Go on, Mr Paton.

HERBERT: Mrs Vivyan has never been married. The name is assumed. Oh God, I don't know how to tell you! Mrs Vivyan, please leave us. I can't stand it. I can't say these things before you, and I must say them. It will be better for all of us if you leave us alone.

LOTTIE: Oh no, you asked me to stay, when I offered to go. Now I want to hear all you've got to say.

HERBERT (*with an effort*): She's the daughter of a vet., Jack. She got mixed up with a man at Oxford, and then came to town. Four years ago she made the acquaintance of Lord Feaverham. And when he got married he settled on her the sum of twelve hundred a year.

(*A pause. Jack has now become calm again, and looks stonily at Herbert.*)

JACK: Well?

HERBERT: What's the matter, Jack? You don't seem to understand.

JACK (*passionately*): Haven't you made it clear, damn you? How can I fail to understand?

HERBERT: Why d'you look at me like that?

JACK (*very calmly and slowly*): You've told me nothing which I did not know before.

HERBERT (*horror-stricken*): Jack, you're mad!

JACK (*passionately*): Confound you; don't you hear! I tell you that you've said nothing which I did not know before.

HERBERT: You don't mean to say you knew what the woman was whom you were going to marry?

JACK: I knew everything.

HERBERT: Good God, Jack, you can't marry another man's cast-off. . .

JACK (*interrupting*): I'd rather you didn't call her ugly names, Herbert, because, you know, she's going to be my wife.

HERBERT: But why, why, man? Oh, it's infamous! You say you're not passionately in love with her.

JACK (*to Lottie*): What shall I say to him, Lottie?
(*Lottie shrugs her shoulders.*)

JACK: Well, if you want the least creditable part of the whole business. . .

LOTTIE (*interrupting bitterly*): He doubtless does.

JACK: Remember that for a penniless chap like me she's a rich woman.

HERBERT (*with horror*): Oh! (*Then, as if gradually understanding*): But you're selling yourself; you're selling yourself as she sold herself. Oh, how can you! Why man, you're going to live on the very price of her shame.

JACK (*almost in an undertone*): One must live.

HERBERT: Oh, Jack, what has come over you! Have you no honour? It's bad enough to marry the woman, yet do that if you love her; but don't take the damned money. I never dreamt you could do such a thing. All the time I was thinking that this woman had inveigled you; and my heart bled to think of the pain you must suffer when you knew the truth.

JACK: I'm very sorry.

HERBERT: Why didn't you tell me?

JACK: One doesn't care about making such things more public than necessary.

HERBERT: No!

JACK (*going up to Lottie*): Why do you listen to all this, dearest?

LOTTIE: Oh, I've had hard things said to me for years. I can bear it, and I don't want to run away.

JACK: You're very brave, my dear. (*Turning to Herbert*): If you'll sit down quietly and not make a beastly fuss, I'll try and explain to you how it all came about. I don't want you to think too badly of me.

LOTTIE: Oh, don't, Jack. It will only pain you. What does it matter what he thinks?

JACK: I should like to say it once and for all; and then I can forget it. Tomorrow we bury the past forever, and begin a new life.

HERBERT (*sitting down*): Well?

JACK: You know, when I was a boy I thought myself prodigiously clever. At Oxford I was a shining light. And when I came to town, I was eager for honour and glory. It took me five long years to discover I was a fool. Oh, what anguish of heart it was, when the fact stared me in the face that I was a failure, a miserable, hopeless failure! I had thought myself so much cleverer than the common run of men. I had looked down on them from the height of my superiority, and now I was obliged to climb down and confess that I was less than the most vulgar money-grubber of them all. Ah, what a lucky chap you are, Herbert. You were never under the delusion that you had genius. You were so deliberately normal. You always did the right thing, and the thing that was expected of you. And now, you see, I'm a poor, broken-down scamp, while you are a pillar of society. And you play golf and go to church regularly. You do play golf and go to church?

HERBERT: Yes.

JACK: I knew it. And you're engaged to a model, upright English girl with fair hair and blue eyes, the daughter of a clergyman.

HERBERT: The daughter of a doctor.

JACK: Same thing; the species is just the same. And she's strong and healthy, and plays tennis, and rides a bike, and has muscles like a prize-fighter. Oh, I know it. Then you'll get married and help to over-populate the island. You'll rear children upright and healthy and strong and honest like yourselves. And when you die they'll put on your tombstone: 'Here lies an honourable man'. Thank your stars that you were never cursed with ideals, but were content to work hard and be respectable. Oh, it's a long, hard fall when one tumbles back to earth, trying to climb to heaven. . . . And the result of it all is, that you have an income and honour; while I, as you remarked —

HERBERT: I didn't mean to be rough on you in what I said just now, Jack.

JACK: No, I know you didn't, old chap; but nothing very much affects me now. When one has to stand one's own contempt, it is easy enough to put up with other people's. Oh, if you knew how awful those years were, when I tried and tried and could do no good. At last I despaired and went to the Cape. But I muddled away my money there as I had muddled everything in England; and then I had to work and earn my bread as best I could. Sometimes I couldn't and I starved.

HERBERT: Why didn't you write? I should have been so glad to help you, Jack.

JACK: I couldn't. I couldn't accept money from you. One needs to have pawned one's shirt for bread before one can lend money like a gentleman. Lottie found out I was in distress and sent me twenty pounds.

LOTTIE: He never used it, Mr Paton. He kept it for two months so as not to hurt my feelings, and then returned it with effusive thanks. I noticed they were the same four notes as I sent out.

JACK (*with a slight laugh*): Well, I managed to get on somehow. I tried farming, I went to the mines, I was a bar-tender. Imagine the shining light of Oxford debating-societies mixing drinks in his shirt-sleeves and a white apron. A merciful Providence has destined me to be one of life's failures.

HERBERT: It sounds awful. I never knew.

LOTTIE: Of course you never knew! People like you don't. You, with your income and your respectability, what do you know of the struggles and the agony of those who go under? You can't judge, you don't know how many temptations we resist for the one we fall to.

JACK: After all, it wasn't so bad – when one got used to it. And I had the edifying spectacle of my fellows. Army men, shady people from the city, any amount of parsons' sons, 'Varsity men by the score, and now and again a noble lord. Oh, we were a select body, I can tell you – the failures, and the blackguards, and the outcasts. Most of them take to drink, and that's the best thing they can do, for then they don't mind.

HERBERT: Thank God you escaped that.

JACK: By no fault of mine, old chap. I should have been only too glad to drink myself to death, only spirits make me so beastly ill that I have to keep sober. . . . Anyhow, now I'm back in England again, and three or four weeks ago I met Lottie.

LOTTIE: At a night-club, Mr Paton.

JACK: Well, we'd been pals in the old days, and she asked me to go and see her. We soon were as great friends as ever. She told me all about herself, and I told her about myself. It was an edifying story on both sides. She spoke of the settlement, and one day suggested that I should marry her.

HERBERT: And you agreed?

JACK: Oh, I was tired of this miserable existence of mine. I was sick to death of being always alone. I wanted someone to care for me, someone to belong to me and stand by me. And it's so awful to be poor, perpetually to have starvation staring you in the face, not to have the smallest comfort or anything that makes life pleasant and beautiful. You, who've always been well off, don't know what a man can do to get money. I tell you such abject poverty is maddening. I couldn't stand it any longer; I would rather have killed myself. I'm tired of all this effort, I want to live in peace and quiet.

HERBERT: And the price you pay is dishonour.

JACK: Dishonour! I'm not such an honourable creature as all that. I've done mean enough things in my life. I wonder what I haven't done! I haven't stolen; but that's because I was afraid of being found out, and I never had the pluck to take my chance.

HERBERT: How can you live together with the recollection of the past?

JACK: Oh, damn the past! (*To Lottie*): You know me for what I am, dear, and you know I have no cause to despise you.

LOTTIE   (*with her hands on Jack's shoulders*): We're both rather tired of the world, and we've both gone through a good deal. I think we shall be forbearing to one another.

HERBERT: I wonder if you can possibly be happy?

JACK: I hope I shall make Lottie as good a husband as I think she will make me a good wife.

LOTTIE   (*smiling*): Was I right, Mr Paton, when I prophesied you would make a fool of yourself?

HERBERT: Perhaps! I don't know. Goodbye.

LOTTIE: Goodbye.

(*He gives his hand to Jack and walks out. Jack turns to Lottie and she puts her hands on his shoulders.*)

LOTTIE: I'm afraid you'll have to do without a best man, old chap. Respectability and virtue have turned their backs upon us.

JACK: Oh, give them time and they'll come round. They only want feeding. You can get a bishop to dine with you if you give good enough dinners.

LOTTIE   (*sighing*): They're so hard, all these good people. Their moral sense isn't satisfied unless they see the sinner actually roasting in Hell. As if Hell were needful when every little sin so quickly brings upon this earth its bitter punishment.

JACK: Let us forget it all. What does the world matter when we have ourselves? Why did you tell Herbert we were only friends? We're so much more than that.

LOTTIE   (*smiling sadly*): Are we? Perhaps we are; but if love comes let it come very slowly.

JACK: Why?

LOTTIE: Because I want it to last for ever.

(*Jack puts his arms round her, and she rests her head against his shoulder.*)

JACK: I will try to be a good husband to you, dearest.

LOTTIE: Oh, Jack, Jack, I want your love so badly.

CURTAIN

A
Rehearsal

Mr Jenkinson, manager of the Olympia Theatre of Varieties, drummed on the table with his fingers impatiently; and Lucien Smith, composer of the new ballet which was to set the Thames on fire, struck sentimental chords on the piano. They sat on the stage, contemplating in turn the back-cloth let down for rehearsal and the auditorium with seats wrapped in white cloths. They waited for the *première danseuse*, the celebrated Mademoiselle Zampa, but she respected herself far too much to arrive with punctuality, and the manager cursed her volubly.

'Why doesn't that woman arrive?' he cried. He was a dark, stout man, with hair redolent of cosmetic and an accent which betrayed at once his Teutonic nationality and his Jewish origin. 'My time is money, my boy; my time is money.'

Lucien Smith was long and lean, with auburn locks through which perpetually, with a dramatic gesture, he passed his fingers.

'Mademoiselle Zampa is the finest dancer in Europe,' he replied, with an ecstatic sigh. 'I would wait all day to catch one glimpse of her.'

In truth, neither Mr Jenkinson nor the composer was much at ease, for though La Zampa had been called ostensibly to rehearse a dance written especially to display her great skill, the meeting, in point of fact, had been arranged to reveal to her for the first time that she would have to discard the conventional dress of the ballet-dancer for skirts and high heels. Neither knew how she would take it, for she was passionately devoted to the conventions of her art, and it was possible that she would refuse absolutely to dance in anything but the costume in which her great successes had been achieved.

Presently the door of the back-scene was flung violently open, and in there bounded a very fat little man, with iron-grey hair cut short and standing straight on end, a moustache of the fiercest description, and a round, red face from which gleamed passionately two small, enthusiastic eyes. It was La Zampa's father.

The Sketch, 6 December 1905. Presented as a curtain-raiser to Maugham's play *A Man of Honour* at the Avenue Theatre, London, in 1904.

'Behold the incomparable, the adorable, the unparalleled!' he cried, with a strong French accent. 'Gentlemen, take off your hats to Mademoiselle Zampa.'

The lady tripped in upon his words; he took her hand, and together they ran down the stage, kissed their fingers to an imaginary audience, and struck an attitude. Mademoiselle Zampa was a little woman with flashing eyes and lovely teeth; she was oddly dressed now in an old ballet-skirt, tights, an ordinary bodice which she wore in the street, and a somewhat battered hat.

'Geneviève!' cried the composer, passionately.

'Lucien!' she answered.

And with one bound they were locked in one another's arms. Monsieur Zampa explained to Mr Jenkinson —

'Love has triumphed over the chaste heart of Mademoiselle Zampa. She has bestowed her little hand on this fortunate young man; and I, her father, have given my paternal blessing to their union.'

'I'm delighted to hear it,' said Mr Jenkinson, amiably. 'And when are they going to be married?'

'Sir!' cried Monsieur Zampa, with extreme dignity. 'The ladies of the family of Zampa do not get married: they contract alliances.'

The dancer smiled upon her betrothed and pressed his hand.

'He is an artist, like myself, and I love him,' she said. 'He will compose ballets for me and I will dance them. Monsieur and Mademoiselle Zampa will go down to posterity hand in hand.'

'But you'll be Mrs Smith,' suggested the prosaic manager.

'Never!' she answered, proudly. 'If I married seven husbands I should remain Mademoiselle Zampa. In our family the husband always takes his wife's name.'

Monsieur Zampa, with a flourish, took up the tale.

'Mademoiselle Zampa, Célestine, the first of that name, danced before the great Napoleon. He offered her his Imperial crown, but she said, 'Sire, I will not sacrifice my art!' And then my deceased wife — she was also Mademoiselle Zampa. All Europe was at her feet, and Kings desired in vain to kiss her hand. I was proud to take her name. I, René-Antoine-Joseph-Marie de Pornichet de la Paule, a scion of the noblest family in France, was proud to call myself Monsieur Zampa.'

He paused to take breath, and mopped his heated brow.

'Bravo, Papa!' cried his daughter. 'Bravo!'

He smiled, and gallantly kissed her hand.

'And Geneviève is Mademoiselle Zampa the third, perhaps the greatest of them all. The ducal coronet and the mansion in Park Lane have been thrown at her feet; the Peerage and the Stock Exchange have contended for that small white hand. But Mademoiselle Zampa will never marry beneath her. This morning a belted Earl came to me for permission to pay his addresses to my daughter, but I said to him, "My Lord," I said, "my Lord, Mademoiselle Zampa can only marry an artist."'

'Geneviève!' cried Lucien Smith.

'My betrothed!' she answered.

And once more, with affecting rapture, they were clasped in one another's arms. But Mr Jenkinson thought it was quite time to get to the work for which they were there assembled, and Monsieur Zampa, clapping his hands, cried, 'To business, my children; to business!' Lucien Smith flung from his fingers one last kiss to the dancer, and, seating himself at the piano, struck a resounding chord. Mademoiselle Zampa took the centre of the stage and threw herself into an attitude. This was the manager's opportunity.

'But you are not going to dance in those things!' he cried, as though he had just noticed La Zampa's costume. 'Haven't you read the book?' The little woman looked at him, completely at a loss for his meaning. '"The Duchess of Kensington comes forward and dances,"' he read, taking up the 'book' of the ballet.

'Well?'

'The Duchess of Kensington can't dance at a royal garden-party in tights and ballet-skirts and those shoes. You must wear heels, my dear. Duchesses always do.'

The effect of his statement was most alarming, for Mademoiselle Zampa gasped and turned perfectly white; she looked at her father and saw that he, a most apoplectic red, was shaking with mingled indignation and amazement.

'It's impossible!' she cried. 'I've never danced in heels. It is contrary to all the rules of my art. I have been Cleopatra, Queen of Egypt, in ballet-skirts; I have been the Queen of Sheba in these very pink tights, and you say I cannot wear them as Duchess of Kensington.' She snapped her fingers contemptuously. 'You make me laugh.'

'Mademoiselle Zampa has danced before all the Kings of Europe without heels,' protested her father. 'And my deceased wife —'

'My sainted mother! Did she wear heels?'

'My child, she would have sooner died!'

Lucien Smith had foreseen the outrage this demand would seem to the sensitive dancer, and saw that the manager's contemptuous indifference only made things worse. He sought to use persuasion.

'I know it's a degradation,' he said; 'but, after all, the public will have realism nowadays. They no longer understand the choreographic art. Won't you try, for my sake, Geneviève?'

He desired to take her hand, but, with a commanding gesture, she bade him keep his distance.

'Never!' she answered. 'Even for you, Lucien, I will not dishonour myself.'

Mr Jenkinson looked at his watch and got up.

'Now, look here. I've got no more time to waste. You'll *have* to wear heels, and, what's more, you'll have to wear a long dress.'

'My noble father, take me home,' replied Mademoiselle Zampa, haughtily, drawing herself to her full height. 'This man is entirely without modesty.'

'Geneviève, you'll ruin my ballet!' exclaimed the composer, in despair. 'You don't love me.'

'If you loved *me* you wouldn't ask me to dishonour myself.'

'Fiddlesticks!' he cried, impatiently.

Mademoiselle Zampa positively shrieked, and she turned to her father. Her eyes started out of her head.

'Oh, did you hear what he said? "Fiddlesticks"! He's swearing at me. Oh, my noble father, will you allow him to swear at me *before* we're married?'

'No, certainly not!' cried Monsieur Zampa. 'How dare you, sir? How dare

15

you? *I* never swore at my wife till we'd been married six months.'

'You'll ruin my career!' cried Lucien Smith.

'I'm not interested in your career,' she retorted, with flashing eyes. 'I will not marry a man who asks me to sacrifice my art. I loved you because I thought you were an artist.'

'What do you mean by that, Geneviève?' he asked, dramatically.

'If I cannot dance the Duchess of Kensington in ballet-skirts I will not marry you.'

'Geneviève, I, too, have my artistic susceptibilities,' he said, tossing back his auburn curls. 'If you will not dance in heels, all is over between us.'

'Then there is the ring you gave me!' she cried, tearing it off her finger and flinging it on the floor. 'Here is your photograph, and here is the lock of your hair.'

Both these articles, the latter neatly done up in tissue-paper, she produced from her bosom and threw at his feet.

'That is right, my daughter!' cried Monsieur Zampa. 'You have acted with spirit.' He scornfully addressed himself to Lucien. 'She has had better offers. The great Moses Cohen, of Grosvenor Square, has implored her to marry him, but I said a ballerina could have nothing to do with a Kaffir Circus. Now he deals only in Consols. I said she did not like his name. He has changed it to Courtenay Howard.'

Mr Jenkinson looked at the pair reflectively and smiled quietly to himself; long experience had taught him the ways of artistes, and he knew that the only passion which overcame professional pride was professional jealousy. He wanted La Zampa for his ballet, and was aware that she hated no one more than her deadly rival, La Ferrari. When he announced indifferently that it was his intention to offer her the part, the contempt of father and daughter was magnificent to see.

'La Ferrari is forty and she weighs seventeen stone!' cried Mademoiselle Zampa, with a little shriek of ironical laughter. 'She is a common woman, while I am a woman of family.'

'She has thirteen children, and she cannot dance for nuts!' exclaimed René-Antoine. 'Her father was a greengrocer, and her mother a charwoman.'

'My mother was Mademoiselle Zampa, and even my father was a gentleman.'

'René-Antoine-Joseph-Marie de Pornichet de la Paule!' he cried.

Mademoiselle Zampa held out her hand for her Papa, and together they marched towards the door. Lucien Smith angrily shrugged his shoulders.

'Of course, it's no good asking people impossibilities,' he said. 'If she refuses to dance with heels, it's obviously because she can't.'

'What!' cried the ballerina, stopping dead.

'Because you can't,' he repeated. 'Because you can't.'

'Oh, my noble father, will you allow this man to insult me?'

'No, my child!' cried Monsieur Zampa, clenching his fists and trembling with rage, but standing all the while at a very discreet distance. 'Villain! Villain!'

'Take care what you say, Monsieur Zampa.'

The fiery old gentleman stepped back two paces, apparently to give greater effect to his eloquence.

'I seize you by the throat, I slap your cheek, I pull your nose, I box your face. *Voilà!*'

'My noble father,' said Geneviève, proudly, 'you are worthy of the name of Zampa.'

But he was not nearly done. He removed his glove and tossed it down.

'I fling my gauntlet at your feet. Here is my card. I will send my seconds to you in the morning. You shall choose your own arms. René-Antoine-Joseph-Marie de Pornichet de la Paule is equally irresistible with pistol and with sword.'

But Mr Jenkinson, thinking the scene grew unduly violent, sought to make peace.

'Now, look here, Zampa, my boy – don't talk rubbish,' he said, soothingly. 'If she can't dance in heels, there's no more to be said.'

'Sir,' replied the other, bounding to him, 'Mademoiselle Zampa can dance in top-boots, Mademoiselle Zampa can dance in snow-shoes.' He turned to his talented offspring. 'Geneviève, I *command* you to put on shoes; the honour of our house is at stake.'

'That is right, my father. I will show these men what I can do.'

She flung out of the room, trembling with rage, and the old man strode backwards and forwards in a fury. The manager tried to pacify him, but he took no heed – his blood was boiling, and for a while all three waited silently while the dancer changed her dress.

'Your wife only had one baby?' asked Mr Jenkinson, presently, to make conversation.

'Sirrah, the ladies of my family do *not* have babies – they have ballerinas.'

'And if they're boys?'

'They never are,' replied Monsieur Zampa, with dignity and scorn.

But the door in the back-cloth was slowly opened, and Mademoiselle Zampa, with downcast eyes and a shrinking manner, appeared. This time she did not trip upon the stage, and all her arts and graces were gone. She stood shyly on the threshold, overwhelmed with confusion.

'My noble father, I am ashamed!' she sobbed. 'To dance in skirts – it is indecent.'

'Courage, my daughter! The artist must sacrifice everything.'

She advanced, and for once in her life forbore to strike an attitude. The unaccustomed draperies gave her a queer sensation of impropriety. She was like an African belle who might feel perfectly at ease in a necklace of beads as her only costume, yet absurdly self-conscious in a ball-dress. When she began to dance, it was nervously and without abandonment; but gradually, very gradually, the music stirred her, it seemed to give an odd fillip to her blood, and anger lent inspiration for new steps; little by little she warmed up, her movements grew more free; she was transfigured, all her terror vanished; now she forgot everything but that the melody tingled through every vein. She gave herself up to it entirely. She danced as she had never danced before; she danced magnificently. She danced as only she in Europe could dance. But when the music stopped, she came to herself suddenly and had no smiles for the rapturous applause of the three men.

'And now, my noble father, bring me my cloak,' she said, quietly.

'But aren't you going to do it?' asked Mr Jenkinson, perplexed and surprised. 'You've surpassed yourself.'

She drew herself up. 'Do you think I would expose myself to an audience in skirts and high heels? I am a modest woman, Mr Jenkinson!'

'Then I must send for La Ferrari, after all.'

'And tell her she may have my leavings.'

Mr Jenkinson, pursing his lips, prepared to play his last card. He took a telegraph-form from his pocket, and read out the words he wrote: 'Ferrari, 14, Gladstone Road, Camberwell. Will you dance new ballet? Principal part. £40 a week. Jenkinson.' He got up and walked across the stage to give the message to a door-keeper. 'She always said I would never be able to do this ballet without her.'

'She said that?' cried Mademoiselle Zampa, opening her eyes. 'Impudent hussy!'

She hesitated a moment, but the manager dangling that telegram in front of her face was too much for her. With an irresistible impulse, she seized it, crumpled it up, threw it on the floor and stamped on it.

'I no longer love that man, but I will not allow his ballet to be ruined by La Ferrari. The descendant of a greengrocer shall *never* dance to the music of Lucien Smith. I will dance in heels and a long skirt.'

'Why on earth didn't you say that before, my dear?' said Mr Jenkinson, with a great sigh of relief.

Lucien advanced with outstretched arms, radiant, but the lady stopped him.

'Stay, sir. You can never be the same to me. Henceforth you are nothing but Mr Smith. You are unworthy of an artist's love. But for what has been I will beg my Papa to forgive you. . . . My noble father, you will not kill this unfortunate young man.'

Monsieur Zampa sighed. 'Since you desire it, my child, he shall live. He would have been my seventh man – a lucky number.'

But Lucien Smith was distracted. He wrung his hands and implored his Geneviève to forgive him; he vowed he could not live without her; he threatened to take poison on her door-step. At last, he turned to his prospective father-in-law —

'Monsieur Zampa, won't you speak for me? I would have been a son to you; you should have smoked my cigars and worn my old hats.'

'And I would have dandled little ballerinas on my knee,' answered the old man, much affected. He looked at his daughter. 'I know you love him, my child.'

'He has insulted me. He said I could not dance in heels.'

A ray of hope flashed across Lucien Smith's despair.

'But I knew you could. I taunted you so as to make you do it. It was only a trick.'

'Is that true?'

'Geneviève!'

'Lucien!'

He clasped her in his arms, and Monsieur Zampa, waving a large bandana handkerchief, cried at the top of his voice, 'Vive La Zampa!'

ON
PLAYERS
AND
PLAYWRIGHTS

CHARLES HAWTREY

I am somewhat embarrassed at the thought of writing an introduction to the memoirs of Charles Hawtrey, since I am conscious after reading them that the main interest of his life lay in a pursuit for which I care little and of which I know less. He was by passion a racing man and only by necessity an actor. I think that he forgot the name of half the characters he played, but never that of a horse he backed. The haphazard manner in which he went on the stage and his desultory training are astonishing when you reflect that he was the most finished comedian of his generation. For the most part men and women adopt the stage as a profession either from vanity, from an erroneous notion that it is an easy life, or (more rarely) from an innate instinct to act; they seldom adopt it, as did Charles Hawtrey, because they must make a living somehow and the chance offers. We hear much nowadays of the training which the actor of the old days received, and the survivor of that period complains at a length which is sometimes tedious that the young people of the present can neither speak distinctly nor move with ease. He shrugs his shoulders with despair, and tells you that there is no hope until they are 'put through the mill' as he was. It is true that the stage is overcrowded with bad actors, and since they know nothing one is inclined to think that instruction might be of use to them. Schools have been established. But Charles Hawtrey seems to have received very little teaching: during his engagement in *The Colonel* he went to a stage manager every morning for an hour or so, and by him was shown how to walk and how to use his hands. Whatever else he learned he learned by playing. The fact is, of course, that he had that natural gift for acting the lack of which is so lamentably obvious in so many of the persons who seek to earn a living by its exercise. Those who practise the arts must resign themselves to the immortal fact that industry and goodwill contend unsuccessfully with talent. Charles Hawtrey had also a good education and a lively intelligence. They are evidently not essential to the actor, but they can never be a disadvantage to him.

He was, of course, an extremely good actor. The public worshipped him, but somewhat ignorantly, for his naturalness deceived them into thinking that there was little more in his acting than charm and ease. They said he was

---

Introduction to *The Truth at Last* by Charles Hawtrey. Thornton Butterworth, 1924.

wonderfully life-like and thought it was due to a happy chance. But the naturalness of the realistic actor is as artificial as the plausibility of the realistic play. The foundation of the stage is illusion and its superstructure is make-believe. The natural actor is as far from the naked truth of fact as the ranting barnstormer. No one could say a line with the naturalness of Charles Hawtrey, so that when you heard him you said, 'He speaks exactly as though he were in a drawing-room, it is not acting at all'; and yet it was acting all the time, art and not nature, the result of his instinctive sense for the stage and his experience; and the line was said not as it would have been said in a drawing-room but as it needed to be said in order to get over the footlights. I remember that once in his own house I made a remark that amused him and he repeated it to the assembled company. But he spoke it as he would have done on the stage, timing it, with the necessary emphasis on the point; so that it was no longer the casual jest that you make at a party but a 'line'. It lost the very thing Charles Hawtrey in the theatre could so surely have given it, naturalness.

I want to dwell a little on the fact that Charles Hawtrey was a polished, versatile, and ingenious actor because there is little in these pleasantly diffident memoirs to suggest it, and the narrow range of parts to which he confined himself tends to obscure it. He had a just, perhaps even an exaggerated, sense of his limitations; but within his scope he exercised more orginality of invention and a greater variety of humorous observation than the public, with its strangely incomplete appreciation of acting, gave him credit for. (It never ceases to surprise those who have to do professionally with the theatre that not only the average audience, but even the critics find it so difficult to distinguish between the actor and his part.) The relation between the author and the actor should be a collaboration on equal terms, but too often the actor is no more than a sleeping partner. He is like a cash register: you press a key which says two and sixpence, and a disk pops up above which also says two and sixpence. He gives what he gets, but adds nothing to it. Charles Hawtrey added as much as he received and often much more. He built up a part, giving it a life of its own, and adding to it his own vitality, good humour and charm.

But he attached no great importance to his remarkable gift, and this gave him a modesty which is not common among the members of his profession. (I hasten to add that writers, with less justification, are as vain.) He knew that he was an admirable comedian, but he accepted the fact in the spirit of comedy. Once when he was rehearsing a farce of mine it was represented to him by a stage manager that he had arranged the scene so that he was himself in no conspicuous position: 'It doesn't matter,' he said, with a laugh in his eyes, 'I can act just as well in a corner as in the centre of the stage.' The nonchalance with which he took a popularity which often intoxicates was due, I suppose, to the circumstance that for him acting was always little more than a means of livelihood. It struck me as singular that a man should excel in an art to which he was after all somewhat indifferent. His real interest was in life. In the course of his memoirs he speaks of it as a game: with many this is but a phrase; with him it meant a great deal. He was at Eton and at Rugby: he adhered all his days and with singular fidelity to the aims, ideals and ambitions of the public-school boy. They are generous and charming, and if it must be allowed that they are a trifle narrow, he tempered them personally

21

with constant laughter. In talking about Rugby he says that his lessons did not prosper very much because he found so many things to laugh at; to the end of his life he preserved an admirable capacity for laughter. He underwent many vicissitudes, but I think that his sense of the ridiculous never deserted him. He took neither life nor himself with unbecoming gravity.

In England laughter is never very respectable; our countrymen give their esteem more readily to those who bore them than to those who amuse. They find a certain pompous tediousness impressive and they can seldom laugh heartily without feeling a little ashamed of themselves. Charles Hawtrey knew this very well and it never failed to cause him a lively and good-natured amusement. He enjoyed himself, and he gave enjoyment to others. I can imagine no more pleasing recollection to leave the world.

FRANCIS DE CROISSET

There are two or three ways of writing a preface. One is to tell the reader what he should think about the book he is about to read; you take him by the scruff of the neck and with authority insist that he shall admire this and that. It is a method that exasperates me. I do not really want to know what anyone else thinks about a book. The only thing that matters to me is what I think about it myself. What do I care if eminent critics acclaim as a masterpiece a work that has nothing to say to me? Another way, and not an unpopular one, is to pick out all the plums from the book for which you are writing a preface. This has two advantages. The first is that it spares the critic the labour of reading the book; from a rapid perusal of the preface he can write a perfectly satisfactory review and thus save himself a little time and a good deal of trouble. Now I have every sympathy with the harassed reviewer. He should be, and often is, a man of wide reading, anxious to discern talent, with a knowledge of the world, eager, indefatigable, and notwithstanding the soul-destroying nature of his work, able to preserve his freshness; and we know that he is paid less well than a skilled artisan in a factory. Of all the forms of literary activity this is the most miserably rewarded. I have reviewed but three books in my life. For the first (it is true my review took up three columns of a now defunct Sunday paper) I was paid two pound ten; for the second I was paid twenty-five shillings; and for the third twelve and six. I could not but perceive that at that rate I should soon be paying the proprietors of papers for the privilege of writing reviews for them, and being a poor man ceased to look for such unprofitable employment. The other advantage is personal. By telling your author's best stories and quoting his best jokes you can make your preface so entertaining that the book afterwards must fall a trifle flat; you gain the credit of having written a brilliant preface to a thin book. I should without hesitation adopt this method but for two reasons. The first is that I do not think the most jaded reviewer will find this book a labour to read, and the second is that if I extracted the plums the preface would be as long as the book.

There remains then not much for me to do but to tell the reader something about the author. This should not be necessary since for twenty years M. Francis de Croisset has been one of the most distinguished dramatists in

Preface to *Our Puppet Show* by Francis de Croisset. Heinemann, 1929.

Europe. But it is. Once I was at a luncheon party and the company was fashionable and cultured; a woman, intelligent and well-informed, turned to a well-known dramatist who was sitting by her side and asked him:

'Are you going to Marie Tempest's new play tonight?'

'No,' he smiled.

'Why not?' she said. 'I'm told it's quite good.'

'You see, I wrote it. I don't go to my own first nights.'

The dramatist was M. de Croisset.

Sufferance is the badge of all our tribe. If a play is bad no one goes to see it, but if it is good people go not to see the play, but the actors who are playing in it. The author, though he has prudently contracted that his name should appear on programmes, hoardings and advertisements, remains practically anonymous. I do not suppose that in an audience one person out of a hundred troubles to look who wrote the play which he is at the moment enjoying.

And so, though M. de Croisset has written plays that have been acted in every quarter of the earth, though he has had success after success, I must delay the pleasure I can promise that you will have in reading this book by telling you that he is a writer worthy of your attention. It is true that he somewhat obscured his fame by his collaboration with Robert de Flers with whom after the death of Gaston de Caillavet he wrote a long series of plays. De Flers had written so many amusing pieces with the latter that when Francis de Croisset took the dead man's place it was inevitable that the public should ascribe to the older dramatist the lion's share in the new partnership. The French dramatists are very fond of collaboration, and I daresay that two writers can make a more workmanlike job out of a play than one; they are unlikely to construct it improperly, they leave no loose ends; but to my mind something valuable is lost. A play purports to be a work of art and the essence of this is the personality of the author. In the give and take of collaboration the individuality of each writer is apt to slip out of sight; the result is often very competent, it is seldom extremely arresting. Francis de Croisset was an excellent dramatist before ever he joined forces with Robert de Flers. To those interested in such matters it is curious to notice the difference in the plays written by de Flers with Caillavet and those written by him with de Croisset. In the second partnership the humour is not so robustious, but the wit is subtler; the more varied characters are chosen from a wider circle and are painted perhaps not with the old dash but with a greater delicacy; the standpoint is no longer simply that of the Parisian, it is that of the man of the world. In fact the plays have the charming qualities of those which Francis de Croisset wrote alone. The pattern is the same. Robert de Flers had a great knowledge of the stage and of the public, good-humour and good sense, tact and vitality. Between them the collaborators wrote plays which achieved exactly what they attempted; they were gay, entertaining, ingenious and clever. It would have been impossible to do better what they tried to do.

And for this reason, much as his friends must regret the death of so charming and amiable a man as Robert de Flers, it is impossible not to realise that the collaboration of these two writers could no longer have been of advantage to either. They had made all the pots they could from the mould; the only thing was to break it. When Robert de Flers died they were engaged on a play and the completed first act was published in the *Revue des Deux*

Mondes. It has all the old brilliance, the sparkling dialogue, the neatness of construction; the foibles of the day are laughed at with the same kindly irony; and you may be sure that it would have run its appointed course with the same amusing dexterity. Francis de Croisset announced that he would not finish it. I think he was wise. For you have the impression that you have seen it all before; you feel that its perfect method can afford you not the slightest surprise. The formula has at last overwhelmed the playwrights.

The small world of the theatre is changing. Francis de Croisset wrote a little while ago a number of articles for *Comoedia* which he has now republished in a pamphlet under the title *L'Invasion au Théâtre*. He points out the lamentable state in which the French drama finds itself. He notices with consternation that whereas five and twenty years ago French plays, good, bad and indifferent, were acted in every country in the world, now with very rare exceptions they are entirely neglected. On all sides the French dramatist hears the foreigner tell him that he no longer counts, and when he exports with pride a sample of his theatre of ideas he is told that they have had that sort of thing in Berlin twenty years ago. But what is worse, the French themselves will not go to see their own plays; they go to see the plays of foreign dramatists, and do not like them, but their dissatisfaction with their own plays is only increased. They want something new, but what they want they do not know. The English dramatist can only sympathise with this dismay, for he is in the same quandary. The English theatre too is in a mess.

There is nothing for the dramatist to do, but to gird his loins and cope with the changed situation. It is useless to rail at the movie. The wise thing is to profit by the lessons it has taught us. It is foolish to try to compete with it and those writers who attempt to do so by a multiplicity of scenes and by violent action are fighting a losing battle. But action is mental as well as physical. Here the dramatist has the field to himself. Francis de Croisset suggests that the French drama has largely concerned itself with psychological observation and analysis; and the perverted public has now no use for this. I think he is wrong; but it wants movement in it. The cinema has quickened the apprehensions of the audience and they can take a point with a rapidity that was unknown to an earlier generation. They can get in three lines, in an interjection, in a look even, what not so very long ago it required a scene to explain. It is not unnatural if they grow impatient when you tell them at length what they have grasped in a flash.

It is true that love has always been the mainspring of the drama and I suppose that on the whole it will continue to be so. But love has changed too. The dramatist too often lives in a world of his own without contact with the world of everyday. He has not yet noticed that the emancipation of women, the war, the spread of athletics have changed our attitude. The eternal triangle is a bore. Jealousy which once was a motive for tragedy became with advancing civilisation only a motive for comedy; now it is merely a nuisance. We look upon the sexual affairs of other people as their own concern and cannot bring ourselves to attach much importance to the fact that some woman or other has left this lover or taken another. I think it has escaped the attention of the French dramatists that these young men who all through the summer at seaside resorts and *villes d'eau* beat the heads off their English friends at lawn tennis, and these girls who with a great open swing drive a golf

25

ball a hundred and sixty yards down the middle of the fairway have acquired a new outlook. They are no longer the awkward boys and the shy, innocent girls, obsessed by sex, whom the dramatists continue to represent in their plays. Are they going to sit in a stuffy playhouse for three hours to see whether some woman is or is not going to bed with some man? They are much more interested in their handicap.

It is easy to say what is wrong with the theatre: it is very difficult to say how to put it right. It may be that the talkies, bringing us back to something like the technique of the Elizabethans, will solve the difficulty. It may be that it needs a new generation of dramatists to cope with the situation. M. de Croisset holds his hand. You will see when you read the following pages that he has good-humour and philosophy. He is too clever to take himself with unbecoming seriousness. Many people have written books on how to write a play; this will not tell you that; but it is a peep into the dramatist's workshop. It is a summary of the observations he has made on the theatre and on life during his career as a writer of plays. I cannot but think it significant that he has called it *Nos Marionettes*.

NOËL COWARD

The day is no longer approaching; the day has come. Henrik Ibsen put his own forebodings into the mouth of his master builder. He foresaw that the younger generation would come knocking at his door and shaking their fists shout: make room, make room, make room. 'Then there's an end of Halvard Solness.' For us English dramatists the younger generation has assumed the brisk but determined form of Mr Noël Coward. He knocked at the door with impatient knuckles, and then he rattled the handle, and then he burst in. After a moment's stupor the older playwrights welcomed him affably enough and retired with what dignity they could muster to the shelf which with a sprightly gesture he indicated to them as their proper place. For my part I have made myself quite comfortable there. The knowing Lucretius in a passage that has given the world a little shiver ever since it was written remarked that it was sweet, when on the great sea the winds troubled the waters, to behold from land another's deep distress; 'not that it is a pleasure and delight that any should be afflicted, but because it is sweet to see from what evils you are yourself exempt. It is sweet also to look upon the mighty struggles of war arrayed along the plains without sharing yourself in the danger.' But I look upon it as a very graceful attention on Mr Coward's part to reach up to my shelf with a volume of his plays and flatter me with the request that I should write a preface to them. I sit up and let my legs dangle in the air. I let myself down cautiously to the floor and give it a stamp to feel that it is really solid under my feet. And now as with a palsied hand I take up my pen I have just the sort of sensation I can imagine a man having who goes to lunch with his former wife and her second husband. It must be curious and entertaining for him to see from another angle circumstances with which he is so familiar and I suspect that he allows himself an inward chuckle when he considers that in a few minutes after he has drunk his coffee he will find himself once more in the open street. But his successor remains behind.

Suave, mari magno turbantibus aequora ventis. . . .

It would be foolish of me to write a criticism of the three plays[1] in this volume. The reader will read them and unless he is very silly he will not let

---

Introduction to *Bitter-Sweet and Other Plays* by Noël Coward. Doubleday, Doran, 1929.

[1] *Bitter-Sweet, Easy Virtue* and *Hay Fever*.

my opinion of them in the least influence him. The critic whose judgment you trust may render you the service of putting you on to a book you would otherwise have neglected, but when he has done that the only thing that matters is what the book means to you. It may be a masterpiece, but if it gives you nothing you have only wasted your time in reading it.

I should like, however, to say a little on a matter that has of late exercised the critics and the dramatists, since I venture to think that it is one upon which the future of the English drama depends. And since there is no one now writing who has more obviously a gift for the theatre than Mr Noël Coward, nor more influence with young writers, it is probably his inclination and practice that will be responsible for the manner in which plays will be written during the next twenty years.

Mr St. John Ervine published a few months ago a little book called *How to Write a Play*. Mr Ervine is a dramatist as well as a critic and his book is pithy and sensible. It is a work that any writer for the theatre can study with profit. He has exploded the fallacy that there is something mysterious in dramatic technique. Ponderous tomes have been written on the subject by persons who did not know what they were talking about. It is evident that people who have no feeling for the theatre will find it very difficult to write a play, just as people who have no ear will never understand music, and I think it may be admitted that to write a play requires a peculiar gift. It is not a very exalted one, for it can exist without intelligence or originality (one of the most distinguished dramatists of the last generation had the mind and the education of a bartender and wrote notwithstanding clever and charming plays); I think it would be better to call it a peculiar knack. I suspect that the whole secret of dramatic technique can be told in a sentence: stick to the point like grim death. But I mention this book of Mr Ervine's now because he has some interesting things to say about dialogue and especially about Mr Noël Coward's. It is in his dialogue that Mr Coward has shown himself something of an innovator, for in his construction he has been content to use the current method of his day; he has deliberately avoided the epigram that was the fashion thirty years ago (when an early play of mine, *Lady Frederick*, was bought by Mr George Tyler he told me that it was not epigrammatic enough, so I went away and in two hours wrote in twenty-four), and has written dialogue that is strictly faithful to fact. It does not only represent everyday language but reproduces it. No one has carried naturalistic dialogue further than he. Mr St. John Ervine attacks it. He finds it commonplace and dull. He gives a passage from *Home Chat* and another from *This was a Man* to make his point and similar passages could certainly be found in any of the three plays in this volume. He contends that the dramatist should 'heighten and lengthen and deepen the common speech, and yet leave it seeming to be the common speech'.

Dialogue has gradually been growing more natural. It was inevitable that some dramatist should eventually write dialogue that exactly copied the average talk, with its hesitations, mumblings and repetitions, and broken sentences, of average people. I do not suppose anyone can ever do this with more brilliant accuracy than Mr Coward. My only objection to it is that it adds greatly to the difficulty of the author's task. It is evident that when he represents dull and stupid people they will be as stupid and dull on the stage as in real life and they will bore us in the same way. When he exposes his theme or joins together the various parts of his story (and I should think it was impossible to write a play in which certain explanations, of no interest in themselves, can be avoided) he will only with difficulty hold the attention of his audience. The author limits himself to characters who are in themselves exciting or amusing and to a theme which is from the beginning of the first act to the end of the last naturally absorbing. It is asking a great deal. I may point out in passing that as Ibsen's dialogue grew more naturalistic he was led to deal with singularly abnormal characters. On the other hand I do not think it can be denied that when a scene is dramatic naturalistic dialogue vastly enhances its effectiveness. You have a very good example in the last scene of the second act of *Easy Virtue*. Its dramatic value is greatly heightened by the perfect naturalness of the dialogue. In the same play the value of the beautifully drawn character of Marian Whittaker is increased by the absolute fidelity with which her conversation is reproduced. I do not know that Mr Coward has ever created a personage more vivid, pathetic, abominable and true than this. When the characters and the theme allow, as in *Hay Fever*, the naturalistic dialogue can produce a masterpiece in miniature. But I have an impression that Mr Coward has gone as far as anyone can go in this direction. A blank wall faces him. There is less difference between Mr Ervine and Mr Coward than Mr Ervine seems to think. One seeks to reproduce dialogue; the other to represent it. I wonder if here too you do not come upon a blank wall. I wonder if the current fashion to be slangy and brief and incoherent has not blinded the dramatists to the fact that a great many people do talk grammatically, do choose their words, and do make use of expressions that on the stage would be thought 'bookish'. It has seemed to me that during the last twenty years or so the increase of reading has affected current speech. If Mr Ervine read a shorthand report of his own conversation over the luncheon table he would be surprised to find how 'bookish' it was. If he spent an evening in a public house in Lambeth he would be surprised to discover how unusual were the words and complicated the phrases, learnt from the Sunday papers and the films, he would hear from the people standing around him. The present mode in dialogue debars the writer from introducing into his play educated people who express themselves in an educated way. It may be true that the English are a tongue-tied people but are they so tongue-tied as all that? Listen to the conversation of barristers, doctors, politicians, parsons, and you will find that they express themselves quite naturally in a way that on the stage would be called absurdly literary. Stage dialogue has been simplified out of relation with all life but that of the cocktail bar. It seems to me a great loss.

It is evident that the cinema has had a great effect on the drama. In the first place it has quickened the apprehensions of the public so that they take a point very rapidly, and what a generation ago would have needed a long scene to explain can now be made plain in a couple of sentences. Further, it has done so many things better than the spoken drama can do them that it has made it futile for the spoken drama to attempt them. I suggest that the spoken drama must from now on look for its material only in places where the pictures cannot compete with it. They have made physical action more than a trifle tame, but the drama depends on action, and so it looks as though the drama must henceforward deal with action that is purely spiritual. Wit and emotion are demesnes that can never be taken away from it. Now wit is artificial. It has been my good fortune to know most of the celebrated wits of my day, but they sparkle very intermittently. No one in private life shines so continuously as a witty character should in a play, he is seldom so pointed, finished and apt. A play of wit demands an elaborate and polished dialogue which has little relation to the conversation of real life. When you come to the play of emotion the situation is more complicated. Mr O'Neill in *Strange Interlude* dealt with it by making his characters say what he thought they would have said under the circumstances and then adding in an aside what they thought. It was an ingenious and interesting experiment, but I do not think that he or anyone else can repeat it. It seems to me plain that if he is seeking to represent states of mind and affections of the soul the dramatist is handicapping himself unnecessarily if he confines himself to the baldness of contemporary speech. I am not convinced that it is true to life, for my impression is that persons under stress of emotion express themselves with more fluency, elaboration, and often with more eloquence than is generally suspected. I do not see why the dramatist should not put into the mouth of his characters what they feel rather than what they say. It is true that for a moment an audience used to naturalistic dialogue would think the words they heard strange, but an audience can be coaxed or driven to accept any formula. After all copying life, representation, is merely an aesthetic procedure like another: naturalism is no more to be preferred to formalism than a leg of mutton is to be preferred to a sirloin of beef. Now that naturalistic dialogue has been carried as far as it can go I cannot but think it might be worth trying a dialogue that does not reproduce the conversation of the day and only very vaguely represents it, but is deliberately and significantly formal. And since the future of the English drama is in the hands of Mr Noël Coward this, as I climb back laboriously on to my shelf, with my blessing is the suggestion I offer him.

THE GALLERY

The wise dramatist takes the gallery very seriously. He expects to find enthusiasm there. People go to the more expensive parts of a theatre for a variety of reasons. Because they are tired and think it will rest them to spend an evening in a playhouse; because they wish to entertain friends and to take them to see a play is the least troublesome way of doing so; because they have an engagement later and must get through the evening somehow; and sometimes because they have absolutely nothing else to do.

But I do not suppose anyone goes to the gallery except for one purpose, and that is to see the play and its players. And if he goes to the gallery he wants to go very much indeed; the seats are not very comfortable and often he has to wait a long time in the cold and wet to get a seat at all.

I suspect that in most cases it means a greater sacrifice to the man who pays his money to go to the gallery than it does to the man who pays his money to go to the stalls.

Yes, in the gallery there must be enthusiasm and it is enthusiasm the dramatist wants. After all, the play is make-believe, but it is too much to ask the author and the actors to provide the make-believe all by themselves; the audience must be prepared to meet them half-way. The audience in the gallery is readier to do this than the audience in the stalls. They start by giving more comfort, time and hard-earned shillings, and they are eager to be rewarded. They feel instinctively that they are more likely to be so if they meet the spectacle put before them with vivacity and tenseness. That is why the author looks with satisfaction upon a crowded gallery. There he can count on a response.

There is something else. People sometimes speak of a play as a stalls play or a gallery play: they say it is all right for the expensive seats, but no good for the cheap ones. And contrariwise. Well, I suppose there are such plays, and I don't see why there should not be. Taking for granted (though I don't know why one should) that the audience in the expensive parts of the house is more sophisticated than the audience in the cheaper parts, it may well be that the author is pleased to write a play that appeals only to one part of his audience. It is his right and no one has any reason to complain. But the best plays appeal

Foreword to *Gallery Unreserved* by A Galleryite [F.T. Bason]. Heritage, 1931.

to a universal audience; all men and women, whatever their class or education, find pleasure and delight in them. The play that only appeals to a clique or class, whether it is a blood and thunder drama or an artificial comedy of manners, may be good in its way, but that is the best you can say of it. The play that is good without any qualification at all appeals to everybody. But it is very hard to write. The applause of the gallery joined to the applause of the stalls tells the dramatist he has done so.

MARIE TEMPEST

When I went to the first rehearsal of my first play in which Marie Tempest acted[1] it was with trepidation. I knew then little about the theatre, and my mind was filled with fantastic notions. Marie Tempest was the greatest comedienne on the English stage. I expected her to be wilful, exacting, petulant and tiresome; I expected her to insist on having her own way and if she did not get it at once to fly into a tantrum. For that I imagined was how leading ladies behaved.

The play was being produced by Dion Boucicault, and his method was to work over the first act with the utmost thoroughness, thinking that thus he could impress upon the cast the mood of the play and enable them to get into the skin of their parts, so that when he came to the second and third acts there would be nothing much for them to do but to learn their words.

I daresay the method was sound, but it was tedious; I think we worked on the act for a solid fortnight. To my surprise Marie Tempest never showed a trace of impatience; she repeated scenes two, three and four times with perfect good humour. She seemed never to tire. She was invariably punctual at rehearsals; she was very soon word perfect. She worked hard. She listened to what Boucicault told her with attention, and did it without question. This was not at all how I had expected a great actress to behave. Of course, she did not slavishly copy him; instinctively, with her wonderful sense of comedy and her mastery of technique, she translated his words into her own language. She took his suggestions, and at once, without any effort that you could see, gave them originality, colour and life. Her vivid personality transformed them into something definitely her own. It warmed the author's heart to see what she made of his lines.

Others will have written of Marie Tempest's wonderful talent, of her charm and irresistible gaiety; I have written this because it may have escaped the notice of many who have admired her brilliant performances that they are due not only to her natural gifts, which are eminent, but to patience, assiduity, industry and discipline. Without these it is impossible to excel in any of the arts. But that is something that not all who pursue them know.

Tribute to Marie Tempest in *Souvenir Programme*. Theatre Royal, Drury Lane, 28 May 1935.

[1] *Mrs Dot*, produced at the Comedy Theatre, London, in 1908.

GLADYS COOPER

I am rather vague about dates, but I think it must have been early in the year 1910 that Charles Hawtrey called me up one morning and asked me to come to the Royalty Theatre in Dean Street where he was producing plays, I believe in partnership with Vedrenne, to see an actress he wanted me to meet. He was about to put on a light comedy which at his request I had translated from the French for him. I forget what it was originally called,[1] but I gave it the name of *The Noble Spaniard*, and as there was nothing much to it, in order to make it more picturesque I turned it into a period piece in the hope that the pretty clothes would make up for the thinness of the intrigue. There was a good part for Hawtrey, but he hadn't yet found an actress for the chief female part.

'I've asked a girl to come here who might just do for us,' he said when I had shaken hands with him. 'She's at the Gaiety just now, in the chorus, but she wants to get on the legitimate stage. She's as pretty as a picture.'

'Can she act?' I asked.

'I shouldn't think so,' he answered cheerily. 'But you wait till you see her. She's a knock-out.'

The words were hardly out of his mouth when a young woman was ushered in. Hawtrey got up and took both her hands in his.

'Darling. This is Mr Maugham. I've just been telling him you're the most beautiful girl in the world.'

She smiled and shook hands with me. She was very simply dressed in a coat and skirt, and singularly composed considering that she was being thought of for her first speaking part and that if I approved of her she would have the chance of playing opposite the most popular comedian of the day. All that Hawtrey had said of her was true. Her beauty was fresh, healthy and spring-like. Perhaps because notwithstanding the calmness of her demeanour she was inwardly a trifle nervous she had a pensive look which reminded me of that beautiful Greek statue, no more than a fragment, alas, of a girl in the museum at Naples which bears the name of Psyche. She had the same delicate features and the same virginal air. I was surprised when Hawtrey asked her how the baby was.

Introduction to *Without Veils* by Sewell Stokes. Peter Davies, 1953.

[1] It was *Les Gaietés du Veuvage* by Grenet-Dancourt.

34

'She's married to Buck, you know,' he told me.

After a few minutes' conversation she left us and Hawtrey asked me what I thought of her.

'She's the loveliest thing I've ever seen in my life,' I answered. 'But how d'you know she can act?'

'It's not a difficult part and I can teach her.'

'All right then. By the way, what is her name?'

'Didn't I mention it? Cooper. Gladys Cooper.'

But it appeared that she was under contract to George Edwardes and he would not release her, so in the end the part was played by somebody else.

I did not see Gladys Cooper again till she appeared in Edward Knoblock's play, *My Lady's Dress*; but she must by then have acquired something of a reputation since she played the lead. The only recollection I have of it is that she wore a number of pretty frocks and looked even more beautiful than I remembered her. Her acting was only just adequate. It had neither ease nor variety. The last time I saw her was in Noël Coward's *Relative Values*. The lovely golden hair was now white, but her figure had retained its youthful slimness and her beauty was undimmed. Her performance was remarkable. It seemed to me that she had never acted better, with greater command of her resources or with greater authority. She had the ease, the variety that she had lacked at one time, immense charm and a surprising vitality. Her gestures, her intonations were perfect.

It is interesting to consider how Gladys Cooper has succeeded in turning herself from an indifferent actress into an extremely accomplished one. I have a notion that her beauty has been at once her greatest asset and her greatest handicap; an asset because without it she would never have gone on the stage, for she is not the born actress who whatever she looks like is impelled by her nature to act (she would have competently run a business or, married to a landowner, managed an estate); a handicap for reasons which I shall now suggest. Of course it is well that an actress should have a certain comeliness; if she is too homely it is hard to persuade an audience, however well she acts, that she may be the object of a passionate love; and though it may not be true that love makes the world go round, love requited or unrequited is in general the mainspring of the theatre; but there is a certain coldness in perfect beauty which is, not repellent, to say that would be an exaggeration, but not alluring. Some irregularity of feature perhaps enables an actress to display emotion more effectively, and unless she is very plain she can with make-up and sympathetic lighting render herself sufficiently attractive. From her portraits we know that Mrs Siddons had a statuesque beauty that was not only imposing but positively awe-inspiring, but we know also that this somewhat restricted the range of parts in which she was at her greatest. We can see her as Volumnia or Lady Macbeth, but we can't imagine her romping through an eighteenth-century farce. Eleonora Duse had fine eyes and an attractive face, but she was not a great beauty; she could play with equal virtuosity Goldoni's *La Locandiera* and D'Annunzio's *La Città Morta*. The point I want to make is that classical features limit the power of an actress to display the variety of emotion which a part may require. Charm is an indefinable thing; it is not often combined with the extreme of beauty.

If Miss Cooper has succeeded in overcoming the handicap of her startling beauty it is to be ascribed, I think, to the passing of the years, to her great common sense and to industry. Age, which has left her beauty almost unimpaired, has given her face an expressiveness which in youth it lacked. From Mr Stokes's book you will get the idea that she created parts, by the light of nature, as it were, without effort. I do not believe that. It is true that when she played in the movies she did not trouble to read the entire script, but was content to learn her own lines and then was able to give a performance so good that she received more than once the awards which Hollywood confers on an outstanding performance. I think in this case her wide experience enabled her to get into the heart of a character by intuition and so play it for all it was worth. But that was the reward for years of hard work.

It was not till after the first world war that she acted in any of my plays. She was then established at The Playhouse, the most popular actress of her day, with an immense and enthusiastic following. She was not only very beautiful, but an extremely competent actress. Mr Stokes appears to think that, with all these advantages, she went her own way indifferent to direction. That is not the impression I got when I watched the rehearsing of my plays. I found her conscientious and eager to do her best. I saw her directed by Gerald du Maurier and Charles Hawtrey. As she very well knew, both of them knew their business. My recollection is that she took their suggestions without question and was able very quickly to do what they required. When either du Maurier or Hawtrey wanted her to do something in a different way she never hesitated to try it, and try it again, till she had satisfied herself and him. One trifling incident occurs to me: in a play of mine called *The Letter*, in order to get a crucial dramatic effect Miss Cooper had on a sudden to fall to the floor in a dead faint. That is not an easy thing to do in a natural manner without hurting oneself. For fear of this, the first time she rehearsed it, Miss Cooper did it with some hesitation, whereupon Gerald du Maurier, by doing it himself, which was his useful way of directing, showed her how it could be done with effect and without danger. She tried it perhaps half a dozen times till he cried: 'That's right!' and ever afterwards she did it exactly as he had shown her.

She was prepared to leave nothing undone that could be done by hard work to make her performance as good as she possibly could. And you could rely on her. She was not one of those tiresome creatures who may give a perfect performance one day and a poor one the next. These plays of mine had long runs and from my point of view as a dramatist not the least of Miss Cooper's merits was that, however long the run was, her performance never varied. Of course she had to be suited. The actress doesn't exist who can play equally well Katherine of Aragon and Millamant, Ophelia and Hedda Gabler. It appears that Miss Cooper was at one time induced to play parts in two of Shakespeare's plays. I am not surprised that she did not please the critics. She is essentially modern. But for all that she has a wide range. She played in three plays[1] of mine and in one[2] that was dramatised by an American playwright from one of my novels. I did not write the plays for her, I wrote them for

---

[1] *Home and Beauty* (1919), *The Letter* (1927) and *The Sacred Flame* (1929).

[2] *The Painted Veil* by Bartlett Cormack (1931).

themselves; but I greatly admired her and it was inevitable that I should bear in mind the probability that she might care to act in them, with the result that the character I invented was more or less unconsciously coloured by this, just as long before the plays I had written with Irene Vanbrugh in mind were coloured by my knowledge of her brilliant talent. The four women Miss Cooper portrayed in the plays to which I am now referring were, unless I deceive myself, as different as the creatures of an author can be (and to some extent an author remains like himself, for himself is all he has to offer), and each of these parts she characterised admirably. For by the time she came to act my plays Miss Cooper, by the hard work to which I have drawn attention and by an unceasing desire to do her best, had become a very fine actress. I owe much to her. And now she has mastered her profession. She cannot go on playing *Relative Values* for ever. Is there no young dramatist to write a play that will give her the opportunity to display her truly remarkable gifts?

ON
PAINTERS
AND
PAINTING

GERALD KELLY

1. A Student of Character

The observer of life, listening in studios and at café tables to the conversation of painters, must have heard often with ironic amusement their contention that it is only the judgment of painters upon painting which has any value. They insist upon the importance of technique and are impatient of the criticism of those who have no practical knowledge of it. No one would make the preposterous claim that only a writer could judge the excellence of *Vanity Fair*, and yet the technique of writing is no less complicated than that of any other of the arts. Of late an exaggerated importance has been attached to technique, and those who practise a particular art have sought to make it into a mystery. Some years ago, owing to the influence of a popular and not undistinguished writer, there was a great interest in technique as such, and people troubled themselves with a needless accuracy; they spoke of steam-engines in the terms of the mechanician and of flowers in the terms of the botanist: they made themselves not only unintelligible but tedious. Art-critics, a timid race anxious to be right – as though to be right were more important than to be sincere – have stuffed themselves with the jargon of the studios, and have judged pictures as though they were painters. But since the technique of painting is very difficult the painter will be inclined to attach too great consequence to it, and the part of the critic is to remind him that technique is no more than a means. Good grammar may be expected from a writer, and he should be able to set down plainly and neatly what he wishes to say; he need not be praised for these qualities and their lack of essential importance is shown by the fact that some very great writers have not possessed them. Charles Dickens wrote often very bad grammar, and Honoré de Balzac was frequently diffuse and clumsy. It cannot be different in painting. You have the right to expect that a painter's values should be correct, and I see no more reason to congratulate him on the fact that he draws well than to congratulate a public speaker on the fact that he enunciates clearly. In none of this does art consist. A work of art must offer two much more important things, namely, entertainment and emotion.

I know little of the technique of painting, and care less, and in this short study of Mr Gerald Kelly's art I have nothing to say about that side of his

International Studio, December 1914.

work. I have called him 'a student of character'. It is through his absorption in this that he gets those qualities of entertainment and emotion which seem to me the essentials of art. (I may make myself clearer by explaining that the peculiar form of entertainment which a picture offers is decoration.) Mr Kelly has painted portraits, he has painted in Spain, and he has painted in Burmah; but his interest in character makes a whole of work which at first sight looks as if it might be divided into three parts between which there is no great connection. His Spanish work, his Burmese work, shows no less an absorption in character than do his portraits of Captain Reeves, R.N., or of Lady Clarke illustrated in this article;[1] but it is an absorption in the character of a people rather than in that of individuals. We who practise the arts know only our own country, and when we paint or describe other peoples' can tell not the truth about them, but the impression they make on us. This art can with difficulty be other than quaint or curious and at the best tell us only how a particular generation regarded a civilisation other than its own. The French painters of the eighteenth century who painted the East – there was an exhibition of their work at the Louvre a year or two ago – looked upon it as a masquerade and offered us an Orient in powder and patch; and the French romantics painted the East of the Byronic attitude: our own generation has been chiefly impressed by the mystery of the East, and it is this which Mr Kelly has painted. His Burmese dancers – there is a long series of them, painted with boldness and great vigour – have a strange impenetrability, their gestures are enigmatic and yet significant, they are charming, and yet there is something curiously hieratic in their manner; with a sure instinct, and with a more definite feeling for decoration than is possible in a portrait, Mr Kelly has given us the character of the East as we of our generation see it. It needed a peculiar sensitiveness; and the same sensitiveness has served him in painting Andalusia. Here again it is the character of a race that he has painted, more intimately than when he painted the Burmese, because the soul of the Spaniard is nearer to us than that of the Oriental, and here again he has shown a rare originality, for Andalusia has meant to the painter, as to the superficial traveller, a land of song and light laughter, of dancing and castanets. It was Théophile Gautier who described the country in these terms, and the world at large has been content to see it through his eyes. It is a vulgar Spain of the Paris exhibition, a Spain at Earl's Court, which fills the imagination of the traveller who visits that country, and since most men take from their journeys only what they bring to them, often enough he comes home again with his impressions unaltered; often, too, finding little of what he expected, he brings back only disillusion. If you look at the pictures which illustrate these pages,[1] *Joaquina, The Black Shawl, Rosa Maria, On the Rocks*, you will see that Mr Kelly has seen Spain very differently. He has painted Andalusia, for it is Andalusia that he has painted in the portraits of these different women just as much as if he had painted street scenes in Seville or the crowd at a bull-fight, with fresh eyes and from an entirely personal standpoint; and they who know the country must realise the truth of his presentment. For Andalusia is a land of passion, and passion is not mirthful, there is always tragedy at the back of the dancing

---

[1] Not reproduced in this collection.

and the laughter which are all the superficial see; and the songs of its people are a melancholy wailing: they deal with unrequited love and death and hunger. *Rosa Maria*, the woman of *The Black Shawl*, with her beautifully painted hand, have eyes heavy with tears, their faces are sensual with a sensuality raised to a strange height of passion. There is the real Andalusia, and the painter who could see it, breaking through a shallow tradition, has gifts of insight which are rare among his fellows.

But there is a wall raised between us and the peoples of other lands; we know our own folk because our childhood has been spent among them; a thousand delicate feelings aid our comprehension; and our description of foreign nations, however subtle, cannot have a complete intimacy.

Character deals with the individual; and the painter of character has full scope for his gifts only when he is portraying his own countrymen. It is when Mr Kelly paints Englishmen and Englishwomen that he reveals himself, patient, acute, and carefully exact, and his sitters with all their foibles and vices, their virtues and pleasant humours. Then he paints not only the character of a people but also of persons. Then his art is penetrating. Everyone who is interested in modern painting will remember his portrait of *Mrs Harrison*, now in the Municipal Gallery at Dublin. It is a portrait of a little old lady, but painted with such sincerity and emotion, soberly with a becoming restraint, that the individual is merged in the type; and you have a picture of graceful old age, insouciant as old age so often, so pleasantly, is, and beautiful. If art must give entertainment and emotion, here indeed is art. Only the mediocre keep always to the same level, and Mr Kelly is not mediocre. Sometimes he sees his sitters without sympathy, which is the essential gift of the portrait-painter, and then his pictures are dull; but more often, instinctively, perhaps, he paints with a true emotion; and then his portraits take a very high place as studies of character. He is not an idealist. He puts down what he sees, and when he sees with sympathy he gives you the very soul of the man, his strength and weakness, his very idiosyncrasies. It would not require a fertile imagination to give a true account of *Captain Reeves, R.N.*, or of *Lady Stanley Clarke*. They are placed on the canvas for the world to see them. Though knowing neither I fancy that I could write an accurate history of each.

Mr Kelly is young still, and life has still lessons for him. When he fails it is through lack of sympathy, and when he learns a more complete sympathy, when he is able to see the point of view of those he paints, discovering how each one of us is right from his own standpoint, he will produce a series of works which will be a true and personal record of the generation in which he lived. Is that a poor thing to do from the peculiar outlook of the painter? I am not a painter and do not know. It is what the great Holbein did.

2. Paintings

I am the last person who should write a preface to this catalogue of Gerald Kelly's pictures, which the public is now invited to see. He is my oldest friend and I cannot be expected to write of them as I would of those of someone whom I did not know. It is nearly fifty years ago that he came to spend one Sunday at a house near Paris which a brother of mine had rented for the summer and where I was staying. Gerald Kelly was then a short, slender young man in his early twenties with a mass of untidy black hair, regular features and fine, eager eyes behind great round spectacles. He had a nervous vitality and that exuberant loquacity which we tongue-tied English look upon as a characteristic of the Irish. He was as violent in his enthusiasm for what he liked as he was violent in his denunciation of what he didn't. He was not one for half measures. But it was obvious that he was extremely intelligent and for his age he was widely read.

I saw him several times during that summer, and I think it was in the following spring that I went to Paris for a year and took a small flat in Montparnasse. Gerald Kelly had a studio nearby and we used to dine every evening along with other painters and writers in a small restaurant in the Rue d'Odessa where they kept a back room for us. We were all young and it was the scene of heated discussions on art and literature which to us then were the only subjects worth considering. My day was spent in writing novels and Gerald Kelly's in painting portraits.

For, from the beginning, it was to that variety of art that he felt himself drawn. Portrait-painters nowadays have to put up with a lot of detraction. Roger Fry, as we know, claimed that advertisement, or publicity, in one form or another has been one of the chief incentives to the production of a painted portrait. He would have been better advised to leave out the word *chief*. Sometimes a patron has his wife or children painted because he is fond of them. Sometimes friends gather together to commission an artist to paint a portrait of someone for whom they have affection or respect. I cannot believe that Philip IV commissioned Velasquez to paint his daughter for any purpose other than his love for that small person. Did Henry James's friends get Sargent to paint his portrait as an advertisement? He didn't need it. He would have refused indignantly to sit for such a purpose.

Portrait-painters, it seems to me, can be divided into two classes, those who are more interested in themselves than in their model and those who are more interested in their model than in themselves. I was once painted by a distinguished French painter who, when the picture was finished, looked at it thoughtfully and said: 'You know, people always complain that my portraits aren't like, I can't tell you how little I care'. The French words were: '*Je ne peux pas vous dire a quel point je m'en fous*'. Now Gerald Kelly, from the outset of his career, has been a portrait-painter who is interested not in himself, except in so far as he has always tried to paint the best pictures he could, but in his sitter.

Preface to catalogue of *An Exhibition of Paintings by Sir Gerald Kelly*, Leicester Galleries, London, 1950.

He has travelled widely and wherever he went he painted. The visitor to this exhibition can see for himself how fascinated he was by the novelty of Burma, its heat and colour, and the strangeness of its architecture. Gerald Kelly has painted in Spain, where he spent several years, and in China. But these productions, interesting and accomplished as they are, to me are in the nature of a holiday he allowed himself from the main business of his life. This has been to set down on his canvas the features of his sitter correctly, to give the impression of the weight of the body under the clothes, to suggest the bones under the face, to get the expression of eyes and the curl of the lips, in short to produce an honest, faithful portrait and at the same time give his picture a decorative quality. I have a notion that if any of his sitters are remembered in a hundred years people will be glad to know that this is just what they looked like. They will know then that this was a painter who was prepared to sink his own individuality and devote himself to the sole purpose of sincerely representing that of his sitter.

A portrait is to some extent a collaboration between the artist and the sitter. If there is nothing to interest in the sitter's personality the painter can do no more than, with his experience and knowledge of technique, produce a portrait which, if he is lucky, will satisfy his client. Like most painters, I suppose, Gerald Kelly is at his best when, as in the *Mrs Harrison*, now in Dublin, the portrait of an old lady, there was in his sitter the grave serenity, tinged with humour, the unassuming assurance of a Victorian gentlewoman, which aroused his emotion; or when, as in the many portraits he has painted of his wife, and in those, not few, he has painted of me, his affection was engaged.

His art is quiet, unobtrusive and distinguished, and it may be that it is an art for the home rather than for a public gallery where it may be overshadowed by pictures which are startling and provocative. His pictures are easy to live with. Strangely enough, considering his Irish origins, they are very English. They fit in comfortably with Chippendale chairs, chintz-covered sofas, and bowls of flowers filled with daffodils in spring or roses in summer. Through the open windows you see spacious lawns and herbaceous borders, and beyond green meadows with here and there a coppice.

MARIE LAURENCIN

I have absolutely no justification for writing a preface to the catalogue of an exhibition of Marie Laurencin's pictures but that I like them and own several. I bought them at odd times and after a while found myself with five. I had by then fully recognised their great decorative value, but this, it seemed to me, was enhanced if you did not mix them up with other pictures. Always charming, they are more charming if they have the field to themselves. At this moment I happened to buy a house on the Riviera, and it occurred to me that it would be agreeable to arrange my dining-room so that I could show these five pictures to the best advantage. It was a room of moderate dimensions. The walls were whitewashed. I reframed my pictures in wooden frames of tarnished silver; my furniture was Italian Louis XVI and I pickled it; I had some little Directoire arm-chairs (all nice people should give you arm-chairs to dine in), and I scraped off the heavy paint that disfigured them and faintly silvered them; I had a couple of mirrors with green glass frames and Venetian candelabra of painted wood and looking-glass. When I looked at my Marie Laurencins in that setting I hugged myself for joy. They looked so gay and fresh. The setting gave an added value to those enchanting and original colours of hers.

I was interested when I found that Lady Cunard had done the same thing as I had. She has a magnificent collection of Marie Laurencins. Hers are more important than mine, but, I hasten to add, not more delightful, for Marie Laurencin very seldom descends from her own high level. These are used to decorate a large drawing-room. They are framed with a thin gold line and then in broad strips of looking-glass so that the frame gives the effect of a panel. They fit in very well with the Adam ceiling and the Aubusson carpets, the crystal brackets and the great crystal chandelier. With their pale blues, their pinks, their mauves, they have an eighteenth-century air that goes very well with the room, but they have also a Parisian sophistication of yesterday that makes the past of powdered wigs and patches an intimate recollection, as it were, of our own experience. They have the remoteness of a faintly naughty fairy-tale. They suggest the dreams of modish debauchery that a young girl

Preface to catalogue of an exhibition of *Flower Paintings by Marie Laurencin*, Mayor Gallery, London, 1934.

might have who had never been out of a convent. So might the great world that she had never seen appear to her ingenuous reverie; and life, guessed at from the novels she read in secret, might have that exciting, enigmatic, charming and aristocratic colour. You do not quite know what these delicious young creatures are doing. With their fair hair and black eyes, with their draperies of delicate hue, they are a little unreal, but infinitely graceful and alluring. You feel that a fantastic adventure is certainly waiting for them round the corner.

And these flowers, to which the reader of these few lines is now invited to give his kind attention, are the fit and proper flowers to be laid at the feet of any one of those slim girls by a slightly Byronic lover. These careless nosegays would give a note of freshness to the faded petit-point of the drawing-room in a chateau at the end of an enchanted avenue.

PAINTINGS
I HAVE LIKED

The most stirring thing that has happened to me during the last few months is one that on the surface might well seem to offer no occasion for excitement. I happened to be in San Francisco when they were showing that collection of French pictures which before the war the Republic, now defunct, had sent to South America with the propagandist intention of displaying to the peoples of its states the fine flower of French culture. I went to see it one Saturday afternoon. The gallery was crowded with young people. They were looking at the pictures with eager attention; they were discussing them with one another, they were pondering over them, and on many a face I saw a happy glow of delight which could be nothing but the outward sign of an inward and true emotion.

Now not all these pictures had an obvious appeal. They ranged from the school of Fontainebleau to those pictures of the modern masters to appreciate which, I should have thought, considerable acquaintance and some education in the art of painting were essential. But these young men and women were taking them, even the most advanced, in their stride; it did not appear to me that they were hostile to what was new and strange, but on the contrary were anxious to understand it in order to receive the communication which I cannot but think they instinctively felt might be of value to them. I do not believe that 30 or 40 years ago a similar exhibition could have attracted such an eager and interested crowd of the very young persons; many of them were college boys from Berkeley and their girls, but many were workingmen from the neighbouring factories, with their wives, who had spent the whole week performing the self-same motions in monotonous toil. It was a deeply impressive sight. I may be grossly mistaken, but I like to think that it indicates an obscure reaction from the mechanization of contemporary life and the glimmering, perhaps even more than a glimmering, of a desire, not yet quite conscious, for the spiritual things that can make life richer and more varied.

Now I must tell you that I do not believe, as most people believed a generation ago, in art for art's sake. I do not think art is merely for delight.

Life, 1 December 1941.

Many works of art have been produced, in painting, in music, in writing, which have no other aim and no other effect than to give pleasure, and they are to be prized because pleasure is good and spiritual pleasure is enduring; but the ultimate value of art lies in its moral value. Unless art enriches the soul and leads to right conduct it is merely entertainment and then is no more estimable than bowls or an ice-cream sundae. But great art does just that; and as I walked about the gallery, looking sometimes at the pictures, most of which I knew well, but more at the people, I could not but be exhilarated, for it seemed to me that their enthusiasm and appreciation, their receptive sensibility held a bright promise for the future of mankind. For in the end democracy depends on the virtue of the individual and great art conduces to virtue. We are the product of many forces and few of us can tell what the influences are that have worked to make us the sort of beings we are. That night, unable to sleep, I wondered what exactly these pictures, some of them so difficult, had meant to those people I had seen studying them and what result the impact might have on a happy few.

Many of us can point to a book we have read at an auspicious moment which has had the effect of a revelation. It may be the Gospel of St. John or the Confessions of St. Augustine, some dialogues of Plato, poems of Keats or Walt Whitman, or even a novel. I doubt whether any picture can have so violent and revolutionary an effect. The influence of graphic art is more temperate. For my own part I have a notion that there are certain pictures that have so profoundly moved me that they have had not a little to do with the sort of man I am; but before I speak of them I should like to say that I think the painters wrong who state that only those can appreciate or speak profitably of paintings who are intimately acquainted with technique. We peaceable citizens use a plane to take us from place to place and it is unnecessary for us to know the processes of its manufacture. That may be a matter of interest to the person of a mechanical turn, but it is not the particular business of the passenger. So a painter has a communication to make and it is this that is our concern; the steps he has taken to express his communication to the best advantage have nothing to do with us.

But whereas great books are within everyone's reach and he can get hold of them with ease and read them at his convenience, most great pictures have in course of time found their way into public galleries. Not many of us are so fortunate as to possess a picture whose appeal makes it a constant source of spiritual enrichment. The only millionaire I ever envied was the late Mr Frick because he owned that portrait of Rembrandt's son which is known as the *Polish Rider*. I fancy that is a picture of which the emotional significance could hardly be exhausted. It is charged with romance. And since the masterpieces must be seen in galleries it can only be a matter of chance what pictures they will be that contribute to the development of any particular person. For it is in early youth that the spirit is most apt to receive those enduring impressions that mould the character and the young have no choice in their place of habitation.

I look upon myself as very fortunate that the circumstances of my life enabled me to frequent the Louvre at an early age and it is because I was so much and so often in Paris that some of the pictures in that rich, ill-kept and ill-arranged gallery have made so stable an impression on what I suppose I must call my subconscious self. I have not by nature good taste. The first room of my own I ever had I decorated with brightly coloured pictures of juicy girls which I got out of the Christmas numbers of illustrated papers and I blush when I think of the pride I took in them. But in due course I grew ashamed of them and replaced them with large photographs of old masters; I can only remember that among them was a reproduction of a somewhat sentimental head by Van Dyck and of a landscape by Hobbema.

But before I was much older I saw a picture at the Louvre that after all these years has not lost its power to move and delight me. I must have seen it often before, but with an unseeing eye, and I cannot tell how it came about that one day it made an impression on me so poignant that it has lasted all my life. This was Titian's *Entombment of Christ*, which is in what they call the *Salle Carrée*. I suppose it is not considered one of Titian's most important pictures, for it is seldom illustrated in the books that have been written about him, and if I continue to find it one of the greatest pictures in the world it must be because there is something in it that says something of importance to me. I will not try to describe it, for pictures are there to be looked at and words are powerless to give a notion that the reader can translate into an image of the thing seen. You might as well try to tell a deaf man what a chorale of Bach's sounds like. Of course this picture has the sumptuous colour which is common to most of the Venetians and it has a flowing rhythm that seems like the very palpitation of life; but it has more than that; the event it depicts is one of the most harrowing in human history, and the weeping women are bowed with grief, and yet it is instinct with beauty. The only thing I can compare it with is with those last pregnant words of Hamlet's: The rest is silence.

Not far from Titian's *Entombment*, in the Long Gallery, is another picture of his that I can never tire of and that is the *Man with a Glove*. Even when I bear in mind Velasquez's portrait in Rome of *Pope Innocent*, I think it the finest portrait in the world. It was painted between 1510 and 1520 and is supposed to be that of Girolamo Adorno, a Genoese, who was ambassador of the Holy Roman Empire at Venice. It is the portrait of a young man. It is so much alive that he seems to abide your question and you ask yourself, as you would of a recluse you had come across casually in some strange city in a far land, what is the poignant secret that his sealed lips withhold. He lived in courts and knew their intrigues and their deceptions. He knew the shallow loveliness of the Renaissance and his thoughtful mien, his disillusioned serenity persuade you that, like many another man of his period, he was learned in the wisdom of the ancients; but it may be that there is in those dark and wistful eyes a presentiment of untimely death and a nostalgia for something beyond the delight of art and letters, beyond the purposeless activity of life, the bustling of seafaring Genoa, the sensual magnificence of Venice, a nostalgia for the peace of the Absolute. He died at 33.

Walking down the Long Gallery in imagination, for alas, with Paris under the brutal heel of the invader and its pictures scattered, for all I know, or hidden, that is the only way you can now visit the Louvre, I stop before one of its most moving pictures. This is Rembrandt's *The Supper at Emmaus*. The incident the artist has chosen to paint is narrated by St. Luke in beautiful words. The two disciples, you remember, were on their way from the city, talking together of the things which had happened and they were joined by one whom they took for a stranger,

> for their eyes were holden that they should not know him. . . . And they drew nigh unto the village, whither they went: and he made as though he would have gone further. But they constrained him, saying, 'Abide with us: for it is toward evening, and the day is far spent'. And he went into the tavern with them. And it came to pass, as he sat at meat with them, he took bread and blessed it, and brake, and gave to them. And their eyes were opened, and they knew him, and he vanished out of their sight.

It is an intensely dramatic picture, but it is dramatic without emphasis so that if you did not know already that Rembrandt was a great artist, a master of light and shade, you might think that he had left the story to tell itself and that it was by a happy accident that he had produced a painting that is so profoundly satisfying to the aesthetic sense. It has none of the sumptuous colour of Titian's *Entombment*, it is quiet in tone and restrained, but it has a sober, glowing richness that uplifts the spirit and I wonder to myself if it is that, or some deep emotion in the painter, that gives this little picture that strange feeling of the supernatural which to me is its most troubling and most appealing feature. It is one of the most deeply religious pictures of the world.

I saunter on, looking for my favourite Chardin, but I know I shall not find it, for it is not in the Louvre, but in the National Gallery in London. Chardin by many people is looked upon as one of the lesser masters. I do not think he is. For one thing he was eminently skilful. He had a wonderful talent for putting on to canvas the play of the light and the savour of colour and because he liked to do this he preferred to paint still life which he could arrange as he chose. He was a very even painter and I cannot think of a single one of his pictures in which he falls more than a little below his own high level.

Now and then he painted domestic scenes, women at their chores, because he had to sell to eat, and it appears that people would not buy his still lifes. The patrons of his day asked for the human interest; it is strange that they did not see that the significance of his still lifes consists not only in their lovely harmonies and in their exquisite delicacy but precisely in their human interest; for Chardin's peculiar virtue is that he was able to see the beauty and the throbbing life that there is in humble ordinary things like pots and pans. You cannot believe he painted them merely because he could make a decorative arrangement of them and a delicate harmony of colour; had that been all, he could hardly have painted them with such tenderness, and you cannot resist the conviction that they were to him somehow symbols of the pathos and the pity, the courage, the endurance, the goodwill and the honesty of the common people.

Some time ago I wrote a novel[1] in which I had occasion to make a character, a Russian refugee, speak of a particular picture of Chardin's; it happened to be the picture in the National Gallery in London which I have just mentioned, but that did not suit me and so, taking the novelist's licence, I feigned that it was in the Louvre. I put into as apt words as I could exactly the feeling it gave me and since I can express no better what I look upon as Chardin's deep significance I shall take leave now to repeat them.

---

[1] *Christmas Holiday* (1939).

It is a tiny canvas on which are painted a loaf of bread and a flagon of wine. And isn't it wonderful, I make my character say, that with those simple objects, with his painter's exquisite sensibility, moved by the charity in his heart, that funny, dear old man should have made something so beautiful that it breaks you? It was as though, unconsciously perhaps, hardly knowing what he was doing, he wanted to show you that if you only have enough love, if you only have enough sympathy, out of pain and distrust and unkindliness, out of all the evil of the world, you can create beauty.

It's not only a loaf of bread and a flagon of wine; it's the bread of life and the blood of Christ, but not held back from those who starve and thirst for them, and doled out by priests on stated occasions; it's the daily fare of suffering men and women. It's so humble, so natural, so friendly, it's the bread and wine of the poor who ask no more than that they should be left in peace, allowed to work and eat their simple food in freedom. It's the cry of the despised and rejected. It tells you that whatever their sins men at heart are good. That loaf of bread and that flagon of wine are symbols of the joys and sorrows of the lowly and meek. They ask for your mercy and your affection; they tell you that they're of the same flesh and blood as you; they tell you that life is short and hard and the grave is cold and lonely. It's not only a loaf of bread and a flagon of wine; it's the mystery of man's lot on earth, his craving for a little friendship and a little love and the humility of his resignation when he sees that even they must be denied him.

I don't know if you can call the ceiling that Michelangelo painted for the Sistine Chapel a picture. It is surely the most impressive piece of painting that exists in the world. However often you see it you are filled with stupefaction. I do not suppose a nobler figure has ever been produced by the hand of man than that of Adam at the moment of creation. Its beauty takes your breath away. And those sibyls who sit brooding over the destiny of man have a stately grandeur that uplifts the heart.

The paintings I have spoken of before make their appeal by stirring the imagination, they speak directly to *you*, but the effect of this ceiling in the Sistine Chapel is, at least on me, somewhat different. It is not the beauty of the design and the sublimity of those superhuman figures that deeply move me, but the genius of the man who conceived and executed this stupendous work. The word genius is much abused; I have seen it applied to the author of a few Broadway successes and to the authors of two or three best-selling novels. But it can be as safely used of Michelangelo as of Shakespeare. When you crane your neck and strain your eyes to look at this ceiling in the end what overwhelmingly impresses you is the personality of the artist. His greatness is evident in every part of this vast fresco. It awes and humbles you and at the same time you are filled with exultation because man with all his weakness, all his shortcoming, is able to reach such heights. How can you think little of him when he is capable of so much nobility and it enthralls you to be assured that the soul of man is of infinite capacity.

These pictures that I have spoken of have a high seriousness and even a tragic cast. That is not unnatural, for the great art I value, that which has a moral implication, is serious; it seeks, whether the mind behind the hand that painted it knew it or not, it seeks to offer a clue to the mystery of being and to shed light on the various soul of man. It deals with momentous things. Life is

51

tragic and in beauty there are more tears than laughter. Man is a very strange animal, he can combine greatness of soul with many petty and discordant traits, but when he comes to produce a work of art it is from the greatness of his tortured soul that he delivers his communication.

Greatness of soul. It is this that gives a painting its deep significance. Take *The Embarkation for Cythera* by Watteau, also in the Louvre. It is a charming picture. Those graceful creatures in their pretty dresses are setting sail blithely for the island of the blessed hidden in the distant blue and in the gold dust of the sun. It is a gay, carefree scene and yet strangely suffused with melancholy, as though even while he painted the painter were conscious that joy was fleeting and unsubstantial and the bright day must end with questions that the delightful pleasures of the moment could not answer. But it is disillusion and regret that the picture suggests and that is not enough; it is a wistful rather than a tragic note, and so in the end the picture offers no more than enchantment to the eye. That is a great deal, but it does not nourish the soul.

I did not come to know modern pictures intimately till I was past early youth, and I have had to grow accustomed to them. I have had no great confidence in my judgment and with the passing years I have often changed my mind. Pictures which at one time I greatly admired have come to seem to me of not much consequence. When I was 18 a friend of mine was given a picture of a haystack and I could not make head or tail of it. It didn't look like any haystack I had ever seen and I thought it horrible. Time went by and I began to think it a very lovely little picture. It was fresh and living and the colour was beautiful. I went on seeing this picture for 40 years and the last time I saw it I found it dull, empty and commonplace. It was painted by Monet. Monet had something to tell that interested a certain period, but it was not a communication pregnant with implications, and so when he had told it and you had profited by it you found nothing more to interest you in him. To me a picture by Monet is as important now as a speakeasy after the repeal of the Volstead Act.

I look in pictures for something to excite my imagination as well as to please my eye, and I do find it in the work of some modern painters, but I am more conscious that now I give as much as I get. By a process of association I enrich them with my memories, my reading and my experience. I do not think that Utrillo is a great painter, he is certainly a very uneven one, but I have occasionally seen a picture of what is called his white period that has wrung my heart. To someone who knows Paris, those street scenes of sordid suburbs, with their air of desolation and their hostile silence, are of an infinite sadness; those humble bedraggled houses are the dwelling places of the God-forsaken and you are oppressed by the horror of their narrow, hopeless, cheese-paring lives. I would not own one of these pictures; it would be a constant reproach to me.

Then there is Gauguin. He is not a great artist either: I think his life and character more interesting than his paintings. I once wrote a fanciful description of a fruitpiece in the museum at Stockholm, but it is in his Tahitian scenes that he is most truly himself. They are deliberately stylized, but they have an idyllic character that does recall those lovely islands of the South Seas and for one who has lived in them they evoke memories of a kind of sensual content and a happiness of the spirit which the passing of time can never quite dim.

There are two artists greater than these, Degas and Cézanne, and there is one picture by each of them that I treasure in my memory. Degas was the painter of the life about him; he painted ballet-dancers and washerwomen, cafés and horse races. There is in the Louvre a picture called *L'Absinthe*, a picture of a shabby-looking man and of a wretched, sodden woman; they are sitting at a café table drinking, and in their attitudes, in their cowed sloth expose the degradation and the despair of vice. It is exquisitely painted, the composition is beautiful and the colour is lovely. It is a tragic picture of real life. It is smelly and dirty, mean and yet with a strange fire – cynical, if you like, grim, unpleasant and yet infinitely pathetic. It is a document of the period.

Now I have only one more picture to speak of and that is Cézanne's picture called, I think, *Mont St. Victoire*. I do not know where it is now. It is a picture of Cézanne's native Provence, a green picture of a hill and olive trees and little red-roofed houses; it is dusty and hot and the torrid sun has soaked up the garishness of the Mediterranean colour so that the greens are wan and the reds are pale; it is Provence. It is of course beautifully composed, for no painter of recent times has had to a greater degree than Cézanne the gift of what I can only call architectural construction, but that to the layman is no matter, he does not need to know what it is that gives him so intimate a satisfaction; to me the point of the picture is its earthiness and at the same time its spirituality, its sober truth and its tender poetry. It is Provence. It is the home of song and wine and laughter, the cradle of an ancient civilization, the land of beautiful memories and a rich culture, and the dwelling place of saints and husbandmen and black-eyed, smiling women. It is France, with its grace, its solid virtues and its love for the soil; it is France that for all its faults, so bitterly atoned for, is deathless.

PETER ARNO

It is just possible that, if I tried hard enough and wrote with assurance, I could produce a piece on the work of Peter Arno which would persuade the indulgent reader that I had the necessary qualifications to write art criticism. I believe that I could discourse upon the decision of his line, his dexterous use of mass and the boldness of his chiaroscuro as impressively as anybody else; but I have a notion that pictures are made to be looked at rather than written about, and of no pictures is this more true than of those of a draughtsman with whom the caption is often an essential element of the composition and whose aim is to make you laugh.

So the first thing I have to say is: look at these cartoons and have fun. But when I consider a product of the creative impulse I am seized with curiosity to discover what I can about the man who has thus expressed himself, and, turning over the pages of this book and studying one witty drawing after another, I have sought Peter Arno to know what he looks like and what manner of man he is. For I must tell you that when I sat down to write this introduction I had not met him.

I had been assured that he is the best-dressed man in New York. But the best-dressed man is the man whose clothes you never notice and so this characteristic gives him an elusiveness which makes the quest infinitely arduous.

I had been told also that Peter Arno is a perpetual frequenter of night clubs. Since I never go to them I felt I would never see him, but even if I went I did not suppose that I should be so fortunate as to chance upon him, for the night club is the perfect hide-out. Every night club is like every other; in the same smoke-laden air the same orchestra plays the same tune while the same couples, like sardines, canned but amorous, gyrate upon the same exiguous floor; at the same bar the same men listlessly absorb the same drinks and occasionally exchange the same wisecracks with the same bar-tender; the same socialites are always just leaving the same table to go on to the same night club a few streets off where they will sit at the same table. Place brings no diversity and when you are in a night club it is all one whether you are in New York, in Paris, in Istanbul or in Tokyo; in fact, with a little imagination you can circumnavigate the globe and experience all the educational advantages of foreign travel by keeping your feet firmly fixed on the bar of any night club in the country. But that of course you can never do, for, as though the Hound of Heaven were after you, you are impelled down the nights and down the days to flee from one devastating sameness to another.

How could I hope to find a man in the labyrinth of that innumerable repetition when his most remarkable trait, I had been told, is that there is nothing remarkable in his dress? It seemed a hope as forlorn as to look for an innuendo in the multiplication table. It occurred to me then that my only chance of finding Peter Arno was in his work, and so, faint yet pursuing, fortified by a diligent perusal of detective fiction, I returned to the study of his cartoons.

A clue presented itself. I noticed that two types often recur in his men. One is a large man with a bald head, a noble, hooked nose and a white moustache. He has a dignified presence and the complacent authority of inherited wealth. In England he would be the colonel (retired) of a crack regiment, but since he is American I take him to be the president of a corporation. Though you see him sometimes in yachting kit or in bathing costume he is more at home in a dinner jacket, but never feels entirely himself except in tails and a white tie. His eyelids, like Mona Lisa's, are a little weary, but his spirit is undaunted and his eyes gleam with concupiscence when they fall on the grapefruit breasts of the blonde and blue-eyed cuties whom a beneficent providence, in Peter Arno's drawings, has created to bring a fleeting happiness into the lives of the leaders of industry. His wife is a Daughter of the Revolution. She is stern of visage, a woman massively proportioned and swathed, under her Paris gown, in armour more to mitigate the exuberance of her charms (back and front) than to protect her virtue. For all his riches her husband stands in awe of her. No one can fail to observe that the cuties, with their vacuous stare and their turned-up nose, who grace so many of Peter Arno's drawings are surprisingly ignorant of physiology, and when they have a baby are often at a loss to account for it. I asked myself, therefore, whether that complacent shadow in the background is not thrown by Peter Arno himself, whether, if he were brought out into the open, he might not have a plausible explanation to offer for the appearance of the little stranger; and then, seized with a wild surmise, I went on to suppose that in this glamorous moustachioed man he has boldly presented his own lineaments. Is this the Peter Arno I sought?

But no sooner did the thought occur to me than I put it aside, for there is another type that occurs even more frequently in his drawings. This is a much smaller man, a man of meagre physique, bald too, but with black hair and a flowing black moustache, with a long thin nose and a bewildered gaze. He also has an eye for blonde beauty, but he is doomed to frustration, and though he likes his liquor he cannot carry it. He is not a man who loves his fireside and yet nature has so formed him that the only bliss within his reach is the domestic. He is the romantic to whom romance is irremediably denied. He is not a bank president, he is the friend of bank presidents; he is not a happy man. But he is the end of my search. The artist is modest. The artist tells the truth. This, I said to myself, this surely is Peter Arno.

And then, having built up this watertight case, this portrait of the man I had never seen, I met Peter Arno. I found to my dismay that the picture my imagination had created was wholly inaccurate. He is well-dressed, yes, but not in the flamboyant manner that would cause a convention of energetic tailors to hurl their dubious laurels at his brow. He is tall, broad-shouldered and lean. His hair is dark and neatly groomed. His manner is frank and engaging. I learned, too, that he detests night clubs and, far from frequenting them, he goes into them only rarely and then usually for the purpose of memorizing a *décor* for a cartoon.

I was a trifle appalled by the real Peter Arno, for this imposing, youthful, witty man was as different from the scraggy, desirous, timid, thwarted little fellow of the cartoons as his own brush strokes differ from those of Leonardo. Having met him, I can no longer feel that the appearance and personality of Peter Arno must remain, like that of the famous Master of the Virgin of Cologne, an insoluble mystery to tantalize the critics of after ages. I cannot help wishing, a shade too wistfully perhaps, that my original hypothesis was right, for there is a pathetic quality in that melancholy lover of the cartoons who, though winning near the goal, never, never kisses, a quality which complements the sardonic humour of these drawings and adds a nostalgic note to their powerful virility.

THE
LADY FROM POONAH

In asking me to respond to the toast of literature the President of the Royal Academy has done me a great honour, but he has put me in a very embarrassing situation. If I were responding to such a toast in another place, at a City banquet for instance, I should feel inclined to say that though in the visual arts, in musical composition, our countrymen have acquitted themselves with honour and distinction, it is in our literature that the genius of our country has found its most brilliant expression. But so that I should not be accused of presumption I should hasten to add that our fiction can do no more than hold its own with the works of the great novelists of France and Russia. But I don't think it is a patriotic bias that makes me claim that since the days of Ancient Greece no nation can boast of such a volume of lovely poetry as we have produced in this small island. The poetry that our poets have produced since Chaucer wrote *The Canterbury Tales* is one of the brightest jewels in the British crown. It is an imperishable monument to the greatness of our race.

But I am sure you will agree with me that to make an address on such lines on this occasion would be highly tactless, so I will content myself with thanking the President of the Royal Academy for the graceful and flattering way in which he has asked me to [respond] to this toast. English literature needs no words of mine to commend it. English literature speaks for itself.

So if you will allow me, I will tell you of an incident that occurred to me two or three years ago in the very portals of this august institution. I came early one afternoon to see the pictures in the summer exhibition and noticed an elderly lady, in well-cut tweeds, who was obviously waiting for someone. A glance told me that she had come up from the country for a morning's shopping and after a frugal lunch at a tea-shop was going to *do* the Academy before catching the 4.57 back to Cheltenham. A second glance told me that after completing her education in England she had returned to India to keep house for her widowed father who was in command of the troops at Poonah.

Maugham's speech given on 2 May 1951 at the Royal Academy's annual banquet in London, in reply to the toast of literature, from the typescript in the possession of The Humanities Research Center, University of Texas. A condensed version was printed in the *News Chronicle*, 3 May 1951.

Then of course I knew exactly who she was. She was the lady whom we have all heard of but very few of us have met. She was the lady who doesn't pretend to know anything about art, but knows what she likes. So of course I lost no time in getting into conversation with her. I found her most affable. She told me she was waiting for her nephew who had promised somewhat against his will to *do* the Academy with her. He'd had a job for a whole year with the British Council in Paris and now he knew all about art. He was very advanced, she added. He'd had to throw Cézanne into the discard because he was really too pretty-pretty and he was terribly worried about Picasso. He'd told her that if Picasso didn't look out he'd have to scrap him too.

'He *is* advanced,' I murmured.

And then, as though they had just occurred to her, she said the words I was waiting for.

'Of course I don't pretend to know anything about art, but I know what I like. What I always say is: A thing of beauty is a joy for ever.'

'Yes,' I replied, 'Keats said that too, but only once, and if he meant, as I think he did, that a thing of beauty is a joy for ever because it retains its beauty for ever, he was wrong. Beauty is as transitory as everything else in this world. Sometimes it has a long life, as the classic Greek sculpture has had owing to the prestige of Greek culture and owing to its representations of the human form which have provided us with an ideal of human beauty; but even Greek sculpture, owing to the acquaintance we have now made with Chinese and Negro art, has with artists themselves lost much of its appeal. It is no longer a source of inspiration. Its beauty is dying. Why d'you think,' I asked the lady, 'that movie directors no longer choose their heroes as they did twenty years ago for their classical beauty, but for their expression and such evidence as their outward seeming offers of character and personality? Because they've discovered that classical beauty has lost its attractiveness. Sometimes the life of beauty is short. We can all remember pictures and poems which gave us the authentic thrill of beauty in our youth, but from which beauty has now seeped out as water seeps out of a porous jar. Beauty depends on the climate of sensibility and this changes with the passing years. A different generation has different needs and demands a different satisfaction. We grow tired of something we know too well and ask for something new. The eighteenth century saw nothing in the painting of the Italian primitives but the fumblings of immature unskilful artists. Were they beautiful then? No. It is we who have given them their beauty and it is likely enough that the qualities we admire in them are not the qualities which appealed to the lovers of art, long since dead, who saw them when they were first painted. The first President of the Royal Academy in the second Discourse recommended Ludovico Caracci as a model for style in painting and compared him with Titian to Titian's disadvantage. Would any of us do that now? Hazlitt was a great critic and a good enough painter to paint a tolerable portrait of Charles Lamb. Of Correggio he wrote that he possessed a greater variety of excellence in the different departments of his art than any other painter. Who can think of him, he asked rhetorically, without a swimming of the head? We can. Now it isn't any good saying that these eminent persons didn't know what they were talking about; they expressed the cultivated aesthetic opinion of their time. Beauty in fact is only that which produces the specific pleasure which leads us to describe an object as beautiful during a certain period of the world's history, and it does so because it responds to certain needs of the period. It would be foolish to suppose that our opinions are any more definitive than those of our forefathers, and we may be pretty sure that our descendants will look upon them with the same perplexity as we look upon Sir Joshua's high praise of Pellegrino Tibaldi and Hazlitt's passionate admiration for Guido Reni.'

I must tell you that by this time I had become conscious that the lady to whom I had made this long speech was becoming increasingly restive and, when I stopped to take breath, she said:

'Do you know, I don't believe my nephew is coming after all. He's as brave as a lion really and he got an M.C. in the war, but I'm afraid at the last minute he funked it. I wonder if you'd *do* the Academy with me?'

'No, I don't think I will if you don't mind,' I said, 'but I'll tell you what I will do. I'll buy you a catalogue and see you safely through the turnstile.'

As we walked upstairs, for something to say, I asked her:

'Have you ever bought a picture?'

She gave me a startled look, almost as though I'd said something improper.

'Oh, no,' she said, 'it never occurred to me.'

'Why not?' I said. 'It's great fun buying a picture.'

'But I wouldn't know how to,' she cried.

'It's the simplest thing in the world,' I told her. 'You see a picture and you fall in love with it and you ask the price and if you can afford it you buy it. It's as easy as falling off a log.'

I'd evidently upset her, for she frowned a little, and then she said rather tartly:

'It's all very fine to talk of falling in love. When my dear old father was in command of the troops at Poonah, I used to get engaged to quite a number of the subalterns, not simultaneously of course, but one after the other, and when I came to the conclusion that I didn't care for them as much as I'd thought I did, I told them so frankly and we always parted good friends. But a picture's different. When you've got it, you've got it for keeps.'

'Not necessarily,' I said. 'If you fall out of love with it, you can always give it away as a wedding present, or if you don't want to do that you can put it an attic and leave it to your nephew in your will.'

'He'd be furious,' she cried. 'You see, I don't pretend to know anything about art, but I know what I like.'

'Yes, I know,' I said, 'but a thing of beauty isn't a joy for ever. Taste changes. There's always a chance, a slim chance perhaps, but a chance nevertheless, that when your nephew in the fullness of time inherits your picture he'll look upon it as the gem of his collection. He'll show it to his cronies and say: "Just look at that. It's the best picture I've got. I've been offered hundreds of pounds for it, but I wouldn't part with it for any money and I'm leaving it to the National Gallery. And would you believe it, my aunt bought it for twenty-five pounds at the Royal Academy. What a flair the old girl had."'

After that I bought her a catalogue as I'd promised and saw her through the turnstile. And even if she didn't buy a picture that afternoon I'm sure she thoroughly enjoyed the exhibition as I trust you will when in due course you are given the opportunity of seeing it.

THE
ARTIST AND THE THEATRE

I began collecting theatrical pictures two or three years before the First World War. It was pure accident. I was at that time a popular author of light comedies, and on the strength of the money they brought me, I bought the lease of a small house in Chesterfield Street. It was built in 1734 and so the lease had over eight hundred years to run. One day Hugh Lane dropped in to see me and told me that he had seen in a shop in Pimlico a theatrical picture by De Wilde which he thought uncommonly good.

'They're only asking forty-five pounds for it,' he said, 'you're a dramatist, you ought to buy it.'

I went to see it. It represented two actors in a scene from *Sylvester Daggerwood*. I liked it and bought it. Not very long afterwards, in April 1914, there was a sale at Christie's which included a theatrical picture that had belonged to Henry Irving, and because I had one I bought another. It was Zoffany's portrait of Garrick and Mrs Cibber in Otway's *Venice Preserved*, and I paid twenty-nine pounds for it; then I acquired a smaller version said to be by Benjamin West of Reynolds's huge picture of *Garrick between Tragedy and Comedy*, which is now in the possession of Lord Rothschild. I forget what it cost me, but certainly very little, for at that time nobody was much interested in such pictures. After that it was all up with me. I began to frequent sales, and whenever a theatrical picture came up which I liked I bid for it and generally got it. Foster's auction room in Pall Mall soon became a rewarding hunting-ground. Every week the walls would be thickly covered with pictures of all sorts, mostly very indifferent; and now and again I came across a single figure of an actor in costume, grimy and badly wanting restoration, but still in its original frame. I was often the only bidder, and the discouraged auctioneer knocked it down to me for a guinea or thirty shillings.

Sometimes, of course, I was unlucky. Once I saw at Christie's a Zoffany which represented Garrick as Macbeth and Mrs Pritchard as his lady, and I set my heart on having it. The bidding started slowly, and I was confident of getting it as usual for a few pounds; but to my surprise I found that a dealer

Introduction to *The Artist and the Theatre* by Raymond Mander and Joe Mitchenson. Heinemann, 1955.

I knew slightly was persistently bidding against me. We bid the picture up to a hundred pounds, to two hundred, to two hundred and fifty, which was more than had ever been paid before for one of Zoffany's theatrical pictures, and then the dealer sent me the message that he was buying the picture for the Maharajah of Baroda and his instructions were to get it at any price. I gave in and it was knocked down for two hundred and sixty pounds. But I did not only frequent auction rooms. I haunted the junk shops, the frame makers, in Soho and Chelsea, and occasionally allowed the owners to sell me for a song a De Wilde, a Hamilton or a Smirke that they had been trying to get rid of for years.

In course of time the dealers came to know that I was a collector, and whenever they came across a theatrical picture let me know. Naturally the price went up and I could no longer buy a picture for a pound or two. I think I was still the only collector, but a casual buyer often purchased one of these pictures that he had seen at a dealer's, who had had it cleaned and varnished, because it was pleasing. These casual buyers purchased the portrait of an actress in costume not because it represented her in a famous part, but because it was a picture of an attractive woman in a pretty dress. (That is why in my collection the single figures are all of men.) They paid fancy prices. It was only by chance then that I got a bargain. One of the last De Wildes I bought cost me six hundred pounds. Three or four years ago a Zoffany was sold at Sotheby's for eight hundred and fifty pounds and shortly afterwards the dealer who bought it offered it to me for two thousand. It was a satisfaction to me to be able to tell him that I already had another version of the picture and had paid two hundred pounds for it.

This may require some explanation. The artists who specialised in this form of art often painted a replica or two of the same picture. The first one I ever bought, John Bannister and Richard Suett in *Sylvester Daggerwood*, is a replica of one at the Garrick Club; and there are three of Zoffany's *Venice Preserved*. Mine is considered to be the original. I don't know how one can account for this except by supposing that when two celebrated actors were painted together each wanted a copy; and it may be that now and then an admirer ordered still another copy for himself.

Theatrical pictures are a variety of genre painting, which, as we know, became popular in the Netherlands in the first half of the seventeenth century; and it is perhaps suggestive that De Wilde, the most prolific of these painters, was himself a Dutchman. Zoffany painted portraits and conversation pieces, and theatrical portraits only as a side line; but De Wilde, so far as I know, painted very little else. Artists before them had painted scenes from plays, and there is in the Louvre a drawing by Claude Gillet which represents such a scene; but before Zoffany only a few artists like Hogarth, Hayman and Wilson had experimented in painting actual portraits of actors in character. I doubt whether anyone can now tell whether the idea of doing this was owing to the pardonable vanity of the actors, who wanted their ephemeral fame to be thus perpetuated, or whether the idea was an artist's. Anyway, it was Zoffany who started the real vogue that quickly spread. George III, who, according to Hazlitt, was fond of low comedy, commissioned him to paint a scene from Frederick Reynolds's *Speculation* in which Quick, Munden and Lewis were introduced.

I have mentioned only a few of the artists who practised this modest form of art; but there were a good many others, of less talent, who took advantage of the prevailing fashion to earn a few honest guineas. The Garrick Club has a great number, I had over forty, and there must be many more scattered here and there in private houses. And it was not only oil paintings that were produced to satisfy the public demand; De Wilde, evidently to suit patrons of small means, produced in quantity single figures of actors and actresses in water-colour. They are full of charm. The Garrick Club has so many that it has been able to paper the walls of a staircase with them. I had thirty-three myself.

One may ask oneself why this vogue should have been so great as to occasion so enormous a production. I can only suggest as an answer that during the period in which these pictures were painted the English took a passionate interest in the theatre. The public was small and there was a constant change of bill. The repertoire seems to have consisted for the most part of Shakespeare, stock plays and farces. Audiences knew the classical plays well, and the farces were seldom of merit; so it was natural enough that they should take more interest in the players than the play. Hazlitt would not have troubled to write now and then a careful analysis of a popular actor's performance in a well-known play if he had not been assured that the subject was of concern to his readers. It is likely enough that this passion for the stage should have made patrons who could afford it wish to have a picture of a favourite actor in a part that he had made his own (there are many portraits by various artists of Garrick as Richard III), and for the less affluent there were the water-colours that could be bought for a few shillings apiece. The vogue died, I surmise, when photography gave the public an even cheaper way of gratifying a very human desire. In my youth there was still a brisk sale for such photographs, and my own chimney-piece was adorned with one of the lovely Jane Harding and one of the incomparable Eleonora Duse. Now that the fan can cut pictures of the stars of the moment from the illustrated papers the demand has ceased. The pin-up girl of today is the last bastard descendant of the theatrical pictures of Zoffany and De Wilde.

My collection was second only to that of the Garrick Club, and I had spent so many years making it that I was grieved to think that it would be dispersed at my death in Christie's auction rooms. Such a collection can never be made again. Now, it had always seemed to me a shocking thing that so great a capital as London should not have a national theatre such as there is in Paris, Vienna and Berlin. Such an institution would be a worthy monument to British drama and would give an opportunity to the foreigners who visit our country to discover that it has produced not only one dramatist of genius but many of no small merit. It might serve also to create a school of dramatists and a school of actors good enough to revive interest, now sadly diminished, in the spoken drama. When at last the long efforts of a number of enthusiastic persons, striving indefatigably year after year to overcome the indifference of governments and the apathy of the public, seemed likely to be crowned with success and a national theatre would be built, it struck me that by presenting my pictures to it I might achieve my object of keeping them together. Theatres in the eighteenth century, with their rococo decorations, with the red curtains to the boxes, with their immense chandeliers, had a glamour which put you in a comfortable state of mind to enjoy the play you were about to witness. The theatres they build now are severely functional; you can see from all parts of them what is happening on the stage; the seats are comfortable and there are abundant exits, so that you run small chance of being burnt to death. But they are cold. They are apt to make you feel that you have come to the playhouse to undergo an ordeal rather than to enjoy an entertainment. It seemed to me that my pictures in the foyer and on the stairs of a new theatre would a trifle mitigate the austerity of the architect's design. I offered them to the Trustees of the National Theatre and they were good enough to accept them. Through the kindness of Sir Leigh Ashton the oil pictures have been admirably exhibited at the Victoria and Albert Museum. I still house the water-colours till the Trustees, whose property they are, find themselves ready to take them.

This handsome volume, to which these words I have written are meant to serve as an introduction, owes its origin to the enthusiasm and formidable industry of two young men, Raymond Mander and Joe Mitchenson. They have put an immense amount of work into it. They have pored over dusty volumes, searched collections, examined innumerable faded playbills, read old criticisms of plays and looked into the records of sales at auction rooms. They have spared no pains to make their information accurate. They have followed clues with all the pertinacity of a detective of fiction; and so have been able to identify an obscure actor in a forgotten play, and in some cases have even been able to quote the very words he was saying at the moment the artist chose to picture the scene. They have corrected mistakes in attribution; they have been able to decide which was the original painting and which the replica. They are true lovers of the theatre, and their labour has been a labour of love. I like to think that it will not have been entirely wasted, for what they have learnt is surely not without interest, since these pictures, which have been so admirably photographed, will eventually find their permanent place in the National Theatre and there, I trust, give pleasure to generation after generation of playgoers.

ON
HAVING MY PORTRAIT
PAINTED

One day, somewhere in the thirties, I received a letter from Marie Laurencin in which she said that she would like to paint a portrait of me. I answered that I should be highly flattered, but felt it only right to remind her that I was not a pretty young thing with the black eyes of a gazelle, a rosebud mouth, and a pink and white complexion, but an elderly party with a sallow skin and a lot of wrinkles. To this she replied that that was no matter, but she would like me to come in a dressing-gown because she didn't know how to paint a coat. A date was fixed for the first sitting, and because I was too timid to walk through the streets of Paris in a bright blue dressing-gown, I carried it over my arm. I sat to Marie Laurencin for four long afternoons during which she told me the story of her life and loves. I have seldom enjoyed myself more. Toward the end of the fourth afternoon she put down her brushes and, leaning back, looked at the canvas on which she had been working. '*Vous savez,*' she said, '*on se plaint toujours que mes portraits ne sont pas ressemblants. Je ne peux pas vous dire à quel point je m'en fous.*' That may be translated: 'You know people always complain that my portraits aren't likenesses. I must tell you that I don't care a —.' I will leave the reader to add the last word himself. Then she took the canvas off the easel and said: 'Here you are. It's a present.' I don't think that anyone could suppose that I ever looked like that, but it was a charming gesture on Marie Laurencin's part and I am grateful for it.

I can't believe that the features of any private person have been more often drawn, painted, etched, and sculptured than mine. By private person I mean someone who has not won distinction in politics, war, on the stage, in films, or by exalted station. If posterity should want to know what I looked like it will have ample opportunity, but it may well be that posterity will have more important things to concern itself with.

It all began many years ago. In 1904 I spent a year in Paris. I was then an obscure but promising novelist. I made the acquaintance of a young Irish painter, Gerald Kelly by name, who had a studio on the Left Bank of the Seine. He was a voluble and amusing talker; I am a good listener. We became great friends. It must have been two or three years later, when we were both again living in England, that he asked me to sit to him for a portrait. I had never been asked to do that before and was delighted. I do not know what happened to the portrait Gerald Kelly painted then; it may be that he was not satisfied with it and destroyed it. The years went by. I was no longer a promising but obscure novelist: I was a popular playwright. In 1908 I had four plays running in London at the same time. Gerald Kelly painted a portrait of me which is here illustrated[1]; of all the portraits he has painted of me, this is that which I like best. Later he did another portrait called *The Jester*, which was bought by the Tate Gallery. In all he has painted eleven portraits of me. I need hardly add that in due course he became president of the Royal Academy and painted the state portraits of King George VI and his consort, Queen Elizabeth.

I have an idea that there are two sorts of portrait-painters, the painter who is chiefly concerned with his sitter and the painter who is chiefly concerned with himself. The object of the first is to produce an exact likeness of his sitter. Supercilious critics condemn portraits of this kind as photographic and claim that they have nothing to do with art. For all I know they are right; but what they forget is that with the passage of time, when the sitter's clothes have become costume, so that the picture has become a period piece, it may have a decorative value which is not without charm. The painter of the second sort is not particularly concerned to produce a speaking likeness of his sitter: to satisfy the client, he may take some pains to describe on canvas the impression the sitter has made on him, but his real use, the sitter's use, I mean, is to provide an essential element in the general pattern which will result in a work of art.

I have twice been painted by artists who had some such idea. One is Edouard MacAvoy (a Frenchman despite his Scottish name) and the other is Graham Sutherland. It was late in the thirties that MacAvoy asked me to sit to him. He made elaborate drawings of my head and my hands, but then war broke out and the sittings were suspended. I did not see him again till after peace was declared. He told me then that he had finished the picture and was going to exhibit it in the Autumn Salon. This he did and it created something of a sensation. I have been told that Braque greatly admired it; he is reported to have said: 'I have only one criticism to make. The left side of the face is slightly realistic.' I own the picture and I find it a very easy one to live with.

It was soon after the war was over that I made the acquaintance of Graham Sutherland. He had rented a house on the Riviera not far from where I live and I met him at various parties. I knew very little about his work, but I had been told that he was talented and I discovered for myself that he had great personal charm. (Oddly enough all the painters and sculptors I have had to do with had it.) I noticed that Sutherland looked at me a good deal, but I paid no particular attention to that, and it was a surprise to me when a friend came to me one day and told me that Graham Sutherland had asked him to inquire

---

[1] A reproduction of it forms the frontispiece of this collection.

whether I would sit to him for a portrait. I gladly consented. He had never painted a portrait before and so this was in the nature of an amusing experiment. His method, again somewhat to my surprise, was the same as Edouard MacAvoy's; he made careful drawings of my head and my hands, which he preferred not to show me, and I saw nothing of the portrait till it was entirely finished. The experiment succeeded, and I think it is no exaggeration when I say that this portrait made Graham Sutherland's fortune. Since then he has painted several excellent portraits, but I do not know that he has ever painted a better one than mine.

On
Selling my Collection
of
Impressionist and Modern
Pictures

You would not have been invited to come here this evening if the owner of a restaurant called La Colombe d'Or on the hills behind Nice had not had a liking for pictures. Painters found it pleasant to work there and it suited them that the proprietor was not unwilling to take a picture as payment for the board and lodging with which he provided them. In course of time he was able to hang pictures on the walls of the large room which served to seat the customers who came from Nice or Monte Carlo to lunch or dine. The food was good and the pictures, so unlike what one was used to, were an attraction. The artists began to be talked about and bold men actually bought their pictures. The owner of the Colombe d'Or was offered good money for those he had, but aware that they brought him customers, he refused to sell.

One morning when he and his staff awoke to enter upon the day's work he had a shock. During the night burglars had stripped the walls and not a single picture was left. The theft caused a sensation. Now, the Mayor of my village of St. Jean knew that I had a collection of pictures and it may be that he thought it would not be to his credit if they were stolen. He called me up and said he would like to come to my house to see what precautions I had taken to keep them in safety. I said I would be glad to see him. He came. I have a large old-fashioned house with French windows and I conducted the Mayor from room to room. When I had shown him all there was to see he smiled and said, 'I have never seen a house that so obviously invites robbers to enter and steal. If you want to keep your pictures you must do something about it'. 'What?' I asked. 'There's only one thing you can do', he answered. 'You must

Preface to auction *Catalogue*, Sotheby & Co., 10 April 1962.

build a strong-room and keep your pictures in it.' I had not bought pictures for thirty years to keep them in a strong-room, but I saw his point and somewhat unwillingly and at considerable expense I turned one of my bedrooms into a strong-room.

I am often away from home, sometimes for a few days, sometimes for several months. Before I leave I have to send for an electrician to take away the top lights, take the pictures out of their frames and put them in the strong-room. It is an irksome business and I don't know that it is very good for the pictures. When I come home the electrician has again to be sent for, the pictures have to be taken out of the strong-room, put back in their frames and hung back in their appointed places. Even if I were only going out to dinner I could not be sure that a thief would not take the opportunity to steal one or two of my pictures. For many years they had given me great pleasure; now they were an anxiety. I decided to sell them. I hope that you will get as much pleasure out of such as you buy tonight as I have got out of them in the past.

ON
WRITERS
AND
WRITING

ON
WRITING FOR THE FILMS

I know very well that it is unbecoming in me to express my opinion on the subject of writing for the screen, since I have busied myself with the matter only for a few weeks. But in these weeks I have learned a good deal and I pretend only to jot down my first impressions. Everyone now allows that the pictures have reached a stage where they can no longer be treated with a contemptuous shrug of the shoulders. If you are of a pedagogic turn of mind – as apparently many authors are in these days – and wish to improve your fellow men, there is no medium which gives you a greater opportunity. You read your newspaper cursorily and what goes in at one eye goes out of the other. But what you see at the pictures impresses you with peculiar force. It may be deplored that the novelist and the playwright should think it their business to preach; but apparently they often do, too often, perhaps; and they are fortunate enough to find many people who are willing to take them with the utmost seriousness. They can certainly expound their views of life more effectively on the screen than between the covers of a book or even within the three hours' traffic of the stage. The screen is an unrivalled method of propaganda. This was widely realized during the war, but the means employed were ingenuous and sometimes defeated their own object. Little allowance was made for the frailty of human nature, and the pill of useful information was so little coated with sugar that the wretched public refused to swallow it. I shall not forget seeing a picture in a remote province of China which showed the President of the French Republic shaking hands with the Minister of Public Works. This was designed to impress the wily Oriental with the greatness of France, but I do not believe it achieved its object. If on the other hand a writer aspires to be no more, and no less, than an artist, the film is not unworthy of his consideration. There is no reason why the picture should not be a work of art.

But on this question the attitude of many of those who are concerned with the production of pictures is somewhat depressing. For if you wander about the studios you will find that some of the more intelligent men you meet are frankly pessimistic. They will tell you that the whole business is no more than a trick. They deny that there can be any art in a production that is dependent on a machine. It is true that for the most part the attempts that are made at an artistic result support this argument. There are directors who desire to be artistic. It is pathetic to compare the seriousness of their aim with the absurdity of their achievement. Unfortunately you cannot be artistic by wanting to be so; but the lamentable results of these endeavours, often so strenuous and so well-meaning, must be ascribed rather to incapacity in those who make them than to unsuitability in the material. You will not achieve art in a picture by composing pompous titles or by bolstering up a sordid story with the introduction of a Russian ballet or a fairy tale. The irrelevant is never artistic. The greatest pest of the moment is the symbol. I do not know how it was introduced into the pictures but I judge that it was introduced successfully; the result is that now symbolism is dragged in by the hair. Nothing, of course, can be more telling, nothing has greater possibilities; but it must be used with tact, appositeness, and moderation. To my mind there is something grotesque in the way in which an obvious symbol gambols, like a young elephant, through the middle of a perfectly commonplace story. No, the gentlemen who direct pictures will not make them works of art in this fashion. I think they would be well advised to set about the matter more modestly. There is a good deal of spade work to be done first. The sets might occupy their attention. They have yet to discover the aesthetic value of simplicity. They will learn in due course that the eye is wearied by a multiplicity of objects. They will not crowd their rooms with furniture and knick-knacks. They will realize the beauty of an empty wall.

Then I think they can profitably occupy themselves with the subject of line. It is distressing to see, judging by the results, how little thought is given to the beauty that may be obtained from graceful attitudes and harmonious grouping. The lover can clasp his beloved to his heart in such a manner as to make an exquisite pattern; but unless he is a very fortunate young man, whom the gods especially favour, he will not do this by the light of nature. I have been amazed to see how often the lovely heroine has been allowed to be photographed in a position that makes her look like a sack of potatoes. I venture to think also that those directors who pursue beauty (I have nothing to say about those who merely want to produce a picture that will bring in a million dollars: I have no doubt they know their business much better than I do) might explore more systematically the photographic possibilities of atmospheric effect. The camera is capable of a great deal in this direction, and the delight of every audience at the most modest attempts in this field, such as scenes by moonlight, show that the public would not be unresponsive. There is immense scope for the director who wishes to make beautiful pictures; but the Reinhardt of the screen has not yet arrived.

It will appear from these observations that I think the director should be definitely an interpreter of the author. Since I am a writer it is perhaps natural that I should have little patience with his claim to be a creative artist. I think he has assumed this impressive rôle because in the past he has too often been asked to deal with material which was totally unsuited to the screen. He could produce a tolerable picture only by taking the greatest liberties with the story he was given, and so he got into the habit of looking upon the story as a peg upon which to hang his own inventions. He had no exalted idea of the capacity of his audience (the commonest phrase upon his lips was: Remember that my public doesn't consist of educated people. It is not a two dollar public it is a ten and fifteen cent public); and – if I may say so without offence – he was no genius. The stories he offered to an eager world were inane. For the most part the motive was absurd, the action improbable, the characterization idiotic; and yet so novel was the appeal, so eager the desire for this new amusement, that the public accepted all these defects with a tolerant shrug of the shoulders. The mistake the director made was in supposing the public did not see that they were defects. The most successful showmen have always credited the public with shrewdness. Now that the novelty of the pictures has worn off, the public is no longer willing to take these defects so humorously. They find them inconvenient. It seems to me that a few years ago I did not see bored people in a cinema: now I see them all around me. They raise their voices in derision. It is refreshing to hear the burst of laughter which greets a pretentious title.

The picture companies are discovering, what the theatrical managers might have told them long since, that no matter how eminent your stars and how magnificent your production, if your story is bad the public will not bother with you. The picture companies have put a bold face on the matter. They have swallowed their medicine with fortitude. They have gone to the highways and hedges and constrained the author to come in. They have brushed aside his pleas that he had no wedding garment: the feast was set.

The story is now all the thing.

It remains to be seen how the author will meet the situation. I do not think it will be surprising if he does not create very great works of art, for they come as the gods will, sparingly, and should be accepted with surprise and gratitude, but not demanded as a right. It is very good to receive a barrel of caviare now and then, but for the daily meal one should be satisfied with beef or mutton. At all events there will be no excuse for the author if his stories are not coherent and probable, if his psychology (to use the somewhat pompous term by which the play of motive is known in the world of pictures) is not reasonable, and his characters and the incidents he chooses to illustrate them not true to life.

In the past probably the worst pictures have been those which were made out of plays. Because there are certain similarities between moving pictures and plays it was thought that a successful play would make a good picture and, what is more eccentric, that an unsuccessful play might do the same. The fact that a play had been acted in London or New York was supposed to be a valuable asset, and for all I know this may be a fact. But it was constantly found either that the play offered insufficient material, or material of a character that was useless on the screen. We have all seen pictures purporting to be versions of well-known plays and found them most outrageous travesties. And what is more, they were dull. The fact suggests itself that the play as a play is seldom suited for the screen. When you write a play you take an idea from a certain angle. You quickly learn how much you have to eliminate, how ruthlessly you must compress, and how rigidly you must stick to your point. But when the result of these efforts comes to the screen only a bare skeleton remains. The director is not to be so bitterly blamed when he claims that he has had to invent a story to clothe these naked bones. The technique of the modern stage is very sharply defined, and to my mind the modern play as it stands has very little to give the pictures. The moving picture much more suggests the plays of the Elizabethans. But of course an idea can be looked at in all sorts of ways and there is no reason why a story which has proved effective on the stage should not prove equally effective on the screen. It must be written entirely anew from that standpoint. I think a writer might make a good picture from a theme upon which he has already written a good play, but he will probably need incidents other than those which he has used in the play, and, it may be, different characters. He is absurd if he expects real invention to be done by the scenario writer to whom the management who has bought his play will entrust the work of arranging it for the screen. That is work that he alone can do. No one can know his idea as well as he, and no one can be so intimately acquainted with his characters.

I think there is more to be said for the screen version of novels, since here the case is reversed and it is not a matter of expansion and elaboration but of selection. I do not see why very good pictures should not be made from novels. They will serve as illustrations for those who have read them, and may induce those who have not to do so. This may be a good enough thing. It depends on the novel. For myself I look forward to the time when, the present dislike of costume having been overcome, all the great novels of our literature are shown on the screen. I hope, however, that the scenarios which must be prepared for this purpose will be devised by a writer who is not only acquainted with the technique of the film but is also a man of letters and of taste.

But in my opinion all this in relation to the screen is by the way. I venture to insist that the technique of writing for the pictures is not that of writing for the stage nor that of writing a novel. It is something betwixt and between. It has not quite the freedom of the novel, but it certainly has not the fetters of the stage. It is a technique of its own, with its own conventions, its own limitations, and its own effects. For that reason I believe that in the long run it will be found futile to adapt stories for the screen from novels or from plays – we all know how difficult it is to make even a passable play out of a good novel – and that any advance in this form of entertainment which may eventually lead to something artistic, lies in the story written directly for projection on the white sheet.

NOVELIST
OR BOND SALESMAN

xxx, Beacon Street, Boston,
The Twenty Third of September,
Nineteen Hundred and Twenty Four.

My dear Mr Maugham:–

I trust that you will pardon a total stranger writing to you and will give a few minutes of your time to answering a question which I am going to put to you. I am sure that you are very busy and I would not take the liberty of asking your advice if I were not fully determined to take it. To cut a long story short my son is about to leave Harvard and has determined to adopt a literary career. His intention is to write chiefly fiction and I should be very grateful if you would tell me in a few words what you would recommend him to do now. I am anxious to do everything in my power to assist him.

Cordially yours,
Frances Van Buren Hale

Hotel Gotham,
New York City,
Sept. 27, 1924.

My dear Mrs Hale:–

Give your son one thousand dollars a year for five years and tell him to go to the devil.

Yours very faithfully,
W. S. Maugham

xxx, Beacon Street, Boston,
The Thirtieth of September,
Nineteen Hundred and Twenty Four.

My dear Mr Maugham:–

I am entirely at a loss to understand your answer to my letter. I do not think that my request was unreasonable and I cannot think it deserved a reply which if I hesitate to call uncivil you will not be surprised if I consider strangely flippant in a writer of your standing in the literary world. I regret that I troubled you and beg to remain

Yours truly,
Frances Van Buren Hale

Hotel Gotham,
New York City,
Oct. 2, 1924.

My dear Mrs Hale:–

I am much grieved that you were displeased with my answer. I had no wish to be impolite and I was very much in earnest; I was brief, which I thought you wished me to be, and I gave you advice which I knew to be direct and which I thought was sensible. Your son is about to leave Harvard and therefore may be presumed to possess at least the elements of a liberal education; I can imagine no better grounding for anyone who desires to be a writer, and from your letter I judge that he has been brought up in easy circumstances. He will doubtless have spent most of his life among ladies and gentlemen. This is a class which from a literary standpoint rests now under a cloud and I daresay it merits the contempt of that large body of writers who do not belong to it; but after all it ventures still to exist (though judging from the plays I have lately seen in New York and the novels I have read you would hardly suspect it) and it is well for the writer to know its habits and customs. It is possible even that he may wish to write about it. I am prepared to believe that life is more significant in a delicatessen store than in an apartment on Park Avenue and that the emotions of a truck driver are more subtle than those of a person of quality; but there *are* persons of quality and there *are* apartments on Park Avenue and the writer is wise who regards nothing human as alien to him.

So far so good.

Your son, I suppose, has led a sheltered life and at his age he can hardly have much knowledge of the world. I do not know how you can better help him to acquire this than by taking the advice I gave you. On a thousand dollars a year he cannot starve, but if he is of an adventurous disposition (and unless he is he will not desire to be a writer) he will often find himself penniless and so obliged to do whatever he can to get his dinner. That is not bad training. On this sum he can travel all over the world, but only under conditions which will throw him in contact with all sorts and kinds of men. He will not be able to afford the luxury of respectability. Besides, in telling him to go to the devil you will have explained to him that you mean him to attach the widest possible

75

meaning to that hackneyed phrase. If he has any spirit he will soon find an infinite number of ways and means to carry out your suggestion and in five years he will have gathered experience and an acquaintance with men and women which cannot fail to be of great value to him as a writer. If at the end of this period he cannot write then you must console yourself with the reflection that he lacks what no thought of yours nor advice of mine can give him: talent.

Yours very faithfully,
W.S. Maugham

xxx, Beacon Street, Boston,
October the Fifth,
Nineteen Hundred and Twenty Four.

Dear Mr Maugham:–

I am sorry if I seemed a little abrupt but I will frankly confess that I could make neither head nor tail of your first letter. Of course I see now that you had no wish to be discourteous or flippant. But all the same I do not think I quite agree with the things you say. Surely it is not necessary for a writer to live in an extraordinary manner any more than it is necessary for a violinist to wear long hair. Miss Austen wrote her admirable novels without ever leaving the respectable circle in which she was born and Mr Henry James whose novels I am sure you appreciate as highly as I do both in England and America never to my knowledge moved in any world but that to which he was entitled by his birth and position. It has been my privilege to know Mrs Wharton for many years and though she has lived so long in France I can vouch from personal knowledge for the fact that she has never ceased to be a refined and accomplished gentlewoman. I cannot help thinking this proves that there is no reason why a writer with talent should not write a successful book without taking such a hazardous course as you propose for my son.

But I daresay I did not put my original question quite clearly. What I really wanted your advice about was more the technique of novel writing if you understand what I mean. This is a matter on which a young writer naturally stands in need of guidance and I can only say on my behalf as well as on my son's that I should be sincerely grateful for any hints you can give him.

Yours most cordially,
Frances Van Buren Hale

Hotel Gotham,
New York City,
Oct. 10, 1924.

Dear Mrs Hale:–

I am somewhat embarrassed to know how to answer your letter, since in the last seventeen years I have written but four novels and so can only look upon myself as an amateur: I am sure that there are a great many people who are much better qualified than me to give your son hints on this difficult matter.

All I can usefully do is to tell you what is my own practice, and the first thing that strikes me is that I have no habitual practice; it seems to me that every novel must be written in an entirely different fashion, and so far as I am concerned each one is in a way no more than an experiment. Each subject needs a different treatment, a different attitude, and even a different manner of writing. The only rule I know which is always valid is to stick to your point like grim death. Much harm has been done to the art of fiction by the opinion widely held some years ago that the novel was a suitable vehicle for ventilating every sort of view and advocating any kind of theory. Writers who wanted to preach sermons, urge reforms, or castigate abuses threw their ideas into the form of fiction. They produced a large number of very tedious novels. I cannot help thinking that to entertain is sufficient ambition for the novelist, and it is certainly one which is hard to achieve; if he can tell a good story and create characters that are fresh and living he has done enough to make the reader grateful. I certainly find in myself no urge to reform, admonish, or instruct my fellow men, and if I desire information about town planning or the Montessori system I shall not look for it in the pages of a novel.

You will not have failed to notice that many novels are written which have every possible excellence and yet are quite unreadable. I hope you will not think it a wilful eccentricity when I tell you that I look upon readableness as the highest merit that a novel can have. They say that it is better for women to be good than to be clever; that is a point upon which I have never been able to make up my mind; but I am quite sure that it is better for a novel to be readable than to be good and clever. I have often wondered what it is exactly that gives a book this quality. I will not tell you all the conclusions I have come to but only one or two points which seem to me to tend to that admirable result.

I think first of all that the writer is wise to be brief. I like a novel which can be read at a sitting and for my part, when I am writing one, I use every device I know to persuade the reader to do this. Then I think he should pay greater attention to his form than English and American novelists – influenced by the heresy that the novel is a rag-bag into which can be thrown any matter that comes along – habitually do. If so many novels nowadays did not start without a beginning and leave off without an ending it would seem absurd to point out that a good novel should have a beginning, a middle, and an end, and all its parts should be duly balanced. A novel should have an inner harmony and there is no reason why the reader should be deprived of the delight which he may obtain from a beautiful proportion. In this connection I strongly recommend your son to read Carl Van Vechten's *The Tattooed Countess*. He will find in it a model of form which alone makes the book a pleasure to read; and he will find also ingenious characterization and an enchanting humour. He cannot read it attentively without obtaining from it valuable instruction, profit and edification. It is a perfect example of perhaps the most difficult book to write: the light novel.

I think the writer is well advised who writes simply. I would have him use the plainest words and put them in the most natural order. I have no patience with the writers who employ bizarre constructions and make a parade of unusual epithets; nothing goes out of fashion so quickly as affectation nor is anything so stilted as the modish phrase of the year before last. I know one eminent novelist who spends much time studying all manner of dictionaries in order to find unexpected words. I cannot imagine a more trivial occupation. I have noticed that the writers who use these odd and extraordinary words do not always know their meaning. I knew another writer, now happily dead and forgotten, who was so eager to be distinguished that he wrote 'ends and odds' for 'odds and ends'. Let not your son be afraid of the hackneyed phrase; it may very well be the most suitable. Above all he should be clear. I do not think the writer has a right to ask the reader to puzzle over his meaning. If he knows it himself he can put it in plain terms; if he is unwilling to do this he must be very sure that it is profound enough to repay the reader's trouble when he has got to the bottom of it. Nothing is so tiresome as the obscurity which envelops a commonplace. But let not your son think that if he writes soberly, clearly, and plainly he must eschew beauty: Swift achieved an admirable style by using the simplest words and by putting them in the most natural order. It is not the resounding epithet which makes good English, but the accurate and sensitive ear.

I am afraid that these suggestions will seem unsatisfactory and haphazard to you. They are what immediately occurred to me; but of course the subject is complicated and you must not for a moment think that I imagine I have said all that there is to be said about it.

> Yours very faithfully,
> W.S. Maugham

> *xxx, Beacon Street, Boston,*
> *The Thirteenth of October,*
> *Nineteen Hundred and Twenty Four.*

Dear Mr Maugham:–

It is very good of you to have written me such a long and careful letter, but since I wrote to you last my son has decided to go into the bond business. I do not suppose that you will leave this country without coming to Boston and when you do Mr Hale and I will have much pleasure in making your acquaintance. I shall be At Home on the first and third Wednesdays of the month all through the winter.

> Yours most cordially,
> Frances Van Buren Hale

P.S. I am surprised at your writing *than me*. Surely it should be *than I*.

ON
PREFACES, CRITICS
AND
A NOVEL

When I considered how to write this preface I discovered that, never having attempted anything of the kind before, I did not in the least know in what manner to set about it. I wanted with a few suitable phrases to put the reader in an amiable frame of mind, so that he should enter in a good humour upon the acquaintanceship of a book which had interested me. A preface should incline him, before he starts, to surrender himself to the author's point of view, and for the moment accept the attitude towards life which is presented to him as true. For this is the demand the author makes; he does not say, This and that are so, but, I see them like this, and my truth, not absolute truth, is what matters, and if you don't like it you can lump it. Well, of course, this claim, reasonable though it is, must be insinuated into the reader's mind with address, and, conscious of my inexperience, I sought for models. The French have a natural gift for such things. I remembered that I had frequently read graceful little prefaces in which some French man of letters had introduced to the public the novel of a younger writer, and I had been taken by the skill with which so often the modest task was performed. But in the remote island on which I write, though the cicadas are making an infernal racket in the olive-trees and the sea is still glittering in the sun, I can find nothing to my purpose, and so am thrown on my own resources. Fortunately, among the books I have brought with me is Borrow's *Bible in Spain*; I had not read it for many years, and it seemed to me that it was just the kind of reading which would suit long mornings spent on the beach. The preface starts with these words·

> It is very seldom that the preface of a work is read; indeed, of late years most books have been sent out into the world without any. I deem it, however, advisable to write a preface, and to this I humbly call the attention of the

---

Preface to *Two Made Their Bed* by Louis Marlow. Heinemann, 1929.

courteous reader, as its perusal will not a little tend to the proper understanding and appreciation of these volumes.

Though I can hardly persuade myself that the perusal of this short note will not a little tend to the proper understanding and appreciation of this volume, I will bear in mind that the preface of a book is seldom read, and therefore take my courage in both hands. It is obviously not my business to offer a criticism of this novel. To read about books is, like playing patience, an agreeable pastime, and if the critic is a man of character or humour (it is not easy to be both) it is often a very agreeable one indeed, but I have never been able to persuade myself that it is anything more than a pastime; for the only thing that matters to me about a book is what it signifies to me. If I think the critic is a man of sense – by which I suppose I mean, if I have found by experience that his judgment on the whole agrees with mine – I am glad to have his recommendation; but all I want him to say is, Read this, or Don't. Why should I bother my head with what he thinks about it besides? I do not want him to come between me and the book; he may have seen in it all kinds of subtle things which I am incapable of seeing, but why should I care? The meaning of a book is what it means to me, and if to this I add the meaning it has for the critic, I am reading another book and not that which the author has written. I am content that a critic should point out the way to me, but I do not wish him to describe the interesting objects I shall see by the wayside. I think we are all hampered in our appreciation of the classics of literature by the consciousness at the back of our heads of what the critics of the past, great and little, have thought of them. It is a curious experience to read one of these celebrated works – *King Lear*, say, or *Don Quixote* – as though one had never heard of it before. The results are often very surprising.

Therefore, before I leave the reader to form his own opinion of this book I will not do more than draw his attention to a point which very nearly escaped me, for, though it is an integral point of the author's scheme, he has touched upon it so discreetly that there is a danger of its being entirely missed. It is as though he had allowed the most important character in his story never to make an appearance before the footlights, but to conduct the action only and always from the wings. The point is the great, the insinuating, and the overwhelming significance of money in the affairs of life. It is the string with which a sardonic destiny directs the motions of its puppets. It is like the monotonous, enervating, and tremulous music to which, in their coloured and splendid dresses, move the Javanese dancers. With their arms and their long slim hands they make quick sudden gestures, as though they sought to escape into freedom, but it is merely the fluttering of leaves on the branches of a tree, and the music, insistent and menacing, chains them to its relentless rhythm.

In most novels the characters live in a world in which money hardly counts, and, even if they are poor, they always have enough to go where they like and come when they want to. The loss of it never seems seriously to affect their behaviour, and they can be ruined without lacking a bus fare. Though the hero, by a realistic touch, may not be able to afford a dinner, this, surprisingly enough, does not lessen the ardour of his passion for the heroine. But here you will find something very different, and something (for what this is worth) very like life, for money matters vitally affect the persons of this story, the relations between them, and their attitude. It is pathetic and grim and terrible to observe how the want of a few pounds can influence, not only their actions, but their feelings. For money is a sixth sense, without which you cannot make full use of the other five. A vast deal of nonsense has been written about the value of money; in this book you will find sense. Here, to my mind, is its interest; here is its originality.

THE HOUSE
WITH
THE GREEN SHUTTERS

The fame of George Douglas Brown rests on one novel. The author of *The House with the Green Shutters* was born at Ochiltree, in the County of Ayrshire, on 26 January 1869; he died in London at the house of his friend Andrew Melrose on 28 August 1902. Shortly after his death a memoir of him was written by Cuthbert Lennox, and it is from this and from the reminiscences of Andrew Melrose that I have gathered the information that I now set before the reader. But it is not easy, either from the memoirs or the reminiscences, to tell what sort of a man he was. George Douglas – it is more convenient to call him by the name by which readers knew him – was ill-favoured. He was short-sighted and wore spectacles. He seems to have taken a pride in the shabbiness of his dress. On one occasion, when he was at Oxford, Dr Jowett, the Master of Balliol, asked him to a breakfast at which James Anthony Froude was present. During the course of it Froude turned to the Master and said: 'Our young friend over there is strangely like our old friend —'. Then, after a while again looking at George Douglas, he added: 'You know, Jowett, we always used to say that — was the ugliest man we knew'. Douglas is said to have closely resembled his father, and his father is described as slight of build, below rather than above the middle height; his features were small and sharp, his hair dark, his eyes black, keen and full of meaing.

Andrew Melrose says that Douglas's conversation was incisive and significant. He seems to have been a great talker, argumentative and dogmatic, with a gift for sarcasm and a Rabelaisian humour. He impressed everyone he met by his intense seriousness. He was reserved and his manner was rough, but when you had got over this you discovered that he lacked neither geniality nor kindliness. A shy, lonely man, he made acquaintances more easily than he made friends. Neither the birth nor the circumstances of Douglas's short life were such as to favour the cultivation of those graces that

---

Preface to *The House with the Green Shutters* by George Douglas. Oxford University Press, World's Classics, 1938.

make human intercourse agreeable. His father was a farmer.

> The farm was one of about two hundred acres. It was worked by a single pair of horses, as it consisted chiefly of rough grazing land. With a byre of about thirty cows, it was, like many of its neighbours, principally a dairy farm, producing milk, butter, and cheese.

George Douglas went to the village school and then, having passed the sixth standard, was put to work. For some time he was employed at the pit-head at Trabbock. Then, hearing that a schoolmate whose parents were as poor as his own had gone to a famous secondary school, Ayr Academy, he suggested that he should be sent to it too. This was arranged, and he stayed there till he was eighteen. A bursary enabled him to go to Glasgow University. At Drumsmudden (the name of his father's farm) a heifer was fattened and sold for him every year and he got the proceeds. During the vacations he worked in the fields. He ended his career at Glasgow by winning the Snell Exhibition. This gave him £130 a year for three years with the obligation to reside and study at Balliol. Here, considerably older than most of his fellow undergraduates, he was ill-at-ease and unhappy. His poverty made life difficult for him. He felt he was wasting his time and should never have come.

On leaving, he settled in London to make his living by his pen. A free-lance journalist, he wrote reviews, fill-ups, poems, short stories, a Life of Kruger for serialization in *The Morning Leader* and under the pen-name of Kennedy King, a boys' book. He seems to have earned enough at least to provide himself with the bare necessities of existence. Meanwhile 'he kept steadily in view his determination to do well in literature'. Hundreds of young men, bred in circumstances not unlike those of George Douglas, come up to London every year, struggle into journalism and have the ambition to write a novel or a play that will bring them fame and fortune. Few achieve it. The difficulty of earning their bread and butter, the press of work in an overcrowded profession, lack of talent and weakness of character prevent them. But George Douglas had energy of mind and strength of will. Now and then a little encouragement heartened him. An article he wrote on Burns was accepted by *Blackwood's Magazine* and a short story, 'How Janet Goudie Came Home', was taken by Wemyss Reid for *The Speaker*. But it was not till he had been in London for five years that he wrote a story of about twenty thousand words which he called *The House with the Green Shutters*. He read it to two of his friends. They thought well of it, but he had packed so much matter into so small a space that they were left with an impression of excessive strain, and they strongly advised him to extend it to a full-length novel. This he agreed to do. A year later he finished the book in the form which we now know.

The public at that time was interested in Scottish stories; the Kailyard School, as it came to be called, was at the height of its vogue, and *The House with the Green Shutters* was taken on its publication to be an effective counterblast to the sentimentality that characterized the group. 'I love the book for just this', said Walter Raleigh, 'it sticks the Kailyarders like pigs.' Their productions are dead now. None of them has the merit of that little masterpiece, Galt's *Annals of the Parish*, which may be regarded as their remote ancestor. But when I set about writing this introduction I thought I must make myself acquainted with some, at least, of these works which in their own day had excited so much attention and which, it seemed plain, had had an influence in making George Douglas write his book in just the way he did. I went to the London Library and asked Mr Cox for certain books by members of the Kailyard School. Everyone who uses that admirable institution knows Mr Cox. For hard on fifty years he has been handing books over the counter to a long succession of authors and readers, and I think it would be difficult to find a subject on which he could not give you the names of the authorities you should consult. You have only to tell him what you want to know about and with a certain deliberation, for he is never fussed nor flurried, he will tell you not only what books you should have, who wrote them and when, but also, roughly yet succinctly, what their value is. Though he is busy, for people are coming in all day long and almost everyone has some question to put to him, he will bear your special interests in mind and when next you present yourself will suggest some work that it has occurred to him will help you. Mr Cox is a man of an agreeable corpulence, with a high colour, white hair, a small moustache which hesitates between the tooth-brush and the walrus, and pale grey eyes alert under somewhat heavy lids. You cannot but think that Manet would have painted a wonderful portrait of him; it would have made a fine pendant to *Le Bon Bock*. I went then to Mr Cox and asked him to give me *The Lilac Sunbonnet, Beside the Bonnie Brier Bush*, and *A Window in Thrums*. Nothing surprises Mr Cox and yet, when I made my request, I thought that I discerned in his pale eyes a momentary astonishment; but their expression is somewhat distorted by the strong lenses of his spectacles, and I may very well have been mistaken; he looked down, his heavy eyelids drooped, and gravely, in his measured tones, he answered: 'You'd better take *The Stickit Minister* as well, sir'. But I thought that was too much. I had a notion that the books I had mentioned would give me such information as I needed. I found them somewhat difficult reading. *The Bonnie Brier Bush* was written by a minister called Watson who used the pen-name of Ian Maclaren and opposite the table of contents are the following two lines:

> There grows a bonnie brier-bush in our kail-yard
> And white are the blossoms on't in our kail-yard.

It narrates the events that occurred in the parish of Drumtochty and describes the characters, dour men with hearts of gold and tender women of simple nobility, who took part in them. We are told that Drumtochty had its own constitution and a special throat disease. It is borne in upon the persevering reader that this particular ailment was a lump in the throat. The author himself was seriously afflicted with it. These strong, but not silent men, for in their broad Scots they are uncommonly loquacious, do not weep, but in moments of emotion, and these moments are frequent, give one another a squeeze of their horny hands under the table. 'Ah me!' cries the author, 'Ah me! the thud of the spade on your mother's grave!' The exasperating thing is that though people are brought to the point of death, or die, for no reason but to give the author a chance to wring your heart, he does this so effectually that before very long you too feel yourself affected with the special disease of Drumtochty and hateful tears rise to your eyes.

The Lilac Sunbonnet is by S.R. Crockett. It is as sentimental as the other, but more sprightly. The heroine's name is Winsome. She lives on the farm of her grandparents and the novel relates her wooing by a young student for the ministry. The love-scenes are of a humorous archness that must be read to be believed. Barrie's *A Window in Thrums* is a little different from either of these. For one thing it is better written. Barrie was not only a sentimentalist, there was a harsh, sardonic side to him too, and there is a chapter in this book in which he reproduces the gossiping of two women, mother and daughter, with a fidelity that is empty of benevolence. It might almost be a chapter from *The House with the Green Shutters* and you feel that Barrie was within a hair's breadth of writing as cruel and bitter a book as that. He could well have done it. But, perhaps thinking better of it, he took a header into the milk of human kindness and the reader, before he reaches the final chapter, is splashed with it from head to foot. But Barrie's personages are made of stuff much less stern than Ian Maclaren's. They greet sair. Separately or in couples they hide themselves in corners to have a good cry. They are, however, no less virtuous and God-fearing.

George Douglas saw his fellow Scots very differently. He wrote a savage book.

I will say little about *The House with the Green Shutters*. There is no obligation on anyone to read a novel. A novel is read for pleasure; some of us take our pleasures in one way, some in another; pleasures may be intellectual or they may be fatuous; and it may be allowed that a novel that gives you an intellectual pleasure is of a higher quality than one that merely excites your laughter or holds you by its thrilling story; but the pleasure it gives you is the only test and so every reader is an ultimate judge. A critic may point out that a novel is well-written, well-constructed, and that it succeeds in doing what the author set out to do. But he can do no more; and if you think *War and Peace* tedious or *Red and Black* unpleasant that is your own affair. You have just as much right to your opinion as he has. He may despise you because you do not share his, but you must leave him, with a shrug of your shoulders, to the harmless enjoyment of his contempt; and you can always console yourself with the reflection that, as the history of criticism shows, the best critics are often very much mistaken.

It would be absurd to class *The House with the Green Shutters* with either of the great novels I have just mentioned. It is a young man's first effort. Its faults are obvious and George Douglas was not unconscious of them. When his friend Melrose pointed them out to him, he answered: 'I believe you are right, but I have a feeling now that this book has got to go as it is'. A writer seldom writes as he would like to; he writes as he can; he is often aware of his defects, but he can rid himself of them as little as he can change the colour of his eyes. They are part of what he is. George Douglas wrote in anger rather than with sympathy. There is not a single character in his novel that is not base, cruel, mean, drunken, or stupid. In fierce contradiction to the characters of the Kailyard novelists who are all white, he made his all black, and in the end the reader believes in them as little as he believes in the others.

Experience of life teaches us that few people are all of a piece; they are an intricate mingling of good and bad. Douglas loaded the dice against the persons of his invention. Even when by their own fault catastrophe has befallen them so that common charity inclines you to commiseration, he takes care to make them so vile in their adversity that you cannot even then feel any pity for them. But they are alive. They are creatures of nightmare, and they have the vividness, the actuality of the people that we see in our dreams. And it must be admitted that the impression of power that the book gives is much heightened by the dark colours in which the characters are painted. They lend it a grim intensity of horror. It is not life that he offers, it is a stylized picture deliberately composed in sombre tones; and such is his force, so swift his narrative, and inevitable the catastrophe which his story leads to, that while you read you are held captive by the author's passionate belief in his own creations.

The House with the Green Shutters is the only novel George Douglas wrote. Its success was in some measure due to Andrew Lang who wrote appreciative reviews of it in a number of papers. Presently George Douglas found himself the most talked-of man in the literary circles of London. For the first time in his life he had a little money to spend. He was thirty-two. A year later he was dead. He had for some time been suffering from a liver complaint, he was then living at Haslemere, and a severer attack than usual made him come to London to see a doctor. The doctor wrote a prescription and told him that he would be all right in a day or two. That night, however, he grew worse and was seen by another doctor next day who found that he had congestion of the throat, but was not dangerously ill. He continued, notwithstanding, to grow worse, and a third doctor was called in. This one confessed himself perplexed, but declared that there was no immediate danger. On the following morning, Tuesday, 28 August, he died. The doctors were much puzzled.

It is vain to speculate whether, had he lived, George Douglas would have written other books of merit or whether, like so many, he was a man who had just one thing to say and having said it could have done no more than repeat himself. He had vigour of mind, acid humour, a gift for so telling a story that the reader is led from page to page by a desire to know what is going to come next (the greatest gift the pure novelist can have) and the power of creating living persons of such idiosyncracy that they remain long in the memory. He wrote, if not with beauty, with correctness and lucidity. He had imagination. His defects, lack of sympathy and lack of insight, a tendency to moralize, were the defects of youth. He had enough strength of character to surmount them. But it was a small world that he described; it may be doubted whether the life he led in London, the life of the Bohemian journalist, with its idle sauntering and interminable talk, its pub-crawling, late hours, and capricious industry, would ever have given him the chance to know the people of an ampler world with the intimacy with which he knew his native Scottish and so the occasion to recreate them with his fierce and trenchant individuality. At the time of his death he was at work on a love story, a romance of Cromwell's time; it is hard to believe that it was a fit theme to exercise his grim power. The news of his death came as a shock not only to his friends, but to the public. It seemed tragic that a writer so young, who after years of struggle had just had such a wonderful success, when the world seemed to lie at his feet, should so suddenly perish. Those who have lived long in the world of letters know how much more tragic is the fate of those who have enjoyed a success that they have never been able to repeat. It may be that his death spared him that bitterness.

MODERN ENGLISH
AND
AMERICAN LITERATURE

One of the minor, but delectable and innocent, pleasures of life is to wander about a well-stocked bookshop, looking at titles, taking up a volume here and there, and turning over the pages; and the pleasure is enhanced if there is in the store an assistant sufficiently well informed to tell you something of a book that has excited your curiosity or to suggest one that you did not know of on a subject that happens to be of interest to you. But this is a pleasure of which the vast majority of the inhabitants of the United States are deprived, for, relatively to the population, bookshops, real ones, I mean, are few and far between. They are clustered for the most part in the great centres of population. I myself know a city of now nearly two hundred thousand inhabitants in which the one place where you can buy new books is a gift shop, and the stock consists only of the season's best sellers. The inhabitant of a small town must be satisfied, if at all, with what reprints he can buy at his local drug store.

The need of the public is, however, further supplied by a number of organizations that have sprung up to sell books by mail to members secured by intensive advertising. These books are chosen for them by judges often of reputation, but of varying literary tastes, and the propriety of their judgement is determined by the number of books returned by customers who do not like them and by the increase or at least maintenance of membership. This is probably as good a way of buying books as can be devised for the large number of persons who are out of reach of bookshops and thus seldom have a chance to look at books for themselve and make their own choice; but it is naturally a limiting way, since you must accept the judgment of three or four persons upon what will afford you pleasure or information, and their judgment in turn is influenced by the necessity of selecting books that will appeal to the average taste and so make it possible to order them on the huge scale that alone makes

Introduction to *Great Modern Reading*, an anthology chosen by Maugham. Doubleday, New York, 1943.

the undertaking profitable. It often happens that a very good book in this way gets a nationwide diffusion, but very good books do not grow on every gooseberry bush, and so, since books must be sent to subscribers at regular intervals, it happens on occasion that books of very indifferent merit are given a diffusion almost as wide.

I do not underestimate the value of the various book clubs that flourish in this country. I have myself profited by their existence. They have done much to spread literary culture and have enabled persons anxious to keep abreast of current production, but unable, for the reasons I have stated, to make their own selection, to read books that otherwise they could not so easily have got. I am convinced, likewise, that those whose business it is to choose the books sent out to subscribers are alive to their great responsibility; with them lies the guidance in taste and culture of a vast number of their fellow citizens; and I am sure they do their best with the material they have to deal with within the limits imposed upon them by the necessity of financial profit.

But however good the choice may be, it is the judges' taste that is imposed on the reader. The reader's opportunity is small to select books that appeal to his idiosyncrasy and personal interest. A challenging title or the sight of a book on a subject that arouses his curiosity will never tempt him to purchase it and so perhaps open up to him a new realm of the spirit. I know, of course, that if you do not like the books a book club sends you, they will send you any one you ask for, but then you are forced to trust to reviews or to the publishers' advertisements in the papers. A very small experience will teach you that this is a hazardous way of buying books.

I do not forget the public libraries; many of these, even in quite small towns, are astonishingly well provided, and the librarians I for my part have come across are knowledgeable and very willing to put their knowledge at your disposal. But books are comfortable things to have about a house: kindly friends who do not reproach you if you neglect them, and when you take them up again are as ready as before to give you what they have to offer of refreshment and diversion. It is very nice to own books. That many people think so is shown by the success of a recent venture. Some little while ago, thanks to the happy thought of the publisher who conceived it and the persistence with which he urged it, the chain stores have given counter space to books. The experiment has proved successful and the enormous number of books that have in one year been sold in one chain of stores alone sufficiently shows that there is in the public at large a healthy desire to possess books that can be bought at a moderate price. It is true that the great majority of these books have been works of fiction, but there has been also a satisfactory demand for works on matters of current interest and for works of information.

It is manifest that there is in the people of this country a boundless curiosity and an eager desire to learn. Every town in the United States that is big enough to have a five-and-ten-cent store will in due course have a book department where all and sundry will have the opportunity, which they have never had before, of purchasing for a very small sum books, new books, that will, according to their desire, afford them recreation or instruction. Since in reading, perhaps more than in anything else, appetite grows with what it feeds on, it may be hoped that they will discover how great may be the delight of reading books, and, as their reading grows more extensive and their tastes widens, learn how much enjoyment may be found in great literature, and through it acquire the breadth of vision, the independence of judgment, the tolerance and magnanimity that will make them worthy inhabitants of the world of the future. It may be that when the toil and trouble of these times are matters of history, this innovation will be looked upon as one of the most important events of our day. It will have brought literature, with its infinite possibilities, within reach of all, and who can tell what consequences may not result from it?

It is for the American people that I have devised this anthology. I am informed that the sale of books in the chain stores has diminished neither the membership of the book clubs nor the takings of the regular bookshops. The book clubs, and the bookshops to a great extent, depend on books published at a much higher price. It looks then as though the purchasers of this immense number of books are buyers who have seldom bought books before; and since it may be presumed that they have been bought to read, the conclusion seems obvious that a great new body of readers has been created, people who had never before acquired the habit of buying books or had the occasion to do so. It occurred to me that it would be useful to them, and I hoped interesting, if I could give them for their guidance, as it were, a bird's-eye view of literary production in England and America during the last forty or fifty years. That is what I have tried to do in this volume. It is imperfect, partly owing to my own inadequacy for the task, since my reading, except in special subjects, has been desultory, and it is only too probable that I have remained unacquainted with certain authors a selection from whose works would have made my picture more complete; but it is imperfect also because my space was severely limited. I wished this book to be published at so low a price that it would strain no one's resources to buy it, and the cost of production set definite bounds to the quantity of material I could include.

But because I have made this anthology for the plain people of this country, for the woman who goes into the store to buy a spool of cotton or a cake of soap, for the man who goes in to buy a pound of nails or a pot of paint, I wish no one to think that I have on that account allowed my choice to be qualified by any consideration that what I was offering these readers might be above their heads. Far from it. With the object I had in mind of giving a survey of literary production during a certain period, I have chosen what seemed to me best and most significant. I believe in people and I believe in their taste. Some time ago in San Francisco I went to an exhibition of French pictures, many of which were such as one would have thought could be appreciated only by an instructed taste. It was a Saturday afternoon, and the galleries were crowded largely with young working men and their wives or sweethearts from the neighbouring armament factories. I could not see that they were repelled or even puzzled by the pictures of Cézanne, Van Gogh, Picasso, Matisse, Braque, and so on; on the contrary, they appeared to be deeply interested in them. They stood in front of them, eagerly discussing them, receptive, and it seemed to me anxious to discover what there was in them for *them*. I had a notion that those pictures spoke to them in a language they instinctively understood.

It would be interesting in this connection to know the number of people who listen in on the radio to serious music compared with that of those who listen to music of a lighter character. When I have been to popular concerts, it has seemed to me that it was the best music that chiefly excited the audience's enthusiasm; compositions of inferior merit, which I take it the conductor had put in as a concession to popular taste, were received with comparative coldness. I have a notion then that people are ready to welcome the best when it is offered to them; what they are not prepared to interest themselves in is the not so good. It is the sophisticated, the cultured dilettantes, the fashionable who are more likely to lose their heads over the second rate; since something other than deep-felt emotion is concerned, they are apt to mistake oddness for originality and speciousness for truth. But the band wagon often topples them over into a ditch.

I am not so stupid as to mean that all people have such naturally good taste that they will always prefer what is best to what is of no great value. After all, we none of us do that, and few of us are so delicately constituted that we can put up with nothing but the first rate. Most of us can very much like things of unequal merit. I know for my part I can get a great deal of pleasure out of an opera of Puccini's; but it is a different sort of pleasure from that which I get out of an opera of Mozart's. There are times when I would rather read the stories of Conan Doyle than Tolstoi's *War and Peace*. I mean only that there are many people in this country, many millions it may be, who are quite as capable of enjoying great music, great paintings, and great literature as those others who have had ampler opportunities to form their taste and confirm their judgment. So in this anthology[1] I have made no compromise. I would not claim that all the pieces in it are great literature; during the last twenty-five hundred years, all the world over, not so much of the literature that has been produced can truly be called great; indeed, we have been told that it can be got into a five-foot shelf, and this is a necessarily incomplete selection from the writing in England and America of half a century. I do claim, however, that none of these pieces can fail to appeal for one reason or another to a curious and intelligent mind.

I have always felt that reading should be a pleasure. Of course to get anything out of it you must give it your full attention, but to a healthy understanding there is nothing disagreeable in the activity of the intellect. It is however the business of an author to make your perusal of his work enjoyable. There are writers who have things to say that are interesting and useful for us to know, but by some unfortunate accident of nature they cannot say them with grace or elegance, so that to read them is a burden. Since this anthology is designed also to persuade people to the habit of reading, I have, so far as I honestly could, left out writing of this sort; I wanted to show that good reading could very well be pleasant reading.

I have followed here the plan I adopted a good many years ago in *The Traveller's Library*. I am inclined to think it is not an unsatisfactory one, since in the meantime other anthologists have used it too. But in that volume I had at my disposal all the space I wanted so that I was able to include three novels which for various reasons interested me. I should have liked to do this again, for it would have given me a better chance of making the survey of the

---

[1] Its table of contents is given in Appendix I.

literature of the period more thorough. It could not be done at the price. For the rest the model is the same. It is a selection of poems, short stories, and what, for want of an equivalent English term, I am forced against my will to call *belles-lettres*.

Some of the pieces are by English authors and some by American, but I have not sought in any way to distinguish them, for I think the time has passed when there was any point in speaking of English literature and American literature; I prefer now to speak of it as one, the literature of the English-speaking peoples. I have arranged my material roughly in chronological order, but against the clock; that is to say, I have started with the writers of our own day and gone backward to those who were writing at the beginning of my period. This I have done because for us who live now the present is our more pressing concern. The literary productions of our contemporaries speak our own language and are dressed in the clothes we wear; they use the conveniences we are accustomed to, the telephone, the motor-car, the radio, the plane, so that when we come to make ourselves acquainted with them, it is with a sense of familiarity which is a help to such of us as have never acquired the habit of reading. Because they deal with a life that is our life they have an immediate interest. That indeed is the one advantage we writers of today have over our predecessors, for they had the first chance at all the best subjects; and all we can do for the most part is by ingenuity to give a new twist to situations that have already been written to death. Think what luck the author had who invented the story of Cinderella, and how fortunate was he to whom it first occurred that he could make a moving tale out of the seduction of a village maiden by a bad rich man. The most striking figures that flit across the human scene, the ruffian with the heart of gold, the bloated capitalist and the virtuous workman, the merry widow, the jealous wife, the deceived husband, the spendthrift, the strong, silent man, have been portrayed in every imaginable guise; and we, dealing with them, if deal we must, only with misgiving, are forced to turn the best of our endeavours to creatures of a sadly colourless complexion. And the past has another advantage over us: the great mass of what is produced is forgotten and only the best remains, and it is with that that we must stand comparison. We could never support the competition if it were not that, writing of contemporary life, we have something to offer contemporary readers that even the greatest masters of a bygone day cannot quite give them. For that reason I have felt justified in making most of my selections from the compositions of the last twenty years. I have put the earlier writers toward the end of this volume because I thought I could thus more easily inveigle the reader to read them. I thought that on coming to them step by step he would discover how small an adjustment of spirit it needed to find in them, notwithstanding differences of manner and usage, something to his purpose; and then, learning to his surprise that even those who wrote in the dark age of the nineties could be entertaining, he might be tempted to go back further still and see what there was for him in the great works that are the outstanding glory of our culture.

People will not read the classics because they have got it into their heads that they are dull. They have formed this impression, I think, because they have been forced to read them in schools and colleges, and the reading prescribed by scholastic authorities is not as often as it should be chosen to persuade the young that great literature is good to read. It is natural enough that when they arrive at maturity many persons should suppose that there is little in the great works of the past that can help them to deal with the anxious and harassing present. But a work becomes a classic only because succeeding generations of people, ordinary readers like you and me, have found delight in reading it. It affords that because it appeals to the human emotions common to all of us and treats of the human problems that we are all confronted with.

I have included in this anthology nothing that to my mind has not a merit of its own, but to fulfil my intention in making it I have put in some pieces of which the literary merit is small because they seemed to me significant of the time at which they were written. I have had on the other hand to leave out some things that I thought both significant and of literary value simply because I had no room for them. For this reason I have been obliged to omit Joseph Conrad's *Youth* and Richard Wright's *Fire and Cloud*. I wish to stress this point because, after I published the anthology called *Tellers of Tales*, I was made aware that some of my fellow authors were affronted because I had not included any story of theirs. One wrote to me very acrimoniously, pointing out that his stories had appeared in anthologies for twenty years and the fact that I had not thought fit to insert one proved to his complete satisfaction that I did not know a good story when I saw it. Well, I had read the stories of this irascible author and had received pleasure from them, but here again my space was limited; I was making a choice from stories written since the beginning of the nineteenth century in the five countries that have cultivated the art to best advantage, and I thought that each country should be adequately represented; though I thought the stories of this particular author good, I could not but know that Jack London had done the same sort of thing, if not better, at least before him, and so it seemed to me unnecessary to give an example of his work. I hope then that no writer will be angry with me if in this brief anthology I have not asked him for permission to print a piece of his. It may be that I would have liked to, but it did not quite fit into my scheme. It is no reflection on his merit. I do not pretend that my taste is perfect, nor do I presume it to be as impartial as that which a professional critic is in duty bound to have. I have my likes and dislikes, and though I am not blind to the merit of what I dislike, and will freely admit it, I do not like it any the better for that.

WRITE ABOUT WHAT YOU KNOW

Instead of writing this article I should be writing a letter; but I hate writing letters, and the prospect of writing this one is peculiarly odious to me because I have written it a hundred times already.

I have just been reading some short stories that a young man, twenty years of age, persuaded me to let him send me. He tells me that he wants a candid criticism; but I know, as he in his heart knows, too, that what he really wants is praise. And that is what I cannot give him. The stories are not badly written; he has at least taken the trouble to learn the elements of grammar, a precaution that young writers, both male and female, too seldom take; and his characters, though shopworn, are sufficiently individualized for the purposes of a short story; but he has chosen to write of subjects which, it is only too evident, he knows absolutely nothing about. That is precisely the error that so many young writers make, and it is because I can do nothing but point it out that I have been obliged to write the same letter over and over and over again.

It is at first sight strange that they should do so, since one thinks it much easier to write about what you know than about what you don't. The explanation, I suppose, is that they find the familiar commonplace and think that romance must be sought in the exceptional. That is why they are so fond of writing about painters, actors, singers, and fiddlers.

In one of the stories I have just been reading, a middle-aged farmer's wife, who, we are told, is a gifted pianist, suddenly writes a remarkable sonata and gets a distinguished conductor to orchestrate it. It doesn't require much knowledge of music to know that even a heaven-sent genius couldn't write a good sonata unless he had studied harmony and composition and if it is a good sonata what would a conductor be doing in transforming it into a symphony? Another story deals with painters in Paris. I would bet a considerable sum that the author has never been to Paris or even stepped inside a painter's studio. I know the paintings he describes as great masterpieces. They were painted half a century ago and now hang in the deserted rooms of provincial museums. Old ladies still think them good.

Good Housekeeping, November 1943.

The fact is that when you write about things you don't know you fall into ludicrous errors. Of course a writer cannot have a firsthand knowledge of everything, but his only safety is to find out everything he can about the subject he proposes to treat. Sometimes he thinks himself obliged to fake things; but to do that with plausibility needs skill and experience, and it isn't really worth doing, for it is seldom completely convincing; and if the writer cannot convince his readers successfully, then he is done.

Now, the only way I have ever discovered he can do that is to tell the truth, as he sees it, about what he knows; and the point of this statement lies in the words *as he sees it*. There are no new subjects (and incidentally there is none so stale as the great singer, the great painter, or the great violinist); but if a writer has personality he will see the old subjects in a personal way, and that will give them an interest. He may try his best to be objective, but his temperament, his attitude toward life, are his own and colour his view of things.

Let me give an example. James Farrell in *Studs Lonigan*, aiming at complete objectivity, has drawn a picture of lower-middle-class life in Chicago that gives an impression of complete verisimilitude. It is photographic, and they say the camera cannot lie. I suggest that another writer with a different personality could take the same environment, and even the same characters, and produce a picture that would be almost completely different.

My point is simple: the value of a piece of fiction depends in the final analysis on the personality of the author. If it is interesting, he will interest. It is true that the young writer cannot expect to have a personality that is either complex or profound; personality grows with the experiences of life; but he has some counterbalancing advantages. He sees things, the environment in which he has grown up, with the freshness and the energy of his youth; he knows the persons of his own family and the persons with whom his daily life since childhood has brought him in contact, with an intimacy he can seldom hope to have with people he comes to know in later years. Here is material ready to his hand. If his personality is so commonplace that he can see this environment and these people only in a commonplace way, then he is not made to be a writer and he is only wasting his time in trying.

It is far from my meaning that he should not exercise his imagination. His imagination will work upon the facts and shape them into a pattern of significance or beauty. His imagination will enable him to deduce new facts from the facts he has observed. A writer need not devour a whole sheep in order to know what mutton tastes like, but he must at least eat a chop. Unless he gets his facts right, his imagination will lead him into all kinds of nonsense, and the facts he is most likely to get right are the facts of his own experience.

But now I must write that confounded letter, and the chances are that this boy will think I'm just an old fool who doesn't know what he's talking about.

VARIATIONS ON A THEME: DOROTHY PARKER

The theme, of course, is Dorothy Parker. Long experience has taught me that, when you set out to write a piece and can't think what to say, the best plan is to leave it to your fountain pen. That invaluable little instrument is wayward and to fool you will often start by writing rubbish, but if you give it its head and take no notice, it will generally settle down and write something that at least looks like sense. It has its pride; it knows that the typewriter can't do this, and it knows that the typewriter, once it starts, goes on and on intoxicated by its own facility. Further, no typewriter has ever learned to spell and will complacently (except after *c*) put *e* before *i* till it comes to *seize* and will then without shame put *i* before *e*. The fountain pen has a singular mastery over this difficult English spelling of ours and if by chance it has made a mistake will give a little start which calls your attention to it and urges you to consult a dictionary.

But this is by the way; it is not the case that I do not know what to say about Dorothy Parker, but that I do not know what new I can say. It is as difficult to say anything about her that has not been said a thousand times before as it is about the Venus of Milo. Who has not praised her wit, her stories and her verse? Her witticisms are famous. With equal efficacy she can wield the bludgeon of an angry cop and the rapier of the gallant D'Artagnan. Helen could make a scholar immortal with a kiss; she can make a fool immortal with a jibe. Wit must have a butt and is ill-constituted to paddle in the milk of human kindness; but I should do her an injustice if I gave the impression that hers is cruel; it can be, but also it can be lambent, as harmless as summer lightning, and tender; it is then the natural expression of her rueful and exuberant delight in the absurdity of the universe. Most humorists require an audience; sometimes in their company you will see by the sudden twinkle in their eye that a joke has occurred to them, and then you become aware that they have decided to keep it for a more favourable occasion. Not so with Dorothy Parker. Her humour bubbles up and overflows and, if there is no one there to enjoy it, it makes no matter. She can no more help being amusing than a peach tree can help bearing peaches. Most of us become writers because we can never think of the apt thing to say till the moment to say it has past. One of the charming things about Dorothy Parker is that when the door of opportunity flies open she is there on the threshold ready to make the most of the God-given moment. She seems to carry a hammer in her handbag to hit the appropriate nail on the head. She has a rare quickness of mind.

Once when I was in Hollywood I was invited to dinner by Miss Fanny Brice. It was by way of being a literary party. Aldous Huxley was there, his sardonic gusto in the horribleness of human beings not yet greatly mitigated by non-attachment and brotherly love. Dorothy Parker was there demure in black silk, but with a demureness fraught with peril to the unwary. I forget who the remaining guests were but they were evidently grand, for at dinner Dorothy Parker and I found ourselves seated together a good way down the table and well below the salt. The food was good, the wine choice, and we were waited on by Russian noblemen or Japanese Samurai. I forget which. After my neighbour and I had discoursed for some while upon the weather and the crops, with fleeting references to Shakespeare and the musical glasses, I said:

'Why don't you write a poem for me?'

'I will if you like,' she replied. 'Give me a pencil and a piece of paper.'

Now I am not one of those prudent authors who keep a little book in their pocket, so, whatever they are, wherever they may be (as I hear my radio announcer remark every evening), they can jot down any happy thought that occurs to them. I too sometimes have a happy thought, but I always think I will make a note of it later and then forget what on earth it was. I had neither pencil nor paper.

'Let's ask for it,' I said, and turned to the Russian nobleman or the Japanese Samurai (whichever the case might be) and told him what we wanted.

He was gone a long time, evidently having some difficulty in finding what we asked for in that sumptuous house, but at last returned with a ragged piece of wrapping paper and a blunt pencil. Dorothy Parker took it and wrote:

> Higgledy Piggledy, my white hen;
> She lays eggs for gentlemen.

'Yes, I've always liked those lines,' I said.

She gave a thin, cool smile and without an instant's hesitation, added:

> You cannot persuade her with gun or lariat
> To come across for the proletariat.

With this brilliant rhyme she gathered Higgledy Piggledy into the august company of Jove's Eagle, Sindbad the Sailor's Roc, the Capitoline Geese, Boccaccio's Falcon, Shelley's Skylark, and Poe's Raven. Chaucer's Chanticleer is her fitting mate.

But enough; I must now speak of Dorothy Parker's published work.

I have an old friend who is by profession a literary critic and going to see him one day I found him somewhat discomposed. I asked him what was the matter.

'I've lost a friend,' he sighed. 'X says he'll never forgive me for the review of his book I wrote last week. I praised it for a columm and a half; I only made a few reservations in a few lines at the end. After all, I am a critic and a critic must criticize. To read his letter you'd think I'd panned the damned book.'

I was concerned to find that a distinguished critic could be so ingenuous. Fancy not knowing that a writer will accept fulsome praise as only his due, but will grizzle and grieve over a hint of imperfection as though his publisher had gypped him, his wife betrayed him and his son gone into the movies. You can butter him up till you are exhausted but one word of censure will turn all your butter rancid. Now I am not a critic and it is not my business to criticize. Nor in the present case have I any inclination to do so. In her stories Dorothy Parker has a sense of form which in these days, to my old-fashioned mind, is all too rare. Whether in a sketch or a story she knows exactly where to begin and where to end and when you have done reading it you have no questions to ask (What happened next? Why did he do that?) for she has told you all you need to know. She has a tidy mind and leaves no loose ends. She has a wonderfully delicate ear for human speech and with a few words of dialogue, chosen you might think haphazardly, will give you a character complete in all its improbable plausibility. Her style is easy without being slipshod and cultivated without affectation. It is a perfect instrument for the display of her many-sided humour, her irony, her sarcasm, her tenderness, her pathos. Perhaps what gives her writing its peculiar tang is her gift for seeing something to laugh at in the bitterest tragedies of the human animal. It is a devastating truth that she has discovered, and a salutary one, that there is something irresistibly comic in our most heartfelt woes. Who can but laugh wryly when he reads 'A Telephone Call', that heart-rending monologue, for which of us has not thus awaited with agonizing suspense a call on the phone, a telegram, a letter or a visit? Only a nitwit — but what a happy nitwit he! I do not want to go through these stories one by one, pointing out the peculiar excellence of each, for here they are for the reader to read and the reader is for himself the only judge that matters. He is silly if he lets anyone else, however well qualified, judge for him. In this volume he will find stories aimed only to make him laugh, and a very good aim too, too seldom attempted and less seldom achieved; he will find stories that are cruel, moving, sardonic, tragic, funny, sometimes separately and sometimes all together. But I should like to single out 'The Standard of Living' for its humorous and tender handling of those two little stenographers as they wander up Fifth Avenue looking into the shop windows. They have all the charm, the impertinence, the pathos and the absurdity of youth.

If you are going to judge an author at all, he has the right to demand that you shall judge him by his best. 'Big Blonde' has all the earmarks of a masterpiece. It is worthy to take its place with the short stories, and very few they are, that men have retained in their memories for many, many years. It displays to perfection all Dorothy Parker's enviable gifts. There are few things more difficult than to write a short story the events of which take place over a long period of time, and yet maintain that unity of effect which is the essence of the short story. In 'Big Blonde' Dorothy Parker has succeeded with peculiar skill in doing just this, so that notwithstanding the passage of years you have the same poignancy as is generally only possible to achieve in the narration of a single incident. I think it is done by a determined concentration on the pathetic, feckless, hopeless, tragic, sloppy wanton who is Hazel Morse. People don't often realize how much luck comes into the writing of a good story. A lot of things have to go right. The heaven-sent idea is waiting at the street corner, but you must chance to pass that way to pick it up; it is only by a fluke that you come across the persons who will suggest the characters you need; you have to be in the right mood; time and place must be auspicious. It is no wonder that few good stories are written; it is only a wonder that as many are. In 'Big Blonde' Dorothy Parker had all the luck on her side.

Only a very mediocre writer is always at his best, and Dorothy Parker is not a mediocre writer. Sometimes things don't go so well with one as they might and in such case one can do nothing about it. A carping critic of these stories might suggest that their author on occasion shows an inclination to imitate Dorothy Parker, but I as an admiring friend would answer stoutly that she could not have a better model.

No such reservation could be made with regard to her verse. Now verse is a matter on which I cannot pretend to speak with any authority whatever. I have never written it; I have never understood the mysteries of prosody and I have never even seen a rhyming dictionary, which I understand is as invaluable to poets as Roget's *Thesaurus* is to us lesser fry. It is a pity, because I have a notion that Dorothy Parker's verse has a technical perfection and I can only speak of it as a delighted reader. (It is true that great poets have unanimously agreed that poetry is for delight, though you wouldn't think so if you read some critics and, still more, some modern poets.) But this I do know, that Dorothy Parker has a beautiful clarity – you never need to rack your brains to ask yourself, now what the devil does this mean? – and she has that great gift of nature, a faultless ear. The felicity of her rhymes is enchanting. In too many poems you get the feeling that a line is there, not because it is necessary to the meaning or adds to the emotion the verse seeks to create, but because a rhyme was wanted. With Dorothy Parker never. Her rhymes are as inevitable as they are often unexpected. I should like to give examples to prove the truth of what I say, but it would be foolish to quote when the pages that follow this disquisition are there for the reader to read. Admirable as are Dorothy Parker's stories I think it is in her poems that she displays the quintessence of her talent. Like Heine, she has made little songs out of her great sorrows; we, heartless readers, endure them with fortitude, for have they not wrung from her these gay, tragic poems? And how fresh and various they are! Though beautifully polished, they have an air of spontaneity, and none can know better than a writer what patient industry is needed to acquire that quality. They reflect her personality in its manifold completeness, and what, I ask you, can an artist give you more or better than himself? I shall never grow tired of asserting that it is the artist's personality, and that alone, which gives the work of art its enduring significance. In a few short perfect lines she presents herself to you, to take or to leave, with her pain, her laughter, her tenderness, her feeling for beauty, her ribaldry and her common sense. Now that I come to consider these affections and proclivities that I have ascribed to her, it occurs to me that we all, except bishops and elder statesmen, possess them; but she possesses them in a heightened, more concentrated form, so that when you read almost any one of her verses you seem to see her as through the wrong end of a perfectly focused telescope. It is a great gift to be able to do so much in such a little space. However lyrical her mood, and when she likes she can be as lyrical as Herrick and Landor at their charming best, her aerial flight is anchored to this pendent world (the phrase is Milton's) by the golden chain of common sense. I think it is her common sense that gives her poems their singular and characteristic savour, and what is it but common sense that makes this uncertain, absurd, harsh and transitory life not only tolerable, but amusing? Notwithstanding what I said a page or two back, for my pleasure I will quote the first and last stanzas of a poem called 'One Perfect Rose'. They fittingly bring to an end what I had to say.

> A single flow'r he sent me, since we met.
>   All tenderly his messenger he chose;
> Deep-hearted, pure, with scented dew still wet –
>   One perfect rose.

* * * * *

> Why is it no one ever sent me yet
>   One perfect limousine, do you suppose?
> Ah no, it's always just my luck to get
>   One perfect rose.

A
PLAN TO ENCOURAGE
YOUNG WRITERS

We are living in troublous times and we are all called upon to make great sacrifices in order to achieve security, to maintain peace and to assure our liberty. You may well think that this is not the proper moment to say what I am going to say. I daresay it isn't. But this is the last time I shall ever speak to you, and I must take the opportunity while I have it. I have been invited to come here today because I am a writer, and it is as a writer I speak. But my course is run, and it is not about myself that I wish to speak to you but about the creative writers who are just starting on their careers. The difficulties that confront them are greater than they have ever been. The costs of production are now such that it is hard for a young author to get the chance of publication. The result is that the young and unknown author finds it more and more difficult to get a hearing. And, even when he does, how is he going to live on the royalties of a book that has probably just paid the expense of publication? He can't. He must add to his income in other ways, by journalism, by writing for the radio and by writing scripts if he is lucky enough to have attracted the attention of the talent scouts in Hollywood.

That means that he must give the best of his energies not to creative writing, which is his proper business, but to work which may well destroy his creative faculty.

You may ask how all this concerns you. I will tell you. You are now the greatest and most powerful nation in the world. Not the least of the glories of a great nation is that is has produced a great literature. Now, I think history shows that a nation produces this when it is at the height of its power and vigour. I don't want to depreciate the merits of the politicians, the generals and the admirals who, with a willing people to back them, created the greatness of my own country. But what is the chief glory of the days of Queen

The major part of Maugham's address at the Book and Author Luncheon at the Hotel Astor, New York, on 30 September 1950. *New York Herald Tribune*, 1 November 1950.

Elizabeth, the defeat inflicted on the Armada by the English seamen or the plays of Shakespeare?

It has always seemed to me that this vast country of yours with its mixture of races has the potentiality of producing forms of art which the world has never known. We British have never produced painters and composers that are more than meritorious. Our glory has been our literature. There is no reason why you should not produce great and original artists in all branches of the arts. Now I am coming to the gist of what I want you to consider. The artist needs help and encouragement. Without it, however strong is his urge to create, he may waste much precious time or the artist in him may be destroyed. Now you do something for painting and musical composition, but what do you do for literature? Not very much.

Of course, you know about the Simon Guggenheim Memorial Foundation. It does an admirable work and it does not altogether neglect the creative writer. I have had the curiosity to count the number of fellowships which were granted during the year 1949. There are 137 of them and of these seven were given to poets, writers of fiction and of plays. It provides an author with a sum of money so that he may be at leisure to write a certain book. The candidate for this grant must submit a record of his or her entire career as a writer and a list of his publications. This, of course, implies that the writer in question has already acquired a certain standing. The committee of selection are not satisfied with promise, they demand performance.

But there is another institution which is designed to offer certain advantages to young artists. This is the American Academy in Rome. It was created in 1905 by an act of Congress to promote the study of painting. Later, fellowships were endowed for landscape architecture, and later still a department of musical composition was added. The fellowships are awarded to men and women of high intellectual and personal qualifications who have already demonstrated unusual capacity for productive scholarship or unusual ability in the fine arts. The fellows live in Rome and I have no doubt benefit greatly by their contact with the artistic riches of Italy. But as you will notice the fellowships are not granted to the creative writer. It seems very hard that he should be left out in the cold.

By creative writers I do not mean philosophers, historians or economists, however much you may think their productions are akin to fiction, but poets, novelists, short-story writers and dramatists.

It is for them I should like to see an institution founded on the same lines as the American Academy in Rome. And I would not ask that the fellowships should be awarded to them, as in the Academy in Rome, for their high intellectual and personal qualifications and because they have already demonstrated unusual ability, but only because they show great promise.

I am going to ask you to have patience with me while I tell you something of how I think such an academy as I have in mind should be conducted. I should like it to be installed in a chateau within a few miles of Paris and as a director I would appoint a man of letters still young enough to be receptive to new ideas, or a professor of English literature in one of the colleges. I don't think it would be necessary to have more than about a dozen fellowships. They should be awarded to persons still under thirty, for if by that age they have not shown a little more than promise they are unlikely ever to do so, and they should be given the opportunity if they want it to stay at the academy for three years, and, besides board and lodging, they should be given a sufficient salary to make journeys not only in France, but in England, Germany, Italy and Spain, in fact, wherever in Europe they may expect to gather experience and acquire knowledge.

You will ask what use this can be to them, besides allowing them to live for two or three years in economic security. I will tell you. In the first place, such an experience can only enlarge their mind and their sympathies. By giving them the chance of becoming acquainted with the art, the culture, the literature of Europe, it will develop and increase their personalities, and when you come down to brass tacks all an author has to give is just that, his personality, and the richer, the fuller, his personality the more he has to give. Of course, the business of the American writer is to write about America. No author really knows enough about a foreign country and its inhabitants to write about them convincingly. You must often have laughed at the portraits English authors have drawn of Americans and at the language they put in their mouths. In the same way we laugh at the portraits American writers draw of the English. In each case, they are seldom other than caricatures, sometimes friendly, sometimes unfriendly, but caricatures, nevertheless. Slang is the great stumbling block, and even so good and observant an author as Henry James, who had lived so many years in England, never quite managed to use English slang in quite the way an Englishman would use it.

The point I want to make is that, in order to know your own country, you must know other countries as well.

Many years ago Kipling asked the rhetorical question: What can they know of England who only England know? The answer is: Not nearly enough. I suggest to you that changing the word America for England the same answer may be made. Such an academy as I have in mind, by giving young writers this great advantage of learning what of value they can from a sojourn in foreign countries, would enable them when they came home to observe the American scene from a fresh point of view, and with a catholicity of outlook, which, given their talent, would make it possible for them to write works which would permanently enrich the literature of this great country.

Now I want to digress for a moment. I had long been struck by the fact that the popularity of English writers in this country has of late years enormously diminished. One reason of course is that during the last forty years you have produced a considerable number of authors of great talent and it is very natural that American readers should prefer to read about the American scene and their fellow Americans. But there is another reason for the decline in the interest taken here in English writers. Too often they have abandoned the subjects of common human interest to concentrate their attentions on the parish pump and the vicar's tea party. I formed the impression that they were become not only insular but provincial, and I conceived the idea that something might be done to remedy this if young authors of promise were given the chance of spending a period abroad so that they, too, might acquire freshness of vision which would help them to see their country from a wider standpoint.

I am not a multi-millionaire, and not even a millionaire, but I was fortunately able to provide the Authors' Society with a sum sufficient for them to hand over every year to a promising young author, man or woman, a sum of money large enough for him, or her, with thrift to spend the best part of a year abroad. No strings are attached to this award. It is left to the good sense of the recipient to make the best use of it. I was well aware that the judges would sometimes make the award to someone who would not do this. I was also aware that sometimes the recipient would not be able to profit by the experience. I did not think that mattered. If once in ten years the experience enables an author to produce work which is an enrichment to our literature, I think the money will have been well spent.

Now this is a very small thing I have tried to do. I only tell you about it because it is an indication of the much larger and more important thing I should like to see you do.

Such an academy as I am proposing can be brought into being only by the munificence of a private person. We all know that the wealthy men of America have never been niggardly of their riches. They have created universities, provided vast sums for research, built hospitals, handsomely subsidized music, erected magnificent picture galleries and furnished them with collections of pictures of unsurpassed beauty, but on the whole they have never done much for pure literature. Yet a great literature, as I said before, is not the least of the glories of a great nation. To found such an institution as I suggest would not require very much money. I think it could be created and endowed for at the utmost three million dollars. I am told that in Texas multi-millionaires are as thick as the leaves at Vallombrosa. Is there not one who for such a noble purpose is not prepared not only to gain imperishable renown for himself but also to provide for writers more than the possibility, the probability, that they will in due course produce a literature which will be worthy of the greatness of these United States?

ON STORY-TELLING

I am in a very embarrassing situation. I have been writing for over fifty years and in that long time I have said pretty well all I had to say. I don't see how I can help saying what I have said somewhere or other before. It will make it easier for me then, here and now, if I take it for granted that no one in this room has ever read a single word I have written, except of course the President of the National Institute of Arts and Letters who has certainly read the letter in which I gratefully accepted both my election to this society and his invitation to dine with you tonight. Otherwise obviously I should not be here. And my gratitude to you for electing me and for giving me this party is very sincere. It is an honour you have done me and an honour you have done my country. It is a proof that notwithstanding the differences we have had in the past, your country and mine, and shall doubtless have in the future, you are confident that we stand together not only in virtue of our common language and our common heritage, but in virtue of our common love of freedom and our common determination at all costs to maintain it.

Having said this I should perhaps be wise to sit down and allow you to go on with your doubtless interesting conversations. But I am not going to let you off so easily. I have something more I want to say to you, only I am going in a rather roundabout way to say it.

We have a weekly magazine in England devoted to life in the country. It is beautifully printed and beautifully illustrated. Every week it has an article on one of those great country houses which taxation has now made an almost intolerable burden to their owners. It has articles from which you can learn about the domestic habits of all kinds of animals from hippopotamuses to chaffinches. It has articles on shooting, fox-hunting, fishing and golf, in fact on all the pursuits which in happier days were the pleasant occupation of the country gentleman. It has also an excellent article on bridge from which, if you are smart enough, you can learn how to make a grand slam with only twelve tricks in the two hands. And since the country gentleman has a wife and

An address given at the dinner of The National Institute of Arts and Letters, New York, on 17 October 1950, on Maugham's election as an Honorary Associate of the Institute. Reprinted from the *Proceedings of the American Academy and Institute of Arts and Letters and the National Institute of Arts and Letters*, second series, number 1, New York, 1951.

daughters with leisure on their hands it has a page devoted to the reviewing of new books.

Some time ago I happened to be reading this particular page, and the critic, dealing with a new novel, started with the words: Mr So & So is not a mere story teller. The word *mere* stuck in my throat and on that day, like Paolo and Francesca on another occasion, I read no further.

The reviewer in question is a well-known novelist, and though I have never been fortunate enough to read any of his works, I have no doubt that they are meritorious. I am told that he has a large and faithful public who look forward to the appearance of his latest novel with the same sort of eagerness as fashionable women look forward to the latest creations of Christian Dior or Fath. From the words I have just quoted to you I can only surmise that he looks upon the telling of a story as a trifling matter and I have little doubt that he would contemptuously lump together all the novels that do this as escape literature. This, as you know, is the hardest thing a critic today can say about a novel. This despised class includes the novels of Henry Fielding and Jane Austen, the *Pickwick Papers* and *David Copperfield*, *Vanity Fair* and *Huckleberry Finn*.

We writers of fiction are very simple-minded folk and we are apt to believe what we are told. When it was borne in upon us a generation or two ago that the novel was not only a medium for the creation of character and the narration of a plausible and interesting story, but might more profitably be used as a platform or a pulpit to instruct or reform our readers we were pleased and flattered. It gave us a new and pleasing sense of importance to look upon ourselves as preachers, teachers and reformers, and we assumed our new role with the alacrity with which, I am informed, the duck takes to water. And so for years now the novelists have been writing novels about the economic situation, the housing problem, juvenile delinquency, the prison system and I know not what. And the public have been reading them under the impression that they were acquiring reliable information. There I think they show a naivety which is surprising. The novelist is not an impartial observer. He loads his dice. His sympathies betray him. The public are very much mistaken if they suppose the information he gives them is reliable. But that is not the worst of it. As soon as the novelist sets out to be a preacher and a propagandist he ceases to be an artist, and we all know what happens to his novel then.

For the novel is a form of art, perhaps not a very exalted one, but a form of art nevertheless. It is not concerned with instruction. It is not concerned with reform. It offers entertainment and if it is a good novel it offers intelligent entertainment. People who are interested in juvenile delinquency, the prison system and so forth would be better advised to read the books written about them by the experts on these particular subjects. The proper aim of the novelist, as I have said, is to create characters and devise a story which will enable him to display them. If you like to call him a mere story teller of course you are at liberty to do so. Hard words break no bones. What to my mind it shows is merely that you don't like novels.

But is there such a thing as a mere story teller? I suppose you would call Rudyard Kipling a mere story teller. Many of you must have read the *Plain Tales from the Hills*. They are very early stories, written for the paper for which he was then working, and as stories they are not very good. But he had a peculiar gift for absorbing the climate of opinion which surrounded him. He accepted it as naturally as we accept the air we breathe. He never thought to criticise. In fact he saw nothing to criticise. I don't believe he had any intention of drawing a moral or offering a warning. He wrote of what he saw. It is a devastating picture. I think a perspicacious reader then might have seen how inevitable it was that sooner or later the British would lose India. And take Guy de Maupassant, another mere story teller. You read those brilliant stories now with dismay. The attitude towards life, the opinions, the behaviour he lends to his characters make you understand how it was bound to come to pass that that great and intelligent French people should suffer in the recent war the defeat which shocked the world. And if you want another example take Chekov. I don't think anyone can read those stories now without realizing that sooner or later a horrible and bloody revolution must take place. A wise statesman might have done worse than ponder over them and take their plain message to heart. Now Maupassant was no moralist and Chekov was not made of the stuff of which reformers are made.

The point I want to make is that the story teller by the nature of his gift, by his peculiar feeling for the circumstances of his time, by his choice of people to write about, by the kind of stories he tells, offers a criticism of life. He may not know he is doing this, it may be far from his intention, but he does it willy-nilly. My conclusion is that there is no such thing as a mere story teller.

Having decided this to my own satisfaction and I trust to yours it is as a mere story teller that I thank you once more for the honour you have done me in making me a member of your distinguished society.

MADAME DE SÉVIGNÉ

Well over a hundred years ago, Sainte-Beuve wrote that everything that could be said about Madame de Sévigné had already been said. Since then, however, a great deal more has been said. Such being the case, the reader of these lines must not expect me to tell him anything new. All I can hope to do is to remind him of certain facts that he may have forgotten. The events of Madame de Sévigné's life have been stated in sufficient detail by Mrs Hammersley in the introduction to her translation of the letters which she has made for the delectation of the English reader, and for these I may refer him to that. I am inclined to think that French, for all its clarity, and apparent simplicity, is probably the most difficult of all languages to translate. To translate literally may land one in absurdities. One difficulty that confronts the translator is that the French word and the English one are often the same and yet are not used in quite the same sense; another is that a word may not have the same associations in English as in French, and so to translate it literally may sadly distort the author's meaning. It is to Mrs Hammersley's credit that she has avoided these pitfalls, and her translation, though, so far as I have been able to judge, faithful, is easy, fluent and idiomatic.

Madame de Sévigné was a stylist of high quality. She was fortunate in the time of her birth. This took place at the very beginning of the second quarter of the seventeenth century. The best prose-writers of the preceding century, Montaigne, for instance, wrote with charm and naturalness; but, as George Saintsbury justly remarked, their prose, 'though exuberant and picturesque, was not planned or balanced, sentences were ill-formed and the periods haphazard. It was a conversational prose and had the diffusiveness of conversation.' Jean Guez de Balzac, who lived through the first half of the seventeenth century, created the literary language of French prose, and (I am again quoting George Saintsbury) 'taught French authors to write a prose which is written knowingly instead of a prose which is unwittingly talked'. Voiture, his contemporary, had a lighter touch than Balzac, and 'helped to gain for French prose the tradition of vivacity and sparkle which it has always possessed as well as that of correctness and grace'.

Preface to *Letters from Madame La Marquise de Sévigné* edited by Violet Hammersley. Secker & Warburg, 1955.

Thus Madame de Sévigné had to her hand a perfected instrument which she had the tact, taste and talent to make admirable use of. Critics have noted that sometimes her grammar was faulty; but style does not depend on syntax, it depends, I venture to suggest, on character; and Madame de Sévigné had charm, unfailing humour, sympathy, affectionateness, common sense and keen observation. She wrote neither a treatise nor an history; she wrote letters, and she knew very well that they must have a personal touch. Hers are as easy, and as apparently spontaneous, as those Jane Austen wrote to her sister Cassandra; but she had the advantage of having subjects to write about of wider interest than had our own Miss Austen.

Newspapers then were few and dull. Letters provided people living away from Paris with the news of the day. Madame de Sévigné was in a good position to give it to her correspondents, since by her birth and connections she moved in high society. The subjects that excited the attention of the world she lived in were the sermons of eminent preachers, criminal trials, and the rise and fall of the King's favourites. When she went to Court she was graciously received. Once, Louis XIV danced a minuet with her, and afterwards she found herself standing beside her kinsman, Bussy de Rabutin. 'One must acknowledge,' she said to him, 'that we have a great King.' 'Yes, without doubt,' he answered. 'What he has just done is truly heroic.' But whether that witty, sarcastic man was laughing at her or at the monarch is not plain. On another occasion, Louis XIV, to the admiration of all present, talked to her for several minutes. But it was not often that Madame de Sévigné went to Court: she depended then for the latest news on an intimate friend. This was the Duc de La Rochefoucauld, the author of the imperishable maxims. He was a highly cultivated man, extremely intelligent, with a wide knowledge of the world. This knowledge had left him with few illusions. Sentimentalists have reproached him because, as a result of a lifetime's experience, he came to the conclusion that self-interest is the mainspring of men's behaviour. There is truth in that, but it is not the whole truth. The extraordinary, and heartening, thing about men is that though, in fact, self-interest *is* the mainspring of their conduct, they are capable on occasion of self-sacrifice, disinterestedness and magnanimity. The picture Madame de Sévigné draws of La Rochefoucauld is that of a good, high-minded and generous man; and she never tires of remarking on his good nature, sweetness, amiability, and on his wish to please and to be of service.

During the seventeenth century in France persons of quality took a laudable interest in literature. They read Virgil with delight, and argued intelligently over the respective merits of Corneille and Racine. They discussed the niceties of style, and were ravished by a well-turned phrase. It was, in fact, a time of high civilisation. La Rochefoucauld was in the habit of passing some hours every day with Madame de La Fayette, author of the charming *Princesse de Clèves*, and in her house, in the Faubourg de Vaugirard, they would be joined by Madame de Sévigné and the witty Cardinal de Retz. In summer they sat in the garden, 'the prettiest thing in the world', with its flowers, its fountains and its arbour. What would one not give to have heard the conversation of those four cultured, brilliant and well-bred creatures! Never can there have been talk of such savour before or since. Conversation in those happy days was cultivated as an art, and to talk well and entertainingly gave anyone, however modest his origins, an entry into that closed, aristocratic society. Voiture, the son of a vintner, was sought after for his caustic humour. The Duc d'Enghien said of him: 'If Voiture were a gentleman (*de notre condition*) one couldn't put up with him.' There was Madame Cornuel, daughter of the steward or agent of the Duc de Guise, who was famous for her wit and so was received in exclusive circles. At this great house or at that, Corneille could sometimes be induced to read an unpublished play, or La Fontaine his latest fables; La Rochefoucauld's maxims would be admired or decried and a recent letter of Madame de Sévigné's be read aloud.

The malicious said that her letters were written for effect. What if they were? If you have something to say, which you know will raise a laugh, or if you have a story to tell, which you think will interest, you put it as effectively as you can. I can see nothing blameworthy in that. Madame de Sévigné knew that her letters were passed from hand to hand, and there can be little doubt that she enjoyed writing them and enjoyed the pleasure they gave others. She could be serious enough when the occasion warranted, as, for example, when she gave an account of the death of Turenne; but she had a wonderful sense of fun, and when she had something amusing to relate, she made, as the humorist does, the very most of it. She did not even disdain a pun. One I have noticed is brilliant, but since it is untranslatable I must give it in French; she had a fine apartment that she wanted to let, but could not find anyone to take; an apartment she said '*que tout le monde admire et que personne ne veut louer*'. She claimed with justice that her letters were not studied. She might well have said what Jane Austen wrote to Cassandra: 'I have now attained the true art of letter-writing, which we are always told is to express on paper exactly what one would say to the same person by word of mouth. I have been talking to you almost as fast as I could the whole of this letter.' Madame de Sévigné's letters were written conversation, and the conversation of a woman who talked with wit, humour and spontaneity.

Most of them, as everyone knows, were written to her daughter, Madame de Grignan, whom Madame de Sévigné idolised in a manner that posterity has found exaggerated. Madame de Sévigné was a good-looking woman, with beautiful hair and a dazzling complexion. The censorious observed that her eyes were of different colours, her nose blunt and her jaw somewhat heavy; but she redeemed these slight defects by the liveliness of her expression. Her daughter was a great beauty. It is a curious indication of the manners of the time that when Louis XIV was tiring of Madame de La Vallière, there was some talk of pressing the claims of Madame de Sévigné's daughter to the place which would shortly be vacant. What Madame de Sévigné thought of the project, we do not know, but Bussy de Rabutin, her cousin, looked upon it with favour. 'I should be much pleased,' he said, 'if the King formed an attachment to Mlle de Sévigné, because the young woman is a great friend of mine and he couldn't have a better mistress.' Nothing came of this and the young woman was married off to a member of one of the noblest families in France. Madame de Grignan had none of her mother's attractiveness. She was cold, avaricious, though wildly extravagant, proud and unbending. The two ladies were, in fact, so different that it is not surprising to learn that when, later, they were together in Paris, as they were on occasion for months together, they bickered a good deal. It was only when they were separated that they did not get on one another's nerves.

Madame de Sévigné had another child, a son, Charles by name, who seems to have inherited much of her charm, humour and good nature. It seems hard that she should have loved him so much less than she loved her daughter. He appears to have thought it very natural. When Madame de Sévigné divided her fortune between her two children, giving Madame de Grignan by far the larger share, he took it in good part. He was a great rake in his youth. Madame de Sévigné was the confidante of his amours, and she retailed them in her letters to her daughter with a surprising frankness. Charles de Sévigné was an unsatisfactory lover, and was soon discarded by the exacting objects of his passion. He complained to his mother that she was to blame for this, since he had inherited from her what is politely known as lack of temperament. Madame de Sévigné, left a widow at twenty-six, was abundantly courted, both, it appears, by men who wished to marry her and by men whose intentions were less serious. She remained a widow and chaste. In an age when marriages were made by arrangement, often when the parties concerned were children, conjugal fidelity was rare, and it was in the spirit of the time to ascribe it rather to natural frigidity than to virtue. Madame de Sévigné was a good Catholic, but she was not bigoted; and when her son eventually married, and became deeply religious (he ended his days in a seminary), she found life with him not a little dull.

She was a great reader, especially during the long periods she spent at Les Rochers, the place in Brittany she had inherited from her worthless husband. She adored La Fontaine, and, indeed, quarrelled with Madame de Grignan because she did not share her admiration for the charming fabulist. She venerated Corneille, but did not much care for Racine. For all her sweetness and amiability, there was in Madame de Sévigné a certain toughness, and she found the tender author of *Bérénice* unduly sentimental. She read Montaigne with delight, Pascal, both his *Pensées* and the *Provinciales*, but her favourite author was Nicole, the Jansenist. His good sense and sound judgement appealed to her, and she delighted in his style.

During one of her sojourns at Les Rochers the peasants and the townspeople of Brittany, downtrodden and illegally taxed, revolted. They were punished by the Duc de Chaulnes, governor of the province, with barbarity. They were hanged, drawn and quartered by the hundred. Men, women and children were driven out of their houses into the street, and no one was allowed, under pain of death, to succour them. Madame de Sévigné wrote:

> The mutineers of Rennes have run away long ago; so the good will suffer for the wicked; but I find it all for the best, so long as the four thousand soldiers who are at Rennes, under MM. de Fobin and de Vins, don't prevent me from walking about in my woods, which are very fine and marvellously beautiful.

And again:

> They've taken sixty bourgeois; they'll begin to hang them tomorrow. This province is a good example to the others; above all it will lead them to respect their governors, not to abuse them and not to throw stones in their garden.

It has shocked Madame de Sévigné's readers to see with what complaisance she wrote of these wretched people's sufferings. It is indeed shocking. It cannot be excused, it can only be explained.

The seventeenth century in France was, as I have said, a time of high civilisation; but it was also a brutal time. Men were hard, cruel and unscrupulous. Fine gentlemen cheated freely at cards and boasted of it when they had cozened a fool out of his money. M. de Lenclos, a gentleman of Touraine and father of a famous daughter, ran the Baron de Chabans through the body with his sword as he was stepping out of his coach and could not defend himself. It is true that he had to flee from France, but I do not know that anyone thought the worse of him for the cowardly action. These cultured aristocrats, these elegant ladies – who were reduced to tears by Racine's pathos, who admired Poussin and Claude, who crowded to listen to the sermons of Bourdaloue and Massillon, who were so delicately sensitive to the sadness and beauty of the country – looked upon the peasants as hardly human. They used them as they would never have used their horses or their dogs. Madame de Sévigné shared the common opinions of her day. That the brutes should be hanged seemed to her only fitting, and when the Duc de Chaulnes was removed from the province to rule another that brought in a larger income, she wrote that she was heartbroken to lose her dear good Duke. I suppose the best one can say is that it is unfair to judge those of one generation by the standards of another. Perhaps it is well not to censure Madame de Sévigné too harshly for her indifference to the sufferings of these ill-used creatures when we remember how short a while ago we discovered that men, supposedly civilised, were capable of the cruelties we know of. It looks as though man, when his interest, his fear, his ambition, his pride, are concerned, remains very much what he always was.

The Comte de la Rivière, a relation of the lady's, and himself a voluminous letter-writer, said somewhere: 'When you have read one of Madame de Sévigné's you feel a slight pang, because you have one less to read.'

BOOK REVIEWS

THE
IONIAN SEA

It is curious that in England men of letters have so seldom attempted to write books of travel, whereas in France no form of art has been more industriously studied. I suppose one reason is that the English mind is peculiarly analytic, while in all description the most needful thing is to seize the impression of the moment and put it down without a second thought. That excellent critic, Jules Lemaitre, has given an instance of what I mean. You pass a tree and hear a bird singing. The writers of the French classic period (I do not quote the exact words, but merely the sense) would say: A bird is singing among the leaves. But there is analysis; the first impression was only of song and leaves, and the description is frigid and commonplace. Madame de Levigne, by a stroke of genius, wrote: How pretty it is to hear a leaf singing. That is the point. The English somehow have not the art of putting on paper exactly what they perceive, it is the moral aspect of things which interests them; and at the same time they have not the courage to write all they feel. Yet it is emotion which gives books of travel most of their value. The success of Pierre Loti, I fancy, comes from his recognition of this fact. Compare him with Flaubert, a master of his own style. In *L'Education Sentimentale* there is an account of the forest of Fontainebleau which is admirable of its kind. It is the work of a semi-divine Baedeker: the names and colours of the trees are carefully noted, the shape of the clouds, the chirping of the birds, the various scents. It is the minutest catalogue from which nothing is omitted, and it is absolutely impersonal; probably nine readers out of ten would skip it. But Pierre Loti, on the other hand, treats nature as dependent on mankind, and mankind is himself; to him sea and sky in themselves are nothing, they seem only to express or emphasise his own emotion. He does not hesitate to recount with unblushing frankness his most private concerns. The world and his wife would look coldly upon the English writer who narrated his amours so minutely, and they would merely laugh if he wept such copious tears.

But Mr Gissing has ventured to give us something of himself, and consequently his book is charming. 'Every man has his intellectual desire,' he says;

By the Ionian Sea by George Gissing. *Sunday Sun*, 11 August 1901.

mine is to escape life as I know it, and to dream myself into that old world which was the imaginative delight of my boyhood. The names of Greece and Italy draw me as no others; they make me young again, and restore the keen impressions of that time when every new page of Greek or Latin was a new perception of things beautiful. The world of the Greeks and Romans is my land of romance; a quotation in either language thrills me strangely, and there are passages of Greek and Latin verse which I cannot read without a dimming of the eyes, which I cannot repeat aloud because my voice fails me.

It puts the reader into a pleasant humour to feel that he has a man of flesh and blood to deal with, and not a vulgar tourist intent only upon filling his note-books for the manufacture of a volume. And I am pleased that he does not affect to despise the good things of this world, that he has an amiable word to say for his food and drink. In one place Mr Gissing has apologised for dwelling on such details, but no excuse was needed. Nowadays, the strenuous have brow-beaten us, so that we are half afraid to confess our appreciation for the meat we eat and the wine we drink; and it is refreshing to find someone who is not loftily contemptuous of such earthly things. Personally, I do not share Mr Gissing's respect for the rough wine of Posilippo, and my own recollection of Calabrian vintages leaves me doubtful as to the excellence of the Muscato dei Saraceni. I should like to ask him whether he knows the true wine of Capri, not that obnoxious beverage which unsuspecting persons drink in London, or even in Naples; but the pure, sweet wine of the grape which you buy on the rocky island from the peasant growers. They make it themselves, in the old-fashioned way in which they have made it for centuries, in very small quantities so that it can only be got with some difficulty. But what a wine it is!

But it is rather a sad story Mr Gissing has to tell of his wanderings in Southern Italy. He utters an almost constant cry that things have changed. The old beauty is disappearing before the advance of civilisation. Everything is becoming vulgar and up-to-date. Here is what he has to say of Naples:

> Sirocco, of course, dusks everything to cheerless grey, but under any sky it is dispiriting to note the changes in Naples. *Lo sventramento* (the disembowelling) goes on, and regions are transformed. It is a good thing, I suppose, that the broad Corso Umberto I should cut a way through the old Pendino; but what a contrast between that native picturesqueness and the cosmopolitan vulgarity which has usurped its place! '*Napoli se ne ba!*' I pass the Santa Lucia with downcast eyes, my memories of ten years ago shining against the dullness of today. The harbour, whence one used to start for Capri, is filled up; the sea has been driven to a hopeless distance beyond a wilderness of dust-heaps. They are going to make a long straight embankment from the Castel dell' Ovo to the Great Port, and before long the Santa Lucia will be an ordinary street, shut in among huge houses, with no view at all. Ah, the nights that one lingered here, watching the crimson flow upon Vesuvius, tracing the dark line of the Lorrento promontory, or waiting for moonlight to cast its magic upon floating Capri! The odours remain; the stalls of sea-fruit are as yet undisturbed, the jars of the water-sellers; women still comb and bind each other's hair by the wayside, and meals are cooked and eaten *al fresco* as of old. But one can see these things elsewhere, and Santa Lucia was unique. It has become squalid. In the grey light of the sad, billowy sky, only its ancient foulness is manifest; there needs the golden sunlight to bring out a suggestion of its ancient charm.

Again, at Cosenza Mr Gissing complains of the squalid railway station and the hideous railway bridge, of the 'craze for building, which has disfigured and half-ruined Italy'. At Taranto 'great buildings of yellowish white stone, as ugly as modern architect can make them, and plainly far in excess of the actual demand for habitations, rise where Phoenicians and Greeks and Romans built after the noble fashion of their times'. Throughout Italy it is the same. At Venice they have built an iron bridge across the Grand Canal, and penny steamboats waddle up and down, with trails of smoke and fat gurglings. At Florence new streets, new houses, have been built to mark the pride of a young kingdom; at Rome things are worse, and progress is making its way quite pitilessly. What would one not give to see those dear places as they were before Italy became a European Power – when the Pope reigned absolute in Rome, and Florence still had its Grand Duke and Naples its Bourbon King. Doubtless it was all very corrupt, but it is very corrupt still; and if it was behind the times it was very comfortable and happy. Ask the average thoughtful Italian whether the people are so much better and more contented now than they were in the wicked old days of bribery and absolutism, and you will see he is not so ready with his answer as you expected.

In Calabria the people seem even more poverty-stricken than elsewhere. They are crushed by taxation.

> In all the south of Italy money is the one subject of men's thoughts; intellectual life does not exist; there is little even of what we should call common education. Those who have wealth cling to it fiercely; the majority have neither time nor inclination to occupy themselves with anything but the earning of a livelihood which for multitudes signifies the bare appeasing of hunger.

It is difficult to imagine the shifts to which poverty drives the Southern Italians; money seems to have become all in all to them, and to get it they will do practically anything. Not the smallest evil of this overpowering desire is the popularity of the State lottery, which leads thousands upon thousands to spend every halfpenny they can scrape together, by fair means or foul, upon a ticket for the lottery. It is a passion which fills their minds so that they talk continually of this number and that, of this and the other combination; their whole aim in life is to draw a big prize, it is their one hope of being rich.

> The common type of face at Cobrove is coarse and bumpkinish – ruder, it seemed to me, than faces seen at any point of my journey hitherto. A photographer had hung out a lot of portraits, and it was a hideous exhibition; some of the visages attained an incredible degree of vulgar ugliness. This in the town which still bears the name of Croton. The people are all more or less unhealthy. One meets peasants horribly disfigured with lifelong malaria. There is an agreeable cordiality in the middle classes; business men from whom I sought casual information, even if we only exchanged a few words in the street, shook hands with me at parting.

That is the greatest charm of the Southern Italians, their extraordinary cordiality. They have in their whole behaviour so much grace, such a charming friendliness, that even though they cheat you right and left, it is impossible to resist them. Return after a long absence, and you will find that everyone remembers you, and is delighted to see you. They shake your hand

and smile with pleasure, and show such an interest in all your belongings that you cannot help loving them. Though I am aware that they lie on every possible occasion, that they keep their eye constantly fixed on the main chance, and are none too honest, I think them the most charming and companionable creatures in the world. Nowhere do I find myself more at home than in that enchanting island of Capri, among the peasants and fishermen, whom I know so well, and now, alas! have not seen for so long. But I know they will not forget me. And when I land again at the marina I shall find quite a little crowd on the tiny pier who will burst into a shout of joyous surprise at seeing me, and thinking I have forgotten them, crowd round me to tell their names, and remind me that we are old friends.

But now I must say something about the manner in which Mr Gissing has written his book. I am delighted with his simplicity; for those who care for plain speech are growing fewer every day, and it is a relief to find a book without purple patches, and all the other abominations of fine writing. In descriptions of scenery it is a great temptation to allow the pen to run away with one, to fill one's page with pompous adjectives, to pile up masses of colour; but Mr Gissing, happily, has striven for simplicity, and, indeed, what he had to describe needed no verbiage to make it beautiful. His style seems to me admirably easy, it is harmonious and clear, and well adapted for the expression of his various moods. Sometimes, perhaps, his phrase is a little hackneyed. I dislike, for instance, such expressions as a 'perfect day', and 'noble trees'. But such conjunctions of words are very difficult to avoid, they come so easily to the tongue; and yet it is just they which must be most rigorously shunned. There is a story of a publisher returning a manuscript with the suggestion: 'Your style is too simple. Read Stevenson and Pater, and fill it up a bit.' One would not have thought the advice could be given often, for most writers of the present time have studied those two authors with desperate energy. If to have influence is the sign of real success in letters, these two, with George Meredith, can hardly complain; for little is written which does not show a more or less profound study of all three. Indeed it is not wonderful that modern writers should seek to write in as highly decorated a manner as possible, when one considers how often everything has been said and how unlikely a man is to hit upon a new idea. It is an old paradox that the chief use of language is to conceal thought, and when the thought is mediocre, concealment is ten times more necessary. There is nothing like a fine flow of words to obscure the triteness of an observation, while on the other hand a limpid style like Arnold's exposes poverty of idea with quite a merciless cruelty. It is well to be cautious. Here is a quotation that you may judge for yourselves how much better is a straightforward simplicity than all their rhetoric:

> A female servant, who occasionally brought me food (I found that she also cooked it), bore herself in much the same way. This domestic was the most primitive figure of the household. Picture a woman of middle age, wrapped at all times in dirty rags (not to be called clothing), obese, grimy, with dishevelled black hair, and hands so scarred, so deformed by labour and neglect, as to be scarcely human. She had the darkest and fiercest eyes I ever saw. Between her and her mistress went on an unceasing quarrel: they quarrelled in my room, in the corridor, and, as I knew by their shrill voices,

in places remote; yet I am sure they did not dislike each other, and probably neither of them ever thought of parting. Unexpectedly one evening this woman entered, stood by the bedside, and began to talk with such fierce energy, with such flashing of her black eyes, and such distortion of her features, that I could only suppose that she was attacking me for the trouble I caused her. A minute or two passed before I could even hit the drift of her furious speech; she was always the most difficult of the natives to understand, and in rage she became quite unintelligible. Little by little, by dint of questioning, I got at what she meant. There had been *guai*, worse than usual; the mistress had reviled her unendurably for some fault or other, and was it not hard that she should be used like this after having *tanto, tanto laborato*! In fact, she was appealing to my sympathy, not abusing me at all. When she went on to say that she was alone in the world, that all her kith and kin were *freddi morti* (stone dead), a pathos in her aspect and her words took hold upon me; it was much as if some heavily-laden beast of burden had suddenly found tongue, and protested in the rude beginnings of articulate utterance against its hard lot. If only one could have learnt, in intimate detail, the life of this domestic serf! How interesting, and how sordidly picturesque against the background of romantic landscape, of scenic history! I looked long into the sallow, wrinkled face, trying to imagine the thoughts that ruled its expression. In some measure my efforts at kindly speech succeeded, and her 'Ah, Cristo!' as she turned to go away, was not without a touch of solace.

I read Mr Gissing's book under the pleasantest conditions. I took it with me to the Kentish coast, and read it in the evenings within sight and hearing of the grey sea, my limbs happily tired after the day's golf. And it was a strange contrast to turn my mind, filled with the brilliant colour of Calabria, to this Northern Ocean, cheerless and cold even in mid-July; the sky was like a vault of slate, hanging very low, and at the horizon joining insensibly with the broad, flat stretch of sea. It is good to read sometimes books which are so entirely restful, just as after the turmoil of London, with its unceasing roar, which seems to thunder away even through one's sleep. It is comforting to come to the barren, marshy coast of North Kent, peaceful in its unbroken monotony; it is good after the more vivid mental exercise which the manifold interests of the day force upon one, to seek repose in such quiet and leisurely reading. It freshens one to travel easily with Mr Gissing to these exquisite places with their memories and regrets. And if at first the recollection of the scenes and people I love with all my heart made me wretched because I must remain yet another year away from them, I comforted myself with the thought that after all it is in reminiscences that people and places have their greatest charm. I swear that in real fact the sight of Vesuvius at night with its glow, or the *pergolas* of Capri, never gave me such exquisite sensations as when I dream of them in the dreariness of London. Alas, I never enjoy the sunshine of Naples and the cool azure of the sea so intensely as when the rain pours down in the English winter, and I look, rather sadly, at the desolation without. When the trees are leafless and the wind sweeps along the dreary road, my mind is filled with the bouyant picturesqueness of the Southern crowd, and I hear their joyous laughter. After all, it is the imagination which gives these things their charm. Italy and Spain and Greece are beautiful because painters and writers have seen them with fresh eyes, and put into them the beauty of their own souls. Yet it is difficult to console oneself entirely. Whatever one says, one cannot crush the longing that arises whenever the well-known scenes are brought back. Against one's will, it is difficult to help feeling that out there, in Italy, in the sunshine, life is freer and more worth living. One has an impression that in the South it is possible to seize more vigorously all that existence has to offer; every minute there seems so much fuller; every experience, every pleasure and pain, seems so much more intense. 'It is better to die in a hovel by the Ionian Sea than in a cellar at Shoreditch.'

GROWING UP

It would be affectation if I pretended that the moment I received this book and scanned the table of contents I did not turn immediately to chapter twenty-four. For chapter twenty-four is all about me. I read it with great interest and not a little astonishment. It is very intriguing to know how you strike other people, and most people are too civil or too shy to tell you, and so you go through life thinking you are this and that while your fellow men think quite differently of you and not one thinks the same as the other. And what among all these different impressions you really are, or whether you are anything at all, or just their sum, who is going to say? I was certainly very much excited to discover that I (who to myself appear a very quiet and retiring person, asking merely to be left alone and not bored) to the gay enthusiasm of Beverley Nichols appear romantic and saturnine and bleak.

But this, of course, is not criticism. I feel that here is an opportunity for me to analyse the attitude of youth in the year nineteen hundred and twenty-five towards the world we live in and the psychology of the generation which is stoutly knocking at the door. If I could I would write many acute and sensible things on the subject. But who am I to concern myself with these difficult and important matters? It has been my privilege occasionally to meet the critics who are famous in the pages of the sixpenny weeklies, and I have been impressed by their flashing eyes and wanton hair, and that look they have of eager determination. I have been awed by their universal knowledge and their confidence in themselves. Once I was asked to dinner by Osbert Sitwell to meet a number of them, and I sat forlorn and strange while they discussed the prosody of James Elroy Flecker. In order to show an intelligent interest in the affairs of the spirit, I asked the least imposing of the group if he did not find it very exhausting to read books for review, and with a smile he told me that he seldom came across a book of which he could not 'tear out the heart' in an hour.

For such a drastic operation I have no facility. The young never ask me for advice, and this I regret, since I have a great deal of excellent advice at their disposal, for I am not so foolish as to confuse precept with practice; and I should recommend them strongly seldom to read a book to the end. Life is

Twenty-Five by Beverley Nichols. *Sunday Times*, 7 February 1926.

short. When I was young I read the first five books of *Paradise Lost* with a passionate interest, and, being unfortunately prevented from finishing it, I have never ceased wondering what happened. Being of a sentimental turn of mind and liking a happy ending, I have always hoped that things turned out well.

But since then I have never started a book without finishing it. Not for me is the precious gift of 'tearing out the heart of a book'; I must read to the bitter end or for ever lose my peace of mind. I have read every word of this one. It is full of fun, agreeably written, with a certain carelessness, perhaps, which for all I know adds to its gaiety, but with a sense of the picturesque phrase and in a cosy, vivid English. It has life and good nature. In short, I have enjoyed reading it, and, for my part, if a critic has enjoyed reading a book and will tell me so, that is all I really want him to tell me. What else he has to say but mildly interests me.

BOOKS
OF THE
YEAR

Lucky Jim (Gollancz) is a remarkable novel. It has been greatly praised and widely read, but I have not noticed that any of the reviewers have remarked on its ominous significance. I am told that today rather more than 60 per cent of the men who go to the universities go on a Government grant. This is a new class that has entered upon the scene. It is the white-collar proletariat. Mr Kingsley Amis is so talented, his observation is so keen, that you cannot fail to be convinced that the young men he so brilliantly describes truly represent the class with which his novel is concerned.

They do not go to the university to acquire culture, but to get a job, and when they have got one, scamp it. They have no manners, and are woefully unable to deal with any social predicament. Their idea of a celebration is to go to a public house and drink six beers. They are mean, malicious and envious. They will write anonymous letters to harass a fellow undergraduate and listen in to a telephone conversation that is no business of theirs. Charity, kindliness, generosity, are qualities which they hold in contempt. They are scum. They will in due course leave the university. Some will doubtless sink back, perhaps with relief, into the modest class from which they emerged; some will take to drink, some to crime and go to prison. Others will become schoolmasters and form the young, or journalists and mould public opinion. A few will go into Parliament, become Cabinet Ministers and rule the country. I look upon myself as fortunate that I shall not live to see it.

If there are still people left who care to read a novel which is not concerned with the pressing problems of the day, but look simply for entertainment, I can highly recommend *Bergère Légère*, by Félicien Marceau (Gallimard; published in English by Arthur Barker as *The China Shepherdess*). The author is a Belgian, and for the most part the scene is set in Flanders. It is gay, lighthearted and extremely funny. The heroine is far from chaste, but she is very much alive, delightful and charming.

'Books of the Year'. *Sunday Times*, 25 December 1955.

The third book I wish to speak about I came upon entirely by accident. I have some three thousand books in my house and now and then, looking at the serried shelves, I realise that I haven't one I want to read. On one such occasion I caught sight of *The Letters of Pliny the Younger* (Loeb Library. 2 vols. Heinemann). I had bought my edition sixty years ago, when I was trying to make acquaintance with Latin literature, but had never read it. For want of anything more tempting, I took it from its shelf and began to read. I found it entrancing. I hasten to add that I read it in the admirable translation which accompanied the Latin text.

Pliny was a Roman gentleman of wealth who flourished during the reign of the Emperor Trajan. He had been governor of a province, but had retired to live on his estates and went to Rome only when duty called. He was house-proud, and his description of a house he had built, with its swimming pool and central heating, is very engaging. He was addicted to writing indifferent verse, which he was overproud to read to his friends. He was very generous, but well aware that his generosity was praiseworthy, and always ready to oblige a friend. He was vain in a childish and rather charming way. The more you read his letters the more you feel at home with him.

He was in fact very like one of those cultured English noblemen of the nineteenth century who, after years in the public service, spent their declining years on their ancestral estates and went up to London only when they felt it incumbent on them to oppose some amendment in the House of Lords. Some of them, too, published now and again a slim volume of light verse.

The Letters of Pliny the Younger can be read with pleasure without any classical learning and with only the most elementary knowledge of Roman history. They make a most enjoyable bedside book.

ON
HIS OWN WORK

HOW
NOVELISTS DRAW
THEIR
CHARACTERS

1 *Do you generally draw your characters from models in real life?*
I think as a rule my characters are suggested by someone I have known, but to say that I model them on definite living persons would be to exaggerate. I find that by the time I have finished with a character which has engaged my attention, very little is left of the original. It seems to me that very few persons stand so square on their own feet as to make them suitable for fiction.

2 *Do characters so drawn seem more real in the story, or to yourself, than those that are purely imaginary?*
I do not believe that such characters as I have modelled on actual persons are any more real to me than those I have devised out of my head for the purposes of my story. I do not see why they should be. On the contrary it seems to me that you will know more about a character that you have invented than you possibly can about one who is partially concealed from you by the stubborness of fact.

3 *Which is your own favourite among all the characters in your books?*
I think these two questions which you have put to me rather dull, but the third interests me, since on trying to answer it I have made a little discovery about myself which has given me a moment's surprise. When I look back upon the characters I have invented I find that I am less interested in those that play a leading part in my various novels than in the subsidiary ones. My recollection lingers with most pleasure on a youth called Gerald Vaudrey in *Mrs Craddock* and on Thorpe Athelny in *Of Human Bondage*. I think I liked them because they are gay, amusing and unscrupulous.

Bookman, May 1922.

A
BIBLIOGRAPHY

When the industrious compiler of this bibliography asked me to write a short preface to it I could not but at once consent, but then, considering the matter, I discovered that I did not in the least know how to set about it. So I went to my booksellers, Messrs Bumpus, and asked one of the gentlemen who are accustomed to my vagueness (for I seldom know the name of a book I want, hardly ever the author's, and never the publisher's, so that they have to guess from my confused description and my inexact recollection of where I read about it, what exactly I am looking for) to show me what bibliographies they had. They brought me half a dozen and I turned at once to the prefaces. But for the most part they were written by the compilers and they had enlarged on the merits of the authors whose works had occupied them in what must be a tiresome and thankless task.

Now it is a little unbecoming for an author himself to draw the reader's attention to the significance of his work and to his importance in the world of letters; so, somewhat discouraged, I put the books down. They were no help to me.

I suppose that no author can forget the thrill with which he handles the first copy of his first book.

This with me was *Liza of Lambeth*. I received six copies from the publisher and it was with exultation that I looked at the neat, rather attractive little books in their pale green binding; it was with pride that in the first one I put the name of a friend who had been the dear companion of my lonely youth. I have not myself owned a copy of the first edition of this book for many years, but when I saw a copy the other day, I could not but feel something of the old emotion.

I think the first edition was of two thousand and therefore copies must be getting rather scarce.

But there is another little book of mine which must be scarcer still. It is the paper-bound edition of *A Man of Honour*, which was issued by Messrs

---

Preface to *A Bibliography of the Writings of William Somerset Maugham* by F.T. Bason. Unicorn Press, 1931.

Chapman and Hall. This was a play published in *The Fortnightly Review* by the late W.L. Courtney, who thought well of it, and at my urgent request the publishers bound up a few copies of the sheets, two hundred and fifty, I think, for sale in the theatre during the two performances which the Stage Society gave it.

I am afraid the venture did not profit them, for I doubt whether fifty copies were sold, and I suppose the rest have long ago been pulped.

I hope this bibliography will prove useful to those for whose use it is intended.

It gives me a shiver to turn its pages, as though somebody were walking over my grave: for it is, after all, a specification as it were of my life's endeavour, and that it should be thought worth while to draw it up suggests to me that my work is nearly done.

When I look at it, well printed and smartly bound, I seem to look at my own tombstone.

OF
HUMAN BONDAGE
WITH
A DIGRESSION
ON THE
ART OF FICTION

You will remember that one of the characters in Dostoevsky's novel *The Possessed* remarks that at a literary gathering, such as this, no one should be allowed to discourse for more than twenty minutes. It is true that he is the most odious character in the book, but there is a lot in what he says. I shall try not to exceed this limit. I start by telling you this in case these typescript sheets I have in front of me fill you with misgiving. A year or two ago I was invited to give a lecture at a great and ancient university, and for reasons with which I need not trouble you I chose the somewhat grim topic of political obligation. I knew exactly what I wanted to say and went into the lecture hall without even a note. It was crowded to the doors. I think I got through the lecture pretty well and I reached my peroration without mishap. But having been at one time of my life a dramatist, I have been inclined to end a discourse with a curtain line. Well, I reached my curtain line with a sigh of relief and began very confidently: The price of liberty is — and then I had a complete black-out and I could not for the life of me remember what the price of liberty was.

It brought my lecture to a humiliating conclusion and, unless in the interval someone else has told them, the students of that great and ancient university do not to this day know what the price of liberty is.

Address to the Library of Congress, 20 April 1946. *The Maugham Enigma* edited by K.W. Jonas. Peter Owen, 1954.

I thought I would not let myself be caught in that way again and I am no longer prepared to trust in the failing memory of the very old party you know I am.

I am very grateful to you for coming here tonight, since you are not only paying me a compliment, but you are paying a compliment to a form of fiction which is badly in need just now of encouragement.

I have never pretended to be anything but a story teller. It has amused me to tell stories and I have told a great many. But as you know, story telling just for the sake of the story is not an activity that is in favour with the intelligentsia. It is looked upon as a debased form of art. That seems strange to me since the desire to listen to stories appears to be as deeply rooted in the human animal as the sense of property. Since the beginning of history men have gathered round the camp fire or in a group in the market place to listen to the telling of a story. That the desire is as strong as ever it was is shown by the amazing popularity of detective stories in our own day. For the habitual reader of them can generally guess who the murderer is before he is half way through, and if he reads on to the end it is only because he wants to know what happens next, which means that he is interested in the story.

But we novelists are on the whole a modest lot, and when we are told that it is our business, not merely to entertain, but to deal with social security, economics, the race question, and the state of the world generally, we are pleased and flattered. It is very nice to think that we can instruct our fellow men and by our wisdom improve their lot. It gives us a sense of responsibility and indeed puts us on a level of respectability with bank presidents. For my part, I think it is an abuse to use the novel as a pulpit or a platform, and I think readers are misguided when they suppose they can thus acquire knowledge without trouble.

It is a great nuisance that knowledge cannot be acquired without trouble. It can only be acquired by hard work. It would be fine if we could swallow the powder of profitable information made palatable by the jam of fiction. But the truth is that, so made palatable, we can't be sure that the powder will be profitable. I suggest to you that the knowledge the novelist imparts is biased and thus unreliable, and it is better not to know a thing at all than to know it in a distorted fashion. If readers wish to inform themselves of the pressing problems of the day, they will do better to read, not novels, but the books that specifically deal with them.

The novelist is a natural propagandist. He can't help it, however hard he tries. He loads his dice. By the mere fact of introducing a character to your notice early in his novel he enlists your interest and sympathy in that character. He takes sides. He arranges facts to suit his purpose. Well, that is not the way a book of scientific or informative value is written. There is no reason why a novelist should be anything but a novelist. He should know a little about a great many things, but it is unnecessary, and sometimes even harmful, for him to be a specialist in any particular subject. The novelist need not eat a whole sheep to know what mutton tastes like; it is enough if he eats a chop. Applying then his imagination and his creative faculty to the chop he has eaten, he can give you a very good idea of an Irish stew, but when he goes on from this to give you his views on sheep raising, the wool industry and the political situation in Australia, I think it is well to accept his ideas with reserve.

But please do not misunderstand me. There can be no reason why the novelist should not deal with every subject under the sun so long as it enables him to get on with his story and to develop his characters. If I insist on the importance of the story, it is partly because it is a very useful rail for the author to cling to as page follows page and it is the surest way for him to hold his reader's interest. The story and the persons of the story are interdependent. They must act according to character or the story will lose its plausibility, but it seems to me that the author is at liberty to choose his characters to fit his story or to devise his story to fit his characters. Which he does, probably depends on the idiosyncrasy of his talent, if any.

I suggest to you that it is enough for a novelist to be a good novelist. It is unnecessary for him to be a prophet, a preacher, a politician or a leader of thought. Fiction is an art and the purpose of art is to please. If in [many] quarters this is not acknowledged I can only suppose it is because of the unfortunate impression so widely held that there is something shameful in pleasure. But all pleasure is good. Only, some pleasures have mischievous consequences and it is better to eschew them. And of course there are intelligent pleasures and unintelligent pleasures. I venture to put the reading of a good novel amongst the most intelligent pleasures that man can enjoy.

And I should like to remind you in passing that reading should be enjoyable. I read some time ago a work by a learned professor which purported to teach his students how to read a book. He told them all sorts of elaborate ways to do this, but he forbore to mention that there could be any enjoyment to be got out of reading the books he recommended. In fact he made what should be a delight into an irksome chore, and, I should have thought, effectively eradicated from those young minds any desire ever again to open a book after they were once freed from academic bondage.

Let us consider for a moment the qualities that a good novel should have. It should have a coherent and plausible story, a variety of probable incidents, characters that are living and freshly observed, and natural dialogue. It should be written in a style suitable to the subject. If the novelist can do that I think he has done all that should be asked of him. I think he is wise not to concern himself too greatly with current affairs, for if he does his novel will lose its point as soon as they are no longer current. H.G. Wells once gave me an edition of his complete works and one day when he was staying with me he ran his fingers along the many volumes and said to me: 'You know, they're dead. They dealt with matters of topical interest and now of course they're unreadable.' I don't think he was quite right. If some of his novels can no longer be read with interest it is because he was always more concerned with the type than with the individual, with the general rather than with the particular.

Nor do I think the novelist is wise to swallow wholesale the fashionable fads of the moment. I read an article the other day in which the author stated that in future no novel could be written except on Freudian principles. It seemed to me a very ingenuous statement. Most psychologists, though acknowledging liberally the value of Freud's contributions to their science, are of opinion that he put many of his theories in an exaggerated form; but it is just these exaggerations that attract the novelist because they are striking and picturesque. The psychology of the future will doubtless discard them and then the novelist who has based his work on them will be up a gum tree. How dangerous to the novelist the practice is, of depending too much on theories that a later generation may discard, is shown very well in the most impressive novel this century has produced, *Remembrance of Things Past*. Proust, as we know, was greatly influenced by the philosophy of Henri Bergson and large stretches of his great work are taken up with it. I think I am right in saying that philosophers now regard Henri Bergson's more striking ideas as erroneous. I suppose we all read with a thrill of excitement Proust's volumes as they came out, but now when we re-read them in a calmer mood I think what we find to admire in them is his wonderful humour and the extraordinarily vivid and interesting characters that he created. We skip his philosophical disquisitions.

It is obviously to the novelist's advantage that he should be a person of broad culture, but the benefit to him of that is the enrichment of his own personality. His business is with human nature and he can best acquire knowledge of that by observation and by exposing himself to all the vicissitudes of human life.

But I have not really come here to give you a discourse upon the art of fiction. Dr Luther Evans asked me to talk to you about *Of Human Bondage*, and if I have so long delayed to do so it is because I have now to tell you that I know very little about it. I corrected the proofs in the autumn of 1914 – thirty-two years ago – in a billet near Ypres by the light of a single candle, and since then I have only opened the book once. That was when, some months ago, I was asked to read the first chapter for a record that was being made for the blind. I did not make a very good job of it because I was moved, not because the chapter was particularly moving, but because it recalled a pain that the passage of more than sixty years has not dispelled. So if you will have patience with me I will content myself with giving you the history of this book.

While still a medical student I had published a novel which had some success and as soon as I had taken my degrees I went to Seville and settled down to write an autobiographical novel. I was then twenty-three. Following the fashion of the day I called it rather grandly *The Artistic Temperament of Stephen Carey*. Then I took it back to London to get it published. Life was cheap in those days, but even then you couldn't live for nothing, and I wanted a hundred pounds for my year's keep. But I could find no publisher who was willing to give me more than fifty. I daresay that was all it was worth, but that I obstinately refused to accept. It was a bit of luck for me, for if the book had been published then – and it was certainly very crude and very immature – I should have lost much that I was able to make better use of later.

Years went by and I became a popular dramatist. But those memories of an unhappy past burdened me and the time came when I felt that I could only rid myself of them by writing them; so I retired from the theatre and spent two years writing the book you know now. Then I had another bit of luck. I had called it *Beauty for Ashes*, which is a quotation from Isaiah, but discovered that a novel with that title had recently been published. I hunted about for another and then it occurred to me that the title Spinoza had given to one of the books of his Ethics would very well do for mine. So I called it *Of Human Bondage*.

It was published in England in 1915 and was well enough reviewed. But we were then engaged in a war and people had more important things to occupy themselves with than the characters of a work of fiction. There had been besides a spate of semi-biographical novels and the public was a trifle tired of them. My book was not a failure, nor was it a success. It did not set the Thames on fire. It was only by a lucky break that it was published in America. George Doran, then a publisher who specialized in English books, brought it back to this country for consideration, but it was very long and nobody read it. Then Mrs Doran got an attack of influenza and on asking for something to pass the time, George Doran gave her *Of Human Bondage* to read, chiefly, I believe, because of its length. She liked it and on this he decided to publish it.

It came out and Theodore Dreiser gave it in *The Nation*[1] a very long, intelligent and favourable review. Other reviewers were more moderate in their praise, but on the whole sympathetic. The average life of a novel at that period was ninety days, and about that time *Of Human Bondage* appeared to die. For two or three years, perhaps more, it was to all appearance forgotten. Then again I had a bit of luck. For a reason I have never known it attracted the attention of various writers who were then well-known columnists, Alec Woollcott, Heywood Broun and the still living and still scintillating F.P. Adams. They talked about it among themselves and then began talking about it in their columns. It found new readers. It found more and more readers. The final result you know. It has now gained the doubtful honour of being required reading in many educational institutions. If I call it a doubtful honour it is because I am not sure that you can read with pleasure a book you have to read as a task. For my own part, I once had to read *The Cloister and the Hearth* in that way and there are few books for which I have a more hearty dislike.

It is because the success of *Of Human Bondage* is due to my fellow writers in America and to a whole generation of American readers that I thought the least I could do was to offer the manuscript to the Library of Congress.

When I asked Dr Luther Evans if he would accept it I told him that I wanted to present it in gratitude for the hospitality I, my daughter and grandchildren have received in this country. I was afraid it would seem presumptuous if I said more. I did not expect this celebration. I thought that if Dr Evans was agreeable to my suggestion, I would make the manuscript into a neat parcel, despatch it by parcel post, and then he would put it on one of the shelves in the Library and that would be that. But since you have been so good as to come here, since I have had a signal honour conferred on me, I am encouraged to say what was really my wish to say at the beginning. You know, we British are on the whole honest people, we like to pay our way and we do not like to be in debt. But there is one debt that we can never hope to repay, and that is the debt we owe you for the kindness and the generosity with which you received the women and children of my country when in fear of a German invasion they came to America. They were lonely and homesick and they were unhappy at leaving behind them those who were dear to them. No one knows better than I how much you did for them, how patient you were with them and what sacrifices you made for them. So it is not only for my own small family, but for all those of my fellow countrymen who found refuge on these shores that I wish to offer this manuscript to you, not as an adequate return, not even

---

[1] This article actually appeared in *New Republic*, December 1915.

as a token payment, but just as an acknowledgment of the debt we owe you. Thank you.

BEHIND THE STORY

A good many years ago, getting on for fifteen, I should think, I wrote a book called *The Summing Up* in the course of which, talking of the historical novel, I said that to write it an author needed a profound experience of men to create living characters out of the persons of a bygone day whose different manners and different notions at first sight make them so alien to us. To recreate the past, I added, needs not only much knowledge, but an effort of imagination that is hardly to be expected from the young. I drew from this the conclusion that the novelist should turn to the historical novel towards the end of his career, when thought and the vicissitudes of his own life have brought him worldly wisdom, and when, having for years explored the personalities of the people with whom he has been brought in contact, he has acquired a sufficient knowledge of human nature to understand and so give life to the figures of a past age.

Well, now I have followed my own advice and it is for the readers of *Then and Now* to judge whether I have in point of fact brought to life the persons with whom I have chosen to deal. This is a novel that I have had in mind for many years, for I have never been able to write either a novel or a short story without mulling it over in my mind for a very long time. Whenever I have set myself to write upon a subject that has recently occurred to me or upon a subject that was of topical interest and so had to be written without delay I have made a mess of it.

It is certainly fifty years ago since I first became acquainted with the main writings of Machiavelli. I found them very good reading and I found myself besides intensely interested in the character of the man who wrote them. I read a long life of him and it was then that I got an inkling that there was somewhere there the materials for a novel. For Machiavelli was no ordinary man. He had no patience with humbug. He was no hypocrite. He was completely devoid of sentimentality and he had a cool sense of reality. *The Prince*, his most famous work, is an analysis of how an ambitious man may make himself ruler of a state. Machiavelli with his acute intelligence saw what means such a man must employ to achieve his ends and indicated them with an admirable clarity and with a characteristic lack of moral scruple. He thus produced a very excellent handbook for dictators. Napoleon studied it and we are told that Mussolini and Hitler profited by its teaching. In passing, however, I may suggest that if Hitler had read it more attentively he would have saved himself from making some fatal mistakes.

The rise of totalitarianism and the power achieved by unscrupulous upstarts revived my interest in *The Prince* and in Machiavelli, and I found my thoughts more and more occupied with the novel I might possibly write. I decided to write it because it seemed to me that there was much that is apposite to the present day in those events that occurred in the sixteenth century and salutory lessons to be learnt from the reflections they occasioned in Machiavelli's lucid brain. It is because the theme is actual that I have called my novel *Then and Now*. But one cannot write a historical novel out of one's head; it needs a lot of hard work before one starts to write a line. I gathered the necessary materials. I read books on the history, the manners and customs of the period, and I read Machiavelli's works. He was a great letter writer and many of his letters have been preserved. I discovered from reading them that he, like all of us, was not all of a piece. He was not only an industrious civil servant and an astute diplomat. He was a jovial fellow, who loved to tell a good story and who liked good living and pretty women. I discovered also that he was an ardent patriot. Thus have I tried to represent him. I have chosen for the period of my novel the exciting months he spent with Caesar Borgia, for it was in great part his experience at the court of that picturesque ruffian that gave him the material which he afterwards used in writing his most celebrated book. The moral he drew from the story, and a very sound one it is, I have given in the last brief speech I have put into the mouth of Machiavelli at the end of my book.

But the first business of a novel is to entertain and a novelist is a fool if he writes something from which he himself does not also get entertainment. I did not want this book to be concerned only with plots, counterplots and political dissertations. I wanted some thread, some intrigue, which would hold the reader's attention, portray those aspects of my hero's character which do not appear in his published works and at the same time amuse me to describe. Fortunately for me Machiavelli wrote plays. One, called *The Mandrake* and very well translated into English by Stark Young, is considered by literary critics the best comedy the Italian theatre has produced. It is very bawdy, but since a pope and his cardinals laughed heartily when they saw it, there is no great reason for us small fry to be shocked by it. Now I also at one time of my life wrote plays and they were generally the elaboration of some personal experience of my own. So I asked myself whether it was not possible that Machiavelli had got the idea of his play from something that had happened to himself and then I set myself to imagining what this thing might have been. What I thus imagined the reader will see when he reads my story. I am practically convinced that I have got the facts straight.

Manuscripts and First Editions

I look upon it as a great honour that the Stanford University Libraries have done me in arranging this exhibition of my manuscripts and the first editions of my books. I have never quite understood why people should collect first editions, but to do so is a harmless pastime, and it may be that the collector, at a loss for something else to do, will take down a book from his serried shelves – and read it. That is all to the good. Though not a collector myself, I look upon those who are with sympathy. To make a collection – it doesn't much matter what – adds an enduring interest to life and when the collector has at last found some rare piece that for years he has been looking for, he feels as proud and triumphant as a general who has won a battle. There must be few objects that at one time or another have not been enthusiastically sought after, postage stamps and cigarette cards, snuff-boxes and walking sticks, old pistols, old pewter and horse brasses. Of all such objects for collection I think that to collect first editions is the most interesting, but that, of course, may be only because I am a writer myself.

Manuscripts are in a category of their own. They tell you something about the writer and give your imagination the occasion pleasantly to roam along the bypaths of fancy. I shall never forget the thrill it gave me when on a visit to the Escorial I saw the manuscript of St. Theresa's autobiography. She is one of my favourite saints and it filled me with a strange emotion to look at the bold, clear script which, so it seemed to me, was so wonderfully characteristic of the brave, resourceful, pious and humorous woman she was. There was not a single erasure and if the manuscript I saw was not a fair copy that she had written herself, she must have known at once (as few of us authors do) exactly what she wanted to say and how best to say it. And knowing what I do about her, I am inclined to think that this was in fact so.

St. Theresa wrote her autobiography some four hundred years ago. I am not so foolish as to suppose that any manuscript of mine will survive for so long or, if it happens to do so, will be of any interest. I must assure the reader of

---

By Way of a Preface to *A Comprehensive Exhibition of the Writings of W. Somerset Maugham*, Stanford University, 1958.

these lines that it is with proper diffidence that I am going on now to speak of my own manuscripts. I think I must be the last professional writer to write everything he has written with his own hand. All authors now use a typewriter. I wish some learned professor of English would think it worth his while to write a brief treatise on the possible difference this may make in the production of literature now that every author uses a machine on which to express himself. Will he write more succinctly or, contrariwise, will the facility which the practiced typist acquires induce him to write more and more verbosely? During the First World War I had a job which obliged me to send in typed reports to my bosses. I wrote them in long hand and then laboriously typed them. I was forced to do this because I could never find a machine that knew how to spell.

For many years I did not bother about my manuscripts and they were lost or destroyed. When later I began to have them bound, some were stolen and the rest, for the most part, given away. Some months ago, however, to my surprise I came across the first two acts of a play called *Lady Frederick* which I wrote in 1905. I was interested to see how greatly my handwriting had changed. I venture to call the reader's attention to it not for that, but because it was written on the back of several pages of typescript. I had not the patience to read them and I suppose they were part of a story or a novel that I had sent to a professional typist to be copied and which for some reason I had discarded. Anyhow, being then very short of money, very short indeed, I could not afford to waste pages of good clean paper and had written my play on them. There was no trace of a last act and I had to look at a printed copy of the play to see what it was all about.

Now I have little more to say. I wish to tender my grateful thanks to Mr Terry Bender for the great trouble he has taken to gather first editions of my books and such manuscripts as are available to make this collection as complete as possible. This collection would never have been made but for my friend Bertram Alanson's gift to the Library of Stanford University of a number of my books and the manuscript of *The Trembling of a Leaf*, a collection of stories, among which is one called 'Rain' which has become somewhat widely known. I gave this manuscript to Bertram Alanson many years ago and it was with pride and pleasure that I learnt it had been accepted by the Library. I should like to think it will be a memorial to a long friendship, a friendship of over forty years, during which his kindness and affection have never failed me.

SHORT STORIES

THE
SPANISH PRIEST

There can be few better places in the world than Gibraltar for meeting odd persons. To stay there is like watching in the act some play of manners crowded with characters, all of whom have special and individual peculiarities. In Gibraltar, that ant-hill of a hundred nationalities, Moor and Christian and Jew rub elbows with one another; a babel of different tongues confuses your ear – English, Spanish, Arabic. Saunter through Waterport Street in the afternoon (it is like the high-street of an English market-town, and the massive grey stone of its houses, with their Georgian air, makes a queer impression under that Southern sky), and you will see many strange things. Sailors of all nations lounge idly by the Spaniards' side, and dark-eyed girls in mantillas, accompanied by dueñas, walk quickly with modest bearing; English ladies, of mature age, ride past with callow subalterns attendant; a British regiment passes with resonant tramp to the playing of fife and drum, while little Arab boys, naked of leg, trot along the curb, whistling, of all tunes, *Rule Britannia*. And in the taverns where Andalusian lasses, in the national dress, are dancing the bolero, the man-o'-war's man drinks his grog, the Scot his whisky, while the Spaniard, smoking the incessant cigarette, sips the light white wine of Manzanilla.

To one of these I used often to go, sitting for hours to watch the faces of all those people, and striving to discern their characters from the way they held themselves, or their expression while they talked. Here I smoked one Saturday night when the place was so full that I could get a seat only at a table where sat another man. I paid no particular attention to him till presently he addressed me.

'Rum lot, aren't they?' he exclaimed suddenly, as though his thoughts went parallel with mine.

I turned round and saw a wiry, sunburned fellow, whose appearance was not a little remarkable. He was about fifty years of age, shabbily dressed with that mixture of English and Spanish clothes assumed by those who have spent many years in the country; and the look of his face suggested that he was a

Illustrated London News, 6 January 1906.

hard drinker. But there was strength there as well, and character. The blue eyes were sharp and alert; his nose was strong, large, and obstinate.

'I see you've lived a good deal in Spain,' I said.

'Thirty years.'

'Engineer?' I asked.

'Mining,' he answered.

At that rate, I thought, the conversation would not proceed rapidly, but I am always interested in talking with an Englishman who has lived long in Spain. It is from men such as these, whose avocations throw them into intimate contact with the people, that most can be learned of that curiously impenetrable race. I offered him something to drink and passed him my cigar-case. I noticed that he added singularly little water to his whisky.

'By George,' he said, 'that's good stuff! Can't get it up in the mountains, you know. Have to put up with *aguardiente* and muck like that.'

He lit the cigar and blew out the smoke in heavy clouds. He looked at it and at me, and I flattered myself the cigar was to his liking. An expression of greater content passed over his restless face, in which there was always a look as if he sought something continually: those sharp eyes of his never rested, but darted across the room over my shoulder as if perpetually on the look-out. But now a certain geniality seized the stranger, and I saw he was disposed to be communicative.

'After all, one hasn't much to complain of when one has a drink and a good cigar, a comfortable place to sit in, and a few dancers to look at.'

'You must have seen some queer things in your time,' I murmured, tentatively.

The engineer turned to me suddenly.

'D'you know that somewhere in Andalusia the biggest fortune in the world is lying ready to be picked up by anyone who finds it? Some day a man will stumble against it, and millionaires will be paupers by the side of him. It's there, waiting, waiting.'

He finished the whisky and called for more.

'You see me,' he added. 'I don't look very prosperous, do I? Well, I tell you that if chance hadn't played me a cursed trick, I should be a richer man than Rothschild.'

'Found a mine?' I asked.

'No, that's just what I didn't,' he answered, with a bitter laugh. 'Would you like to know about it?'

'Fire away.'

'Well, I was manager of a mining company in Seville – you know that the mines in Spain are all run by foreigners. I suppose it's the richest country in the world in the way of mineral resources, take it all in all. When people wake up to the fact that the earth out here is just a mass of ore, well, they won't go out to the Cape.'

'What were your mines?' I asked.

'Copper pyrites. They brought in a good deal of money, I can tell you. Anyhow, I was sitting in my office one day when a clerk came in to say that a priest wanted to see me. He wouldn't give his name nor his business. I had a good deal to do, and I answered that I was too busy to see him. In a minute the clerk came back and told me the priest had sat himself down and insisted on waiting till I was free. They told him I might be engaged all day; but he said it didn't matter, he would wait still. I know what these fellows are, so I had him brought in.'

'How long was this ago?'

'About ten years. Well, the priest appeared. He was a tall man for a Spaniard, about sixty years old, I should say, with grizzled hair and a three-days' growth of white beard. He'd got a long, lean face, something like a horse, yellow as though he suffered from a chronic jaundice; and he was as thin as if every day in the year were a fast. He wore a shabby black cassock, threadbare and almost green with age; here and there it was untidily patched, and it was all frayed at the bottom. His great sharp bones seemed to stick out of it as if they would pierce through. I've never seen a thinner man in my life. He took off his hat when he came into my office, and apologised for troubling me. The words seemed to come out of his mouth without any movement of the lips, and he spoke with a sort of hesitation as if he were deadly frightened.

'"Upon my soul," I said to myself, "this is a queer card. I wonder what he wants."

'I found the priest was taking me in pretty thoroughly. His eyes started at my feet and travelled slowly up till they met mine, and then they stopped still. All the time he was there he never took his eyes off me. When I turned they followed me suspiciously; they watched every movement of my hands; and all the while his long, yellow face remained without any trace of expression.

'"Won't you sit down?" I said. "What can I do for you?"

'For a moment he didn't answer, and I wondered if he was a bit wrong in his mind.

'"Am I right in thinking you're a mining engineer, Señor?" he asked, at last.

'"You are."

'"You're the manager of the company?"

'"Yes."

'He paused again and his eyes seemed to gather themselves together, as it were to look more keenly into me. But I grew impatient.

'"Look here, I've got no end of work to do. I suppose you didn't come here just to pass the time of day. If you've got any business to do, do it; if not, you'd better clear out."

'He took no notice of my speech.

'"You must know all that's to be known about mines and mining," he said very slowly.

'"Well, I know a good deal," I laughed.

'He hesitated, and then the question slipped out of his lips in that odd way, so that I might have thought somebody else, whom I couldn't see, was talking.

'"Would you know a piece of ore if you saw it?"

'I started, and looked at him with more interest. It struck me the old man might have hit upon a mine. I'd heard of that sort of thing before in Spain. I didn't answer, and the priest got up; he lifted his long black cassock and from some inner pocket took a rather bulky parcel wrapped in a common red handkerchief. He undid it slowly, with trembling fingers, and all the time his strange eyes watched me closely. He came forward to the table, and laid on it a great lump of stuff about as large as my two fists put together.

'"By Jove, what's that?" I cried.

'I had expected to see copper pyrites or some iron ore of sorts, for that is what we chiefly go for in Southern Spain. I knew the look of them, and this was neither. But it was ore right enough, though I didn't for the life of me know what. I looked up at the priest and I saw that his sallow cheeks were red and he breathed heavily; his keen eyes sparkled as they watched my astonishment.

"It's ore, but I don't know what; do you?"

'An expression of indescribable cunning passed over his face.

"I know nothing of mines. How should I? Can't you find out what it is?"

'I turned it over thoughtfully. I was certain he knew very well, but for some reason wouldn't say.

"I shall have to send it to London."

"Very well. Do so."

"Yes; but hadn't you better explain a bit? How did you come by this? Where did you find it?"

"Ah, that is my secret. I will show you the place when you know what the ore is. And we must have a little agreement. I want half of everything you get – do you agree?"

"Is it a mine, then? Whereabouts? You can surely tell me that."

"It's not very far from Granada. I found it when I was wandering about the mountains. It's an old Roman mine, but it's hardly worked at all. I've studied ores all my life, and I *know* what that is. But you shall see for yourself." He spoke still in the same even tones, without haste, thought I saw he was enormously excited. "And I tell you the ore is just lying there on the top of the earth. You can pick it up as you walk along."

"D'you think there's much of it?" I asked.

"Much? There's enough to pay the National Debt of Spain ten times over."

'I thought it over for a minute or two.

"Well, look here, it's all very extraordinary, but it's no good our going into the matter till I've had this examined. I'll send it along to England at once. Leave me your address, and in three weeks I shall be able to let you know exactly what it is."

'He put his hand on mine quickly.

"Remember, I'm to have half," he said.

'I nodded, and gave him a pen and a piece of paper to put his name down. He wrote painfully, like a man unused to writing, and his large scrawl was scarcely legible. I looked at it, and found the priest was called Vicente Oria y Mazallon; he lived in Granada, in the Calle Alfonso Trece, number seven. I put the slip of paper in my pocket-book and showed him to the door. When we shook hands he told me that if I wrote to that address he would come to Seville at once, and then, the agreement between us properly signed, he would lead me to the mine. I went back into my office and turned over the jagged piece of ore; I wondered what it was, and whether the mine, if such really existed, could be profitably worked.

"Who knows?" I said to myself. "Perhaps the old man's right and I may be on the highway to making my pile."

'I packed it up myself and sent it to England that night. I was overwhelmed with work at that time, and the whole matter slipped from my memory, till, some three weeks later, among my letters I found one from our analyst. I opened it without much curiosity. At first I could hardly believe my eyes. My heart began to beat so violently that I thought I should faint. My head swam. For that piece of ore contained – *gold*, gold in such quantity that the mine from which it came must be the richest in the world. I began to laugh, hysterically, like a woman, and the air grew suddenly so thin that I could scarcely breathe; I seemed to walk upon mountain heights. But I pulled myself together. After all I was a business man and it was stupid to be so overcome. As methodically as I could, I took from my pocket-book the old priest's address and I felt sure now that he knew all the time this secret of fabulous wealth. I went to the post-office myself, and wired him to come to Seville at once. I returned to my office and tried to go on with my work, but my thoughts were no longer under my control. How could I pay attention to humdrum affairs when there lay within my reach a fortune so enormous that the world itself was at my feet? Then it occurred to me that the priest might not have money for the journey, and I went to the post-office again and sent him a note for a hundred pesetas.

'Knowing at what time he could arrive, I went to the station to meet him; I resolved not to let him out of my sight till he had told me where exactly the mine was. I was consumed with the desire to see it with my own eyes. Gold, gold, gold! With feverish anxiety I watched the people get out of the train, and he was nowhere to be seen. I cursed the Spanish dilatoriness which had made him linger. No other train arrived for twelve hours, and I did not know how to bear my impatience. I telegraphed again, bidding him hasten, and again went to the station. Once more I endured that agony of expectation and a bitter disappointment. I met a third train and still he did not come. I began to grow seriously alarmed. I could bear the suspense no longer. There was a train just starting for Granada, and I jumped in. I shall never forget the endlessness of that journey and my desperate excitement as each station brought me nearer. I had no luggage to hamper me, and when at last we arrived I took a cab at once and drove to the Calle Alfonso Trece. It was a poor street, and the house in which the priest lived was a great, ramshackle building, originally perhaps the residence of some nobleman, but now inhabited by a score of shabby families. I asked the first person I met for Don Vicente, and was told he lived in one room on the top storey.

'"Is he in now?"

'"*Puede ser*, it may be. I've not seen him for several days."

'A little boy led me to the attic and with wildly beating heart I knocked. At last, at last! There was no answer. I knocked again and from another room a woman came out.

'"D'you want Don Vicente? He went away a fortnight ago."

'A sudden blackness came before my eyes, and I could scarcely restrain a sob of disappointment.

'"But I've written and telegraphed to him."

'"Ah, yes, I have the letters here."

'She brought me the three telegrams I had sent, and the letter, all unopened.

'"And where has he gone?" I asked desperately.

'"God knows," she answered, shrugging her shoulders.

'Feeling as though the earth were giving way under my feet, I walked slowly down the stairs. What could I do but wait till it pleased the fool to come back? And there the gold was lying and any day some peasant might stumble against a piece of ore, take it to Granada, and give the secret away. The only thing that suggested itself was to go to the bishop and ask if anything was known of the priest; but at the Chancellery they told me he was unattached to any diocese, and no one knew where he was gone. Then I cross-questioned his neighbours. They could tell me nothing, for Don Vicente had been used to live in great seclusion, and even the woman next door knew no more than his name. I asked whether she had a key of his room, but she told me no one ever entered it but himself; and the door confronted me coldly, maddeningly; perhaps behind it, in some note-book or other, lay the secret of the mine.

'I was obliged to return to Seville, and hoping against hope, I thought the priest might be waiting for me there. Again I was disappointed. Then I became convinced that he was wandering about in the neighbourhood of the mine, and the awful thought seized me that the idea of so much gold had turned his brain, as it was almost turning mine; and he had lost all recollection of me and of his own identity. It would be horrible if, when at last I found him, he was a gibbering lunatic from whom I could get no word of sense. I put advertisements in all the Spanish papers, asking Don Vicente Oria to come at once to a certain address where he would hear news to his great advantage. There was no result. Then I offered a reward for anyone who could tell me his whereabouts. This I thought must bring something, for all Spaniards read the ill-printed flimsy rags which pass here for papers, and there was no periodical in the remotest province which did not contain, day after day, my announcement. I advertised so much and so often that the Press grew interested, and wild rumours flew about with regard to the cause of my anxiety to discover this strange priest; presently Don Vicente Oria became as well known a name as any in Spain. The whole population was on the alert to discover him, and yet there was no trace.

'Meanwhile, that lump of ore, promising gold in fabulous quantities, stared at me day and night. Except for this I should have been inclined to think the whole thing an illusion, and that I had merely dreamed of the priest's visit. I resigned my post in Seville, for I wanted a free hand, and my salary was not worth considering beside the prospect of that vast wealth. I went to Granada, for though I had given up hope of ever finding the priest, I thought there might be among his papers some clue to the position of the mine, and I had devised a scheme for getting into his room. Going to the landlord of the house, I asked if I could have lodgings there; as I expected, he told me the place was full.

'"But why shouldn't I have Don Vicente's room?" I asked. "He must be dead or gone to the devil. You're not going to keep it empty for ever."

'The landlord was willing enough to let it, but somewhat feared difficulties with the police if Don Vicente's belongings were tampered with.

'"Don't be a fool," said I. "No one will trouble about you. Don Vicente's property can remain where it is, and if ever he returns he can have it."

'To quieten his fears the landlord asked an outrageous rent, but I agreed to it gladly, and within an hour a locksmith had gained me admission to the room. It was scantily furnished with a bed, a chair, and a table; round the walls books and papers were piled up, dusty and untidy. I looked at the books eagerly, and found they consisted in part of devotional works, but the most were technical treatises on mining. First I examined carefully all the papers with which the floor was littered, and you can imagine how my heart beat. I can see it now, that cold, musty room, and myself feverishly turning over each scrap of paper in the hope of finding some clue. Nothing. I took the books one by one, and sought for a stray sheet on which might be written the name of a place or a map. Nothing. I scrutinized the boards of the floor, and the walls, for signs of an opening in which the secret might be hidden. Nothing. My brain reeled, and I thought if I did not gather myself together I should go mad. Again I examined the books, this time for their contents; for days I worked like a slave, with not a shadow of hope to encourage me. I began to despair, but I would not listen to the voice within me. I determined never to rest till I had discovered this mine. After all, it was absurd; there it was without doubt, less than fifteen miles from Granada, and setting my teeth, I swore I would find it. At last I came across a little faded Spanish book, all worn with age and discoloured, thumbed and dirty; it was an account written in the seventeenth century of the mines exploited by the Romans in Andalusia. My heart leaped, for here, evidently, was the source from which the priest himself had proceeded, and I studied the shabby volume as I never studied printed matter before. Here I found the first trace of his writing, for now and then the name of a place was lightly underlined. I made a careful note of all these, and determined to explore them one by one. I would go to work as the priest had done, and if I went in his footsteps, surely I should arrive at the same result. Then my heart gave a great bound, for I realised that now the mine would belong to me alone, and I need share my wealth with no one.

'It seemed to me that I was on the scent at last, and it was with a light heart that I set out next morning.'

The speaker stopped and laughed bitterly. He called for more liquor and drank it at one gulp.

'It was the first of many fruitless journeys among the mountains of Granada, and that light heart of mine grew so heavy that I could scarcely bear the weight of it in my body. For three years I wandered about those desert places, suffering hunger and cold and thirst. I explored every inch of the country; I found disused mines, but they were worthless. I asked everyone I met whether they remembered an old, tall priest who used to come often to those parts; but never did I meet a soul who had seen him. He had vanished from the face of the earth, and even the remembrance of him was gone. They thought me mad, but I did not care; I went on and on, perpetually looking for my gold.'

'And you never found anything?' I asked.

He paused for a long while before he answered.

'Yes, at last. One day I was walking through the most desert part of the Sierra, where I think no man had ever been before, and I was wishing with all my soul that I'd never set eyes upon that cursed priest. It was bitterly cold, and suddenly the snow began to fall. I looked about for shelter, and saw the opening of a little cave behind some brushwood. I pushed my way through, and thought myself lucky to get into a fairly comfortable place. I struck a match to light my cigar – and then I cried out with horror. I really felt as though my hair stood on end, and I trembled in all my limbs. The match fell from my fingers, and with shaking hand I lit another. Something black was lying at my feet, something ghastly. I touched it. The black cassock of a priest. I'd found Don Vicente at last. Shrivelled like a mummy, a skeleton of skin and bone, but recognisable still, he lay there at my feet, with his secret locked eternally in his breast.'

A shudder passed through the man as he thought of that awful sight. For a while he was silent.

'I suppose he had been there for three years or more. He must have gone to that place immediately after I saw him. Death came upon him suddenly.'

'But surely his presence there . . . ' I began.

'I thought it meant something. I sought again, I sought restlessly, I never tired. I traversed every inch of the land for ten miles around, till my youth was gone and my hair turned grey. I never found anything, never! And still there lies within five leagues of Granada a mine rich with gold, waiting to make some lucky fool the richest man in Europe.'

THE
MAKING
OF
A MILLIONAIRE

Mr Rose came down to breakfast, impatiently threw aside the circulars that sought to engage his interest, and turned to his *Financial Times*. He was a tall, stout man, with grey hair and a heavy moustache. His clothes were made by a military tailor, and he wore them with the dashing erectness of a retired soldier; his eyes had the good-humoured twinkle, his expression the frankness, which often characterise those whose lives have been passed in the easy companionship of mess-rooms. Mr Rose had been for some time a volunteer. He looked up at his wife as she passed him his coffee, and then his glance fell on his son's vacant seat.

'The young scoundrel's very late again,' he said, with a smile of good nature.

At that moment the sluggard came in, and his father turned to him jovially.

'When I was your age I was up by seven every morning. It's lucky you don't have to earn your living as your energetic father did.'

'My dear father, you've made a fortune by shady practices on the Stock Exchange,' answered the young man, with a laugh. 'It's fit and just that I should cultivate an honest incompetence.'

Mr Rose gave his son a quick glance, and immediately laughed heartily.

'You young rascal! You can afford to make fun of the way in which I've scraped together enough to pay your outrageous bills.'

Leslie Rose began to read his letters. His father watched him with fond eyes. He was very proud of this handsome son, whose success at Oxford had been just of the sort which a modest parent might boast of in the city. He had done creditably in the schools; but his athletic prowess had brought his name into many papers, and when the boy got his blue, Mr Rose was as jubilant as when he floated the New-Lyons Gold Mine. Leslie was shortly to marry Janet Blissard. He had made her acquaintance in Shropshire, where the eminent financier had bought an estate. Mr Rose was delighted with the match, for he realised the importance in the county of Colonel Blissard; and remembering his own antecedents, it pleased him to think that Leslie should take a step up in the social scale.

The young man opened his last letter, and the indifferent expression on his face suddenly changed. He frowned, and read the letter again.

'What's the matter, Leslie?' asked his mother, who had caught his puzzled look.

'It's from Colonel Blissard. You know, I was to come up for election at Gann's tomorrow, and he's on the committee. He says that he's forced to leave London on business, and as he won't be able to attend the meeting, I'd better take my name off the list of candidates, as without a committee-man to support one, election at a club like Gann's is very uncertain.'

'Let me look,' said his father shortly, stretching out his hand for the letter.

Leslie stared at him while he read it.

'I suppose it means that I shall be pilled if I don't do as he suggests.'

'Obviously.'

'But why can't Colonel Blissard put off his journey if his presence is essential for Leslie's election?' asked Mrs Rose, anxiously. 'I think it's very selfish of him. He must know how much it means to a young man to be elected to a good club.'

'Don't be silly, Betty,' answered her husband, sharply. 'It's plain enough that he doesn't want to put Leslie up. After all, there are other clubs.'

'But I'm going to ask him what he means,' cried Leslie, quickly. 'It must be some mistake. It's absurd that his son-in-law shouldn't be good enough to be a member of his club.'

'Are you very fond of Janet?' asked Mr Rose.

Leslie reddened to the roots of his hair.

'My dear father, what are you talking about? Of course I am.'

'Would you be very much upset if the marriage were broken off?'

For a moment Leslie was silent. When he spoke it was with a certain bashfulness, as though the words were dragged out of him and he was ashamed.

'I think it would break my heart,' he said.

Mr Rose leaned back in his chair, and looked at his son gravely. The good-humoured frankness had disappeared from his face, and it wore instead an impenetrable expression which was rather impressive.

'Then you had better go and see Colonel Blissard at once. If you start immediately, you'll probably catch him before he goes out.'

'But what on earth can be the matter?' asked Leslie impatiently, and his handsome face was clouded by anxiety. 'Surely you must have some suspicion. I've done nothing that Colonel Blissard can object to. He can only want me not to be a member of his club because he wishes to break off my engagement with Janet.'

'I wouldn't worry myself too much if I were you,' replied Mr Rose. 'Gann's is a very old-fashioned place; it may well be that the committee objects to you because you're my son. There's a certain prejudice against persons of my profession.'

'Yes, but it isn't as if you were an ordinary financier. I daresay there are some who are nothing better than swindling sharpers, but everyone knows that you're the very soul of honour. No one has ever dreamed of accusing you of anything shady.'

The flicker of a smile passed across Mr Rose's eyes.

'Anyhow, you have no time to lose,' he answered.

Leslie got up at once, and in a moment they heard the front door slam behind him. Mr Rose pushed back his chair, and lit a cigar. He held his paper in front of him, but did not read. His wife seemed to occupy herself with trifling things, but she watched him carefully. At last she went up to him.

'D'you know anything of this, Frederick?' she asked quietly, breaking the silence that had lasted since Leslie left them.

'Of what?'

'I think you know quite well what I mean.'

'My dear, I have much more important things to think about than that old fool's refusal to put Leslie up for Gann's.'

'Have you been doing anything that may make him wish to break off Leslie's engagement?' she persisted.

He threw down his paper and met her eye, steadily. He smoked for a moment in silence.

'Colonel Blissard has only seen the soft side of me yet,' he answered. 'If he tries to put a spoke in my wheel, it will be very much the worse for him.'

A look of despair came over her face, and she turned away to conceal a sob.

'You promised that you'd never again do anything that wasn't above-board. Do you want to ruin the boy's happiness?'

'My dear, women don't understand business. You look after your house, and I'll look after the rest.'

When he left her to go to his office, Mrs Rose turned over in her mind many things. Her heart was tortured with anxiety. She had trained herself never to think of certain matters, but now shuddered with fear when she considered how to answer her son if, on his return, he asked inevitable questions. She saw nothing of him all day. He had not come in when she went upstairs to dress for dinner. She heard her husband come, but he went straight to his room. When they met in the dining-room, she asked him if he had seen Leslie.

'I hear that he came to my office, but I've been out nearly all day. I've been extremely busy.'

'He's not come in yet.'

'It's useless to wait for him. Will you order dinner to be served at once?'

They sat down, and Mrs Rose watched her husband eat his soup with gusto. He was abstracted, but had lost none of his jovial good-humour. In a moment her quick ear caught the sound of a key being put into the front door, and she turned to a servant.

'There's Mr Leslie. Ask him not to dress, but to come into dinner as he is.'

The words were hardly out of her mouth when the youth appeared. He bent over to kiss her, and slipped into a chair. He took no notice of his father.

'Good evening, young man,' said Mr Rose, heartily. 'You must hurry up, or your fish will be cold; and you'll find the soles are not to be despised.'

Leslie did not answer. His mother saw that he was pale and haggard. He seemed to hold himself together by a great effort of will. He drank a mouthful of soup and then pushed his plate away. His glass was filled with wine, and when he raised it, she noticed that his hand was trembling.

'Is anything the matter, Leslie?' she asked, in a low voice, leaning towards him.

'I can't tell you now,' he answered, and his tones had in them a ring of passionate despair which she had never heard before.

She looked down, trying to eat her food, trying to show the servants that she was not suffering an indescribable torment. Two hot tears rose in her eyes, blinding her, and they rolled slowly down her cheeks. She realised that her son knew the hideous secret which all his life she had struggled to conceal from him. To her the dinner seemed never-ending; but Mr Rose, thoroughly enjoying the good things of life, ate with hearty appetite. He sought to engage his wife and son in conversation, seeming not to notice their agitation; but since they were uncommunicative, with a slight shrug of the shoulders he surrendered himself to his own reflections. At last the coffee was put on the table. Mrs Rose sighed with relief when the butler closed the door behind him.

'What is it, Leslie?' she asked quickly. 'I've hardly known how to bear my anxiety.'

'I'm sorry you should have thought it necesary to make exhibitions of yourselves before the servants,' interposed her husband.

'Colonel Blissard refuses to allow me to marry Janet,' said Leslie, in a low voice broken with fatigue and wretchedness. 'He gave me a letter from her, saying she was very sorry.'

'But why?' asked Mrs Rose.

Leslie looked down as though the words he had to speak ashamed him. They appeared to issue from his mouth without movement of the lips, and though his voice was very low, they were extraordinarily distinct.

'He says my father's a swindler. He made me read an article in which my father's career was accurately described. It appears that there may be a prosecution.'

Mrs Rose gave a cry, but her husband put up his hand.

'Let Leslie go on,' he said, quietly.

'At first I couldn't believe it. I told Colonel Blissard I was as sure of my father's honesty as of my own life. He gave me proof upon proof. He showed me an old *Times*, in which I saw that twenty years ago my father was prosecuted, and only escaped penal servitude by the skin of his teeth. The Colonel told me he had only just discovered all this, and he would have said nothing because Janet and I loved one another, only at this very moment my father is engaged in a gigantic fraud. The New-Lyons Gold Mine hasn't got any gold in it, and he knew it hadn't. He seems to have used all sorts of cheating methods to deceive the public, and thousands have been ruined. The whole story is out now. There's going to be a meeting of the company tomorrow, and God knows what will be the result of it. I can't expect Colonel Blissard to let me marry his daughter when in a few weeks my father may stand at the Old Bailey.'

Leslie finished speaking and all three were silent. At last, with an impatient gesture, Mr Rose got up. He went over to the chimney-piece and lit a cigar.

'Colonel Blissard's an old fool. You may be quite sure that I've kept within the limits of the law. It's a precious fool who can't, for they're wide enough, in all conscience.'

'Even then, it won't be any the more honest.'

'The morals of the Stock Exchange are not the morals of private life. It's true that I floated a gold-mine, and when the shares stood high I sold my stock. What do you suppose shares are run up for, except to let the inside ring get out? If a good many people have lost their money, I'm very sorry; but some one has to lose the money that some one else gains. Only fools speculate on the Stock Exchange. I have no sympathy with a parcel of old maids and retired colonels who try to make money without working for it.'

Leslie did not look at him. It seemed as though he could not bear to meet his father's eyes. He spoke in the same dull, expressionless tone.

'You knew there wasn't any gold in the mine.'

'One can never be quite certain of that,' returned the financier, with a laugh.

'It seems to me no better than sordid theft.'

'I'm sorry that my methods of making money don't meet with your approval. If you go into the city, they'll tell you that I'm a very good sort – sharp, if you like, as sharp as a razor; but I've never done a man a bad turn nor abandoned a friend in distress. In business every man's hand is against every other's, and it's only because I've been able to adapt myself to the current morality that you enjoy every luxury you can possibly desire.'

'I'd rather eat dry bread and know that it was honestly come by.'

'That's very easily said,' replied the financier, scornfully.

'But I mean it. If I continue to live on the proceeds of your – operations, I'm just as guilty as you are. I've made up my mind to go away. I shall see if I can't make a living in America.'

'Don't be a young fool,' cried Mr Rose. 'Say something to him, Betty. Try and make him reasonable.'

'I think he's quite right,' said she quietly.

'D'you mean to say you're going to let him go off alone to make his own way?'

'No; I propose to go with him.'

'What on earth d'you mean?'

'Don't you remember that once before, many years ago, I made up my mind to leave you? It was after your prosecution, and though you were acquitted, you were hopelessly dishonoured. I couldn't bear that my son should grow up under your influence. You implored me to forgive you, and you promised that if I stayed you'd never again do anything that wasn't absolutely honest. I brought up my boy with the idea that you were the very soul of honour. The money rolled in, and I was tortured by the fear that it wasn't rightly come by. But it was too late then, and for Leslie's sake I held my tongue. Why should I stay, now that he knows everything? I hate and loathe all this money you've made; for I know that to the very core you're dishonest.'

Again silence fell upon them, but at length the financier went up to his wife. His voice was changed, and he seemed really to be under the influence of strong emotion.

'You can't leave me now, Betty, after all these years. I shall be so lonely without you. Don't you know that I love you still, devotedly?'

She did not answer, but drew herself away slightly, so that he should not touch her. He looked at her steadily.

'Do you really mean what you say?'

'I can only stay with you on one condition.'

'I'll do anything you choose,' he cried.

'Heaven knows how all the rest of your fortune was made; but what's done is done, and the harm you've caused is irreparable. But this last transaction is different; you can still pay back the money you've tricked out of these wretched people.'

'What on earth d'you mean?' cried the financier.

But Leslie had quickly caught his mother's suggestion, and he went to his father eagerly. His face was suddenly lit up.

'Oh, father, if you care for us at all you'll do that. You know we're fond of you, both of us. You can redeem everything by that one step, and it'll wipe out all the horrible past. Tomorrow at the meeting you can offer to buy back all the shares.'

'You're a pair of idiots,' cried Mr Rose, angrily. 'Why, they're not worth sixpence. You don't suppose I'm going to throw two hundred and fifty thousand pounds into the gutter.'

'It's only on that condition that I'll stay with you,' said Mrs Rose, in a low voice, but with complete firmness.

'Then you can both go to the deuce for all I care,' cried the financier, beside himself with passion. 'Go to America and see how you like living on ten dollars a week. Wait till you find out how hard it is to make money, and then you won't turn up your noses at me. I have no patience with you.'

He flung out of the room, and slammed the door behind him. He looked at his watch, and since it was late, went straight to bed. He could not sleep; he heard his wife and son go to their rooms, and he tried to subdue the anguish he felt at the thought of them. For he loved them both, and he did not know how to face life without them. He knew his wife well enough to be certain that she would carry out her threat. He raged impotently as he thought of her unreasonableness. He had built up his fortune slowly, and now he had made a magnificent stroke, which gave him influence with the great financiers of the time. He was a man to be reckoned with. It was true that hard words would be used in connection with him, but the glitter of his vast wealth would soon blind the eyes of those who disapproved of the means whereby it was won. In six months his astuteness would be forgotten and only his ability remembered.

He went down to breakfast next morning, but the room was empty. He made no effort to see Leslie or his wife. He was unhappy, but he sought to put away disquieting thoughts, for he had before him a difficult and a busy day. No one could doubt now that the New-Lyons Gold Mine was worthless, and he must face the shareholders that afternoon. Resolutely he set himself to devise a speech whereby he might extricate himself from all blame. Mr Rose had a good deal of practice in dealing with angry shareholders, and he flattered himself that no one could make them gracefully accept the inevitable with such persuasive skill as himself.

When he reached his office, Mr Rose found a number of letters awaiting his attention, and he began to read them methodically. Presently a clerk came in, laid a telegram on his table, and went out.

'Confound the thing, it's in cypher,' muttered the financier, as he opened it.

Then he started on noticing it was from the manager of the New-Lyons

Mine. He wondered what on earth he could have to say that should need so long a cable. Mr Rose took out his code and wrote down the meaning of each word as he looked it out. Presently the nonchalance with which he performed this operation gave way to an extraordinary emotion. His heart began to beat faster. The words made sense, but their meaning was so unexpected that he thought he must have made a mistake. He looked out again the more important words, but they were quite correct. There could be no doubt that the impossible had happened. He shivered; then a curious glow went through him. Finally he began to laugh, and the laughter grew so that he bellowed with loud guffaws. His hilarity was unrestrained. The clerks in the adjoining room thought he was suddenly gone mad. At last he controlled himself, and with his head between his hands, considered with the greatest precision what he must do. In five minutes he got up, pushed aside the letters that were still unread, and took his hat. His cab was at the door, and he drove to three different brokers whom he could trust implicitly, and told them to buy in quietly all the New-Lyons shares they could possibly get hold of. This done, he drove home, and though his mood was jubilant, he took care to preserve an expression of complete gravity. He found his wife in conversation with Leslie.

'You were neither of you visible this morning,' he said. 'I want to know whether you've made up your minds to do anything.'

'We did that last night,' answered his wife, after a pause. 'Nothing can ever alter my determination.'

'I'm proposing at this afternoon's meeting to take back at par the shares of everyone who's willing to part with them.'

Mrs Rose gave a cry. She went up to her husband, and looked into his eyes to see if he was serious. He took her hand quietly and smiled.

'I can't face the prospect of your leaving me. I have no one but Leslie and you in the world, and I only want to make you both happy.'

A look of immense gratitude came over Mrs Rose's patient face, and she burst into tears. She hid her weeping eyes on her husband's shoulder.

'You'd better come to the meeting,' said the financier at last. 'And Leslie might go to Colonel Blissard, and beg him to come, too. I should like him to know that I'm not the dishonest scoundrel he thinks.'

All that Mr Rose suggested was done, and in the afternoon both wife and son waited among the angry shareholders for the directors of the company to appear. Colonel Blissard had been told what to expect, and he sat by their side. It was with wildly beating hearts that these three listened to the chairman's eloquent speech. His wife had never admired him more. He refuted all the charges that had been made against him, and showed with great speciousness that he had acted in perfect good faith. He declared that he was an honest man, and if he had made a mistake in his estimate of the mine he was willing to suffer for it. Mr Rose paused a moment to give effectiveness to the climax of his speech, and then, calmly, as though it were the most natural thing in the world, he offered to take back all the shares of the company. At first the audience was dumbfounded; but when they realised his meaning there was a scene of enthusiasm which brought tears of grateful pride to Mrs Rose's eyes. When the financier at last retired into the private room of the directors, Colonel Blissard, still thrilling with the sight he had witnessed, followed him.

'My dear fellow, I think your action is truly noble. I daresay you've done some foolish things in your day, but upon my word, this makes up for everything.'

'I did it for Leslie's sake,' answered Mr Rose. 'I want him to marry your daughter.'

'Send the young scoundrel to me this evening, and I daresay we can arrange matters.'

The financier did not reach home till late, but his wife was waiting for him. She put her arms round his neck.

'I shall be grateful to you all my life, Frederick,' she said. 'And if we're poor I don't mind. We have nothing to reproach ourselves with.'

'We shan't be so poor as all that, my dear,' he smiled.

He kissed her with real affection, but when he went to his room to dress he chuckled to himself. He took out the cable he had received that morning, and gloated over it. In six months all these shares that he had bought for a song would be worth ten pounds a-piece, and he would be twice a millionaire. For the impossible had happened. In the mine which he himself had all along thought was quite worthless, gold had been found, gold in incredible quantities. And it was impossible for any one to know that when he made the shareholders his quixotic offer he was in possession of this precious information.

'They say that honesty is the best policy,' he muttered.

And then the humour of the situation seized him, and he laughed again. He laughed till the tears ran down his cheeks.

A
TRAVELLER IN ROMANCE

For six and thirty hours snow had fallen in the valley of the Engadine. It was not the soft snow of England, which flutters down in heavy flakes like the petals of roses overblown, but a blinding storm, tenuous as a Scotch mist, driven by the wind from the Alpine heights. I had taken a place in the post-chaise that went from St. Moritz into Italy, and when I reached the office I found waiting already a closed sleigh, gaudily painted in yellow, drawn by four horses. Three persons had taken their seats, and it held but four. The driver mounted his box, and the postman climbed up beside him. We carried the mails to Chiavenna and to the villages by the wayside. Leaving St. Moritz, with its fashionable gaieties and its vast hotels, we descended the hill silently. Below was the lake, frost-bound and covered with snow; while all around, like a vast amphitheatre, were the white mountains.

The driving snow blurred all the outlines. But my contemplation of the desolate prospect was interrupted by my companions, who insisted on closing the windows. I had brought with me, to avoid the possible tediousness of the journey, a volume of Casanova's memoirs: that amusing libertine is the best of all travelling companions; and, strange though it may appear, he has in this respect a certain quite moral value, for none can read him without learning the lesson valuable to all, but especially to the wanderer, that life gives its fullness only to those who are willing to take risks. It persuades one to cultivate a spirit of adventure, without which travel is but a tame affair, and with his example one at least resolves to make the most of passing moments. But my fellow travellers were talking too loudly to allow me to read, and closing the book I sought to gather some amusement from their conversation. A stage-coach is imbued with the romantic spirit, and he must be dull indeed who does not feel a singular thrill when he travels in one. I called back to my mind the descriptions which Casanova has left of his journeys in such conveyances, and wondered what profit he would have drawn from my present company. There were two stout men of middle age, who appeared to have a business connection, for they discussed the sale of some piece of land in a mixture of bad

German and worse Italian, and the fourth passenger was a woman who, without previous acquaintance with the others, joined vigorously in the conversation. To her, I feel sure, Casanova would have addressed himself immediately, and within an hour the pair would have been on the best of terms. I reproached myself because I had not even the inclination to whisper the appropriate nothings. It is true that she was hard upon fifty, stout and ill-favoured, but I am not convinced that the fickle Venetian would have hesitated on this account. So many fair ladies crossed his path that I cannot help supposing their beauty lay mostly in his own passionate imagination.

At Kampfer we stopped and my fellow passengers got out. I hoped for the rest of the journey to have the carriage to myself, but just before we started a man entered. He gave me a glance and bade me good-morning in English. He was a fellow of immense size, with massive bones and large hands. He had a huge nose and a strong square chin. In his tie was an imitation diamond of considerable size, and on his fingers were rings whose imposing stones had never seen the mines of South Africa or Brazil. I put him down as a commercial-traveller; and this in fact he was, for, beginning to talk as soon as we set off, he told me that he had been in St. Moritz to get orders from hotels and was now on his way to Milan. Since the carriage was full he had been forced to come as far as Kampfer in an open sleigh. He talked very quickly, very fluently, but in broken English that was often difficult to follow. I did not know to what nation he belonged. I set myself to improve the shining hour, and I learnt various things about the traveller of commerce which I trust will be useful for me to know. He seemed to like to hear himself speak, and there was a curious grandiloquence in his phraseology which did not fail to entertain me.

We stopped again, this time at Maloggia, and still the snow swept on. It is a place where tourists go in summer, and the vast hotel, with its shuttered windows, looked singularly cheerless. It seemed as though the sun could never shine in that deserted spot. It was luncheon time, and we went into a little inn, but the driver told me he could only wait five minutes. It was too brief a time to appease my hunger, so I hit upon the ingenious device of ordering a bottle of wine and asking the driver to drink with me. Each time he wiped his mouth with the back of his hand and looked doubtfully at the horses I filled his glass, thus gaining sufficient time to eat the food I had brought with me.

As he stepped back into the carriage my friend the traveller waved his hand somewhat dramatically towards the Switzerland we were abandoning.

'Adieu, degenerate land of hotel-keepers,' he cried. 'Adieu!'

I stared at him, and, smiling, asked if he did not like the Swiss. He shrugged his shoulders with impatient scorn.

'Of the peasants I know nothing, but the others, pah! they have souls of shop-walkers. They're extortionate and mean; overbearing and insolent to their inferiors, servile towards their betters. I loathe above all the reptile soul of the manager of a first-class hotel.'

Though not indisposed to agree with him, I surmised that my friend had not done good business in the country we were leaving. I confess I had suspected, however, that the politeness of the gentlemen who conduct these caravanserais is barely skin-deep. It must be pleasanter to be one of their guests than one of their waiters.

157

But we had done with climbing, and now began to descend a winding road. It was very steep, and quickly we came to such a level that the snowy mountains all about us towered still more impressively. On their slopes were forests of fir-trees covered with snow, and their dark jade contrasted astonishingly with the surrounding whiteness. Above, the sky was heavy still with snow. Presently we were driving among the fir-trees, and they clustered thick around us. It was like one of those enchanted woods of fairyland which goblins haunt and where beautiful princesses inevitably lose their way. When we came out of the forest the mountains in front seemed to divide, and I hoped that when we turned the corner we should find ourselves in the magic land of all desires.

'There is our gateway into Italy,' I suggested.

But my traveller put his hand impressively on my arm.

'It is ten times more than that. It is the doorway of Romance.'

I looked at him with astonishment, but made no remark. It occurred to me that this was not an article upon which he could hope to make large percentages, and his failure with the Swiss hotel-keepers was comprehensible if he offered them such a commodity. The conversation was interrupted by our arrival at Vicosoprano, where we changed the sleigh for a trim diligence. We had come to the end of the snow, and the rest of our journey was conducted amid the rattle of wheels on the hard high road. A different driver conducted the four horses, and instead of German gutturals, he addressed them in Italian. He called on San Antonio when they stumbled. The monotonous fir was no longer the only tree that covered the mountains, snow-capped still, for there was now the mountain ash, and presently the hill-side was planted with vines. But they seemed shrivelled by the cold. In their leaflessness they looked like giant spiders set in rows in some naturalist's museum. Still we wound round the mountains, and each turn, instead of the expected plain, brought another huge rugged peak; they stood like sentinels of stone as if to guard the way into Italy. My friend watched the scene with gleaming eyes, and presently, as though by special favour of the gods, the sun broke through the clouds and touched the snowy summits with gold. The traveller pointed with a disdainful thumb at the boxes which contained his samples.

'Those goods I sell are but a pretext,' he said. 'I travel in Romance. I am a Pole, and when I left my country in my boyhood, they placed me in an office in Liverpool. My soul soared above the writing of letters and the casting of accounts, and at nights I read of Italy and Greece.' He lit a really execrable cigar, and with a fine gesture passed his fingers through his hair. 'At last my chance came, for my firm wanted a traveller. I saw that I could earn bread to eat and at the same time seek the Romance which was as dear to me as life. And look, you see in front of you a mountain and nothing more, but I see the plain of Lombardy and the Venetian lagoons, Tuscany and the Umbrian Hills.' His eyes glittered and he blew the smoke from his mouth in heavy clouds. He rolled out a list of names, pell-mell, as though their sound gave him exquisite pleasure: 'Leonardo, Caesar Borgia, Ariosto, Boccaccio. It is true that for a few brief hours in the day I deal with sordid merchandise, but when my work is done I turn to the great ones of the past. And I have the sunset, and the Tuscan wine, and the white teeth of the women of Rome. I am a traveller in Romance.'

At last, exhausted by incessant talking, he fell asleep with a smile upon his lips. It seemed to me, indeed, that he had more in him of Casanova's spirit than most of us can boast of. Presently we came to a little town, grey, dull, and cold, surrounded by the mountains. It was one of those places that depress one utterly because existence there seems inevitably narrow and dreary. Our journey had ended, for this was Chiavenna.

THE
BURIED TALENT

When Convers arrived at Penang and the Resident, coming to meet him, told him that a culvert on the line to Bangkok had been swept away by a flood so that unless he flew he would not be able to go for three or four days, he received the news with equanimity. He decided to wait till the line was repaired. The Resident asked him to stay with him, but with proper expressions of civility Convers chose rather to go to the hotel.

He was now having breakfast on the verandah of his room and he looked forward to spending a lazy day wandering about the pleasant town. He frowned slightly when a letter was brought in to him. On the evening of his arrival he had attended a large and dull dinner party at the Residency and on the day following another at the Club. He guessed that the letter was an invitation to a party of the same nature and he wondered whether there was any means by which he could politely refuse it. But though it was an invitation it was not of the sort he expected. The letter began abruptly.

> *I hardly know how to address you. I'm not quite sure if it's fitting to address His Britannic Majesty's Minister Plenipotentiary to the King of Siam as Teddie and I'm not quite sure if now you're so grand you will want to know an obscure doctor's wife whom you have not seen or heard of for more than twenty years.*

Convers interrupted his reading.

'Who the devil is this?'

He looked at the signature: Blanche MacArdle. It meant nothing to him at all. He went on.

> *I see that you are at Penang and if I know anything of the P.W.D. they won't get the trains running for at least three days, and I am wondering if for old times' sake you would come over to dinner and spend the night. It will only take you a couple of hours to get here by car. Considering the difficulties one has to contend with, I have a rather nice garden. It might amuse you to see what one can do in the East if one tries. I should like to talk to you about poor Charmian.*

Nash's Magazine, March 1934.

Then of course he remembered. It gave him quite a turn. He didn't know much anatomy, but he felt that there was a loose string in his heart, dangling there, and someone had just given it a painful tug. The letter went on to say if he would telegraph, a car would be sent for him and would bring him back next day. Convers got up from his chair, went into the room and wrote out a telegram.

GREATLY REGRET. ABSOLUTELY IMPOSSIBLE. CONVERS.

Then he came back and proceeded to finish his breakfast.

It was useless to renew an acquaintance that had ceased so many years ago. What was the sense of reviving painful memories and probing old wounds that had long been healed? Blanche must be a middle-aged woman by now. MacArdle? He had forgotten that this was the name of the man she married. He remembered him vaguely, a tall, big-boned solemn Scot; he smiled when he thought how Charmian and he had begged her not to marry him. What young fools they were then! And Charmian was dead.

Of course Blanche had done the wise thing and the right thing. Convers wondered what she looked like now. He wondered if she were as tidy as ever. She was a handsome creature, in those days, with fine eyes and a good profile, and in her bearing, although she could not have been more than twenty-four, something already of the tragedy queen. And what had become of the magnificent contralto? When quite unexpectedly she told them that she was giving up her singing to marry, and was going to the F.M.S. with Andrew, he remembered how Charmian and he had besought her not to throw away the glorious instrument that nature had given her. Charmian had wept. There was nothing so rare as a contralto and at the Conservatoire they held out to Blanche hopes of a splendid career. It was already decided that she should make her début in Gluck's *Orfeo*.

It was strange how it all came back to him, the memory of the past, and poor dead Charmian; he had scarcely thought of her for years. What a success she had had and in what shame ended! Convers read Blanche's letter again.

He remembered the room in a pension that he had lived in – he was learning French for his examination – and the studio that Blanche and Charmian had in a street that led out of the Boulevard Raspail, and the Closerie des Lilas, which was their favourite café. Good heavens, how it all came back! After all, why shouldn't he go to see Blanche? He wondered whether she had kept in touch with Charmian after her marriage. For a moment his thoughts lingered with the dead singer; he gave a sigh.

He had been married for [nineteen] years, happily married, and he had two sons of whom he was proud; after falling out of love with Charmian he had fallen in love again before falling in love with his wife; but thinking it over calmly it seemed to him that his love for Charmian, wretched as it had made him, was unique. It had a spiritual quality, a sort of idealistic eagerness, that transfused sensual desire with some beauty not of this earth.

'I've never loved anyone as I loved Charmian,' he pondered, but he was no sooner conscious of the reflection than he felt a warm, grateful glow as he thought of his wife. He smiled affectionately in her absent eyes.

He returned to his room, tore up the telegram form and wrote another.

WILL COME TO DINE AND SLEEP TONIGHT. DON'T BOTHER ABOUT CAR. HIRING. TEDDIE.

His diplomatic career had taken him to several of the capitals of Europe, to Brazil and to Guatemala, but he had never been East and he viewed the passing scene with pleasure. But he saw it with the eyes of his head only; at the back of his mind – more vivid than the interminable plantations of rubber trees and the Malay villages, half hidden by fruit trees, that he drove through – he saw the streets of Paris, noisy, crowded and romantic, and Montparnasse, with its prim air of a town in the provinces and yet with an alertness that set the blood racing through one's veins. The world then was thrilling, and you could not walk down those wide, leisurely streets without a feeling that at every turn the unexpected awaited you. Anything was possible. Art was the only thing that mattered and everyone was young.

He had come from his own respectable pension near the Bois de Boulogne to a party given in his studio by an American painter, and there had met Blanche and Charmian. They were both studying singing and presently their host asked them to sing. Blanche sang some old Gaelic songs and her rich contralto gave them a lovely sadness. Then Charmian sang the great soprano aria from the *Marriage of Figaro*. She had a voice of exquisite purity, not very powerful, but of great sweetness. She was a lovely creature, with a very white skin, a little straight nose and large shining eyes. But it was not her voice nor her beauty that most captivated you; it was an urge of youth, a charming gay exuberance that seemed to shed a material radiance. She seemed to pour life forth as a lamp pours light.

Teddie Convers, a good-looking boy then, in Paris for the first time in his life, fell in love with her at first sight. He sought her society and Charmian seemed to like his. But she knew a good many people on the other side of the river and was often engaged; then Blanche and he would dine together and talk about her by the hour. Sometimes the three of them would go to Versailles and once they spent an enchanting holiday in the Forest of Fontainebleau.

Blanche, older than either of them and of a more serious nature, was in charge of Charmian and kept a watchful eye over her, but she liked the clean young Englishman and felt that Charmian was safe with him. Life was free and easy in the Latin Quarter. None of them had any money, but they enjoyed their work, they enjoyed their play and they were happy.

Of course they had their moments of difficulty, Charmian was careless and extravagant, and when she wanted something the last thing that occurred to her was that she could not afford it. One could not imagine what would have happened if Blanche had not been there. She pinched and saved. Charmian laughed at her prudence, but accepted whatever Blanche did for her with light-hearted insouciance. She managed to make it seem the most enchanting thing in the world to be privileged to do her a service.

Once Convers told Blanche that he thought her the most unselfish woman he had ever known.

'Because of what I do for Charmian?' she smiled. 'It makes me so happy. I love her.'

'Why aren't you jealous of me?'

'Because you love her too? Of course you love her. I should hate you if you didn't. We shall never either of us ever meet anyone quite like her. I think she's going to be one of the great singers of the world. I've got a feeling that some day we shall see that to have known her was the great experience of our lives.'

'You know we're not lovers, don't you?'
'Of course.'
He flushed. He was only twenty-two.
'I think I love her too much for that.'
'I know.'

It was a comfort to him that she understood and did not think him ridiculous. Common friends took it for granted that Charmian was his mistress; it did not dawn on them that his passion for her had a quality that made the thought of sexual union an offence. Charmian had a flower-like beauty that he felt it would be desecration to touch; her purity was so exquisite that it gave him a sort of mystical elation. He asked her to marry him and naturally she refused; she wanted her freedom, her career came before everything. He was prepared to wait. He thought he would love her to the end of time, and he had a kind of inner conviction that one day she would consent to be his wife. He adored her as the saint adores his God.

And now leaning back in the car that sped along the straight road, smoking a pipe, a middle-aged man with grey hair and a keen, intelligent face, he remembered that ecstatic feeling with precision and he was glad to have had it. He had gone through many experiences since then, he had loved, married and begotten children, he had made a success of his career and could look forward to greater success to come, but that ecstasy was a possession that neither time nor circumstance could take away from him. It had given him the sense of immortality.

But at last he was obliged to leave Paris. The second language he was taking for his examination was Spanish, and he was to spend some months in Seville. Charmian promised to write to him. They made plans for her and Blanche to come down and see him at Easter.

It was just then, on the eve of his departure, that Blanche broke the surprising news that she was giving up her career as a singer to marry the big Scotsman who had come over to Paris now and then to see her and whom they knew she refused to marry every time he came. She was going with him to Singapore as soon as they were married. It seemed a terrible thing that with such a glorious voice and the possibility of a great future she should bury herself in a distant country. But after all it was her business and the thought of leaving Charmian made Convers too unhappy for him to bother himself very much with other people's concerns.

Charmian saw him off at the station and she wept bitterly at parting from him. It was he who had to console her by telling her that the time would soon pass and they would be reunited. When the train steamed out of the station his heart was heavy and his eyes were blurred with tears. But his love, and the feeling he had that Charmian loved him also, filled him with a deep serenity. His mind busied itself with the future. He did not know that he was never to see her again.

But now they arrived at a considerable town. The chauffeur stopped in front of a large white handsome bungalow and Convers got out. A big stout woman with grey hair came down the steps with outstretched hands.

'Teddie,' she cried.

It was a shock to him. He would never have recognised her and in order to cover his confusion assumed an effusive cordiality.

'How do you do?' he cried. 'By George, I am glad to see you. What a long time!'

She had still the handsome dark eyes that he remembered, but a heavy jowl and bags under the eyes; her skin was coarse and sallow. She wore a sort of tea-gown, in white silk, and on her ample bosom hung three or four strings of coloured beads. She was an old woman.

'Come in,' she said, 'and I'll give you a drink. I want you to see the garden before it gets dark. Andrew is out. I told him not to come in till dinner so that we could have a good talk.'

She led him into a large sitting-room – overcrowded with furniture, among which he noticed a grand piano – and gave him a whisky and soda.

'I can't tell you how thrilled I was when I saw that you were the new Minister to Siam. At first I wasn't quite sure if Sir Edward Convers and Teddie Convers were one and the same. You see I never thought of you but as a dear little boy just down from Oxford. But then I thought it must be the same. Ought I to call you Sir Edward?'

'Only if you want to make me feel a damned fool.'

'You've got on, haven't you? I suppose you'll be an ambassador next.'

'If I'm lucky.'

She took him into the garden, and as gardeners will, talked to him of this that did well in that climate and of the other that wasn't worth the trouble it cost you. It was a small coco-nut plantation, a square plot of land fenced in, and Blanche had left the regular lines of tall trees undisturbed; she had sown grass and mown it. Along the fences were flowering shrubs; and here and there, seemingly at haphazard, grew clumps of cannas, yellow or flame-coloured. It was exquisitely romantic. Artifice and nature were combined to make a pattern that appealed to the eye and the fancy. The ordered beauty caught the heart with an ecstasy that was almost pain. Then as the light was failing they went and sat on the verandah that overlooked the garden. They made themselves comfortable in long chairs and the boy brought out whisky and soda and a bucket of ice.

'You must be very happy here,' said Convers.

'You're married, aren't you?'

'Yes.'

'Have you any children?'

'Two boys.'

'I envy you that. I never had any children. Will your wife join you in Bangkok?'

'Of course. I'm lost without her. She didn't come with me only because she thought she ought to stay with the boys till they went back to school.'

'I always imagined you'd make a very good husband.'

'It's not difficult to be a good husband when you've got a wife like mine.'

'That sounds as though you were very fond of her.'

'She's a very nice woman.'

'How long have you been married?'

'Nineteen years.'

'I've been married twenty-six.'

'I know.'

She gave a little laugh and he glanced at her, for there was in her laugh a harshness that surprised him. He smiled good-naturedly.

'My dear, I was twenty-two when I was in love with Charmian. You wouldn't have wished me to cherish a hopeless passion for her all my life. I suppose there are people who fall in love only once in their lives, but I think they must be exceptional.'

Blanche turned to him with a smile full of friendliness.

'And yet how indignant you'd have been if anyone had told you that your love for Charmian would die away and in three or four years you'd marry somebody else and live happily ever after!'

'I shouldn't have been indignant, I should just have thought it ridiculous. Whoever loved that didn't think his love would last for ever?'

'It seems rather sad that a passion that was so pure, so intense, so beautiful, should die and leave not a trace behind.'

'Oh, but that isn't so. My love for Charmian was unique in my life. It is an imperishable and lovely memory. All the bitterness I endured is forgotten and I remember only the happiness it gave me. If it didn't sound so pretentious I'd say it enriched my soul.'

They were silent for a while. They thought of that beautiful, gifted creature who attained such heights and ended so tragically. The world moves quickly nowadays and the singer whom half the world so ecstatically applauded is forgotten. But here and there you can still find elderly people who remember Charmian's début in Brussels.

She had changed her good English name of Pelter to that of Pelletier. She made her first appearance in *Thaïs* and the Belgian public went mad over her. She was young and beautiful, she acted well, and her voice, though not very powerful, had a springtime purity and a sweetness that were enchanting. She was never a great artist, but nature endowed her with wonderful gifts and there was a spontaneity in her singing, a deep sincerity in her acting, that disarmed critical opinion.

The following season saw her début in Paris and her success far surpassed expectation. She was launched on the path of glory. But it is a dangerous path and it cannot be trod too warily. Charmian was weak. She squandered her gifts with a spendthrift's improvidence. She would not listen to the counsels of prudence. She was determined to wrest from life every possibility it afforded. She became notorious for her extravagance, the beauty of her clothes, the splendour of her jewels and the magnificence of her establishment. Rich men were glad to satisfy her whims and she flung their money away with the indifference of a wanton child.

She behaved as though her voice were an instrument that could be treated without concern and as though her radiant beauty were imperishable. Things began to go wrong. Now and then she gave a performance so bad that she was hissed. Once the curtain at the Opéra-Comique had to be lowered because she was too drunk to finish the scene. Her voice lost its silvery tone. She put on weight. The fall was as rapid as had been the ascent.

Although so much money had passed through her hands she was overwhelmed with debts. She fell ill. There was a spectacular sale of her effects. Two or three years more went by and she began to sing in second-rate companies at watering places and seaside resorts. Her voice was but a shadow of what it once had been. She continued to pursue pleasure with the same mad frenzy. She fell upon men who exploited and robbed her.

She sank lower and lower till a last she was glad to get engagements in provincial music halls of a doubtful character where she sold herself to coarse and vulgar men for a hundred francs. Any money she could get hold of she spent on drink and drugs. At last even this means of earning failed her.

She was fished out one morning from the harbour at Toulon with a knife thrust in her back. Her death gave the papers some welcome copy; her past triumphs were recalled and industrious journalists traced the course of her final degradation. The last few months of her life had been passed in sordid squalor. She was forty-three when she died.

Blanche sighed. The night had fallen. The fronds of the coco-nut trees made a florid pattern against the starry sky and in the garden the fire-flies, swaying deliberately upon the still air, were like the wavering lights of fairy boats that rose and fell on an unquiet, invisible sea. After the heat of the day the coolness was very grateful.

'Did you never see her again after you left Paris?'

'Never. At first I wrote to her every day and now and then she sent me an untidy scrawl in answer.'

'She never came down to Seville after all?'

'No. At the last minute she sent a wire to say she couldn't. I'd been looking forward to it so much, the disappointment shattered me. When I passed through Paris I couldn't find her. She'd left the studio and the concierge didn't know where she'd gone. I went back to London. I met new people, I had new experiences. I was very young.'

'You fell in love with somebody else.'

'Yes.'

'Did you never have the curiosity to go and hear her sing when she was at the height of her fame?'

'No. I didn't want to revive the old dead feeling. After all it would have been madness. I knew then how she was living. I'd loved her too much to be able to suffer the idea of the rich South American who provided all the luxury I'd heard about. I was older then. I didn't think she'd have much use for an obscure clerk in the Foreign Office. I wanted to keep my recollection undisturbed.'

'And you've done that notwithstanding all that happened afterwards?'

'Yes. My love for Charmian was a perfect thing. I shall always be thankful for it.'

Blanche sighed.

'I suppose it never occurred to you to ask yourself why I threw over the career that seemed open to me and sacrificed my ambition to marry a doctor and come out to the Far East. You weren't much interested in me, were you? I was the prim, prudish Scotswoman who was always in the way. You thought me rather absurd because I tidied up and kept accounts and tried not to run into debt. I'll tell you why I married Andrew. I was afraid.'

Convers did not speak. He waited for her to go on.

'We'd known one another all our lives. He'd asked me to marry him a score of times. He was a good fellow, I knew I could trust him, but I wanted to be a great singer, I wanted fame, and I wanted to lead a full and various life. I knew I had a good voice; of course I was a contralto, but voice for voice mine was finer than Charmian's. I was prepared to work like the devil to make the most of it. In my mind's eye I saw vast audiences held spellbound by the wonder of my singing and I heard the thunder of their applause. I know I should have realised my ambition.'

'I think you would.'

'I adored Charmian. I adored her beauty, I adored her careless gaiety. She was everything that I could have wished to be. I knew she was wilful and loved pleasure, but I was convinced there was no harm in her. My character was stronger than hers and I made up my mind to watch over her and guide her. I was as ambitious for her as I was for myself. When she told me there was a chance of her making her début in Brussels I was as excited as she was.

'I couldn't help boasting about it to one of the girls who were studying with us. She sniggered. I thought she was jealous and I was rather short with her. She lost her temper. She said that if Charmian got this engagement it would be for her looks rather than for her voice. I snapped back at her and we had a row. She said Charmian had been to bed with half the students at the Conservatoire; I don't know what she didn't say. Of course I didn't believe a word of it. I went straight to Charmian. I expected her to be as indignant as I was, but she only giggled; I was so taken aback by her attitude that for a moment I was beside myself.

'She didn't seem to realise the awfulness of the stories that were being told of her. She came up and kissed me and told me not to be an old prude. Then it all came out. She confessed everything, without shame, without reluctance, with a brazen callousness that horrified me. She simply could not understand my horror. I cried with shame for her and it only made her laugh. She mocked me. She sneered at my coldness; she said I would never become a great singer until I let myself go. She called me a constipated virgin.

'I thought I knew every thought in her heart and now I realised there was an abyss between us. She said she wasn't prepared to wait for her chance, she wanted it now; a rich Belgian had promised to get her into the Opera at Brussels and she wasn't going to be such a fool as to miss the opportunity. Of course she would have to pay him his price. Well, what of it? She asked me if I thought one got anything without paying for it. I had a sudden revulsion of feeling for all that world of singers and musicians and impressarios.

'You see, although I was horrified, I saw her standpoint, I was young then and not bad-looking; men now and then had tried to be familiar with me, I wondered whether the time would come when I should go the way she had gone. It was such an easy way. I was frightened. And I was angry that she'd made such a fool of me. I think I had some sort of crazy feeling that by sacrificing everything I cared for I was revenging myself on her. I wired for Andrew and when he came told him that I was ready to marry him.'

Blanche gave a ghostly laugh and turned to Convers.

'You'll hardly believe it, but almost my first thought then was of you. I was as sorry for you as I was for myself. I couldn't bear that this first great love of yours, so pure and ideal, should suffer that awful shock. You were to go in a fortnight. I knew nothing would come of it and I wanted you to believe in her to the end.'

'That was kind of you.'

'Except for you I should have left her at once. On your account we pretended that we were as great friends as ever.'

'You pretended very well.'

'After she'd seen you off she came back to the studio and we parted for ever. My luggage was packed and Andrew was waiting to take me to the station. I was very sad. I loved her still. When I said goodbye to her I couldn't help crying. I know how weak she was. The last thing I said to her was, "Mark my words, it'll end badly"; she smiled and kissed me and answered, "I shall have had my fling."'

But at that moment came the sound of a heavy tread in the sitting-room, a voice called, and Dr MacArdle thumped out on to the verandah.

'What are you sitting in pitch-darkness for?' he cried in a loud cheerful tone.

He turned on the electric light and Convers, getting out of his long chair to greet his host, found his hand heartily grasped by a big stout man with a great deal of curly white hair and a white beard. With his red cheeks he looked the picture of jovial health. The dour silent Scot that Convers remembered had turned into a chatty old fellow with a pleasant word for everybody. He carried his bedside manner into ordinary life and you felt it was his willing mission to cheer and encourage the ailing.

'Glad to see you, sir,' he cried. 'This is a real treat for my mem. You've worn well, upon my word. We're none of us so young as we used to be. Well, you're no end of a swell now, it appears, and I'm just what I was thirty years ago. Still, we mustn't complain. Dinner's ready, my dear. Would Sir Edward like to wash his hands before the cocktails come in?'

'I don't think you need call him Sir Edward.'

The doctor laughed aloud as though he or she had made a joke.

Presently they sat down to dinner. Andrew talked of Siam and asked Convers questions about the previous posts he had filled. He talked about the Federated Malay States and about rubber. He was well-informed. He liked to hear himself speak. He was obviously a good fellow, competent, jolly, who liked his life and was satisfied with what it had given him. It was plain too that he had the greatest admiration for his wife.

'You shall hear her sing after dinner,' he said. 'Her voice is better than ever.'

'What nonsense you talk, Andrew,' Blanche smiled good-naturedly.

'It's a fact. I'm not a bad doctor, though I say it myself, but I'm known from Penang to Singapore as Mrs MacArdle's husband. She's in demand, I can tell you, and if I didn't put my foot down she'd be gallivanting about the country from one year's end to the other. Why, they'll come to hear her from fifty miles around. D'you know she collected over two thousand pounds for the Red Cross during the war?'

They lingered over their coffee and presently Blanche sat down at the piano. She sang that great aria from *Orfeo* which it had once been her ambition to sing at Covent Garden. Her low notes were as magnificent as ever, but the high ones were harsh and strained. She sang two or three more songs. Then Andrew looked at his watch.

'I'm afraid I must leave you. I've got a patient to go and see.' He turned to Convers. 'If I'm not back before you turn in I'll see you in the morning.'

'All right.'

When he had left them Convers asked:

'Do you ever sing those old Scottish songs that you used to sing? D'you remember you sang them the first time I ever saw you?'

'I haven't sung them for years.'

She looked through her music and found the book. She sat down again at the piano and tentatively began an accompaniment. They were tunes gathered among the peasantry of the Northern Highlands and arranged by a sensitive musician. She sang one and then another. They had the melancholy of primitive music and in that warm silent night these songs of women wailing for their men killed in battle and of maids mourning their faithless lovers had a grave plaintiveness that was deeply moving. They did not seem out of place in that distant country; you felt that this music born amid mists and barren mountains had a subtle relation with the land of palm trees and wide rivers. There was a tragic quality in Blanche's voice that gave them a troubling and enigmatic significance. You listened with a feeling of awe for you knew not what and you seemed carried back to ages long ago.

'Let's go into the garden,' said Blanche suddenly.

She got up from the piano and went out. Convers followed her. The moon had risen and [in its] light the garden [was] like a closed garden of a king's palace in the *Arabian Nights*. The coco-nut trees in their regular lines had a hieratic solemnity. Night-flowering shrubs scented the air with a heavy perfume. With silent steps on the close-cut grass they walked down the central avenue.

'Do you know that Charmian wrote to me two days before she died?' Blanche said suddenly. 'I'd read in the paper of her horrible end and it was a shock to me when I recognised her writing. I'd never had a line from her since we'd parted that evening in Paris after you'd gone to Spain. It was written on a common sheet of paper with the name of some café in Toulon and it was in a flimsy, cheap envelope.'

'Did she know your address?'

'It had been sent to my old home in Scotland. It's a miracle I ever got it.'

'What did she say?'

Blanche stopped and even though it was night he could see that she was frightfully pale.

'It was only one line, with her name at the bottom. *It's been worth it.* That's all.'

'I wonder if it was true.'

'I'm sure it was true. But how strange that she should write to me after all those years and how horrible that I should get it when she was dead. It was like a voice from the dead. It's haunted me ever since.'

'Yes, it is strange.'

'I'm glad that she never forgot me entirely. I wonder what was in her mind.'

'Perhaps she was drunk.'

'I don't believe it. I believe that she had a presentiment that her end was near. I think she looked back on her life and she thought of her triumph and her fame, and the love she'd inspired and the love she'd suffered, and her fall, her shame, her disgrace, and she was glad to have lived it all. And she wanted me to know, because I'd run away, because I'd buried my talent in the ground, because I'd made nothing of the gift God have given me and had crept shivering with fear into a hole where I could be safe.'

'I don't see how you can say that you buried your talent in the ground.

You've given pleasure to a great many people. And what about those two thousand pounds that Andrew says you made for the Red Cross?'

'What is that?' she cried with a bitterness that startled Convers. 'I've sung cheap ballads to people who could appreciate nothing else. I've sung in drawing-rooms after dinner to people who wanted to play bridge. D'you remember what my voice was like twenty-four years ago?'

'But you've been happy here. You've had the love of your husband.'

'Oh, yes, I've been happy. I'm fond of Andrew. I've been comfortable. My life has been a sober jog-trot. Dull, mediocre, aimless. And that brief note of Charmian's asks me a question all the time. It asks me: Can you say as much, can *you* say it's been worth it? And the answer is No. I made a mistake. I oughtn't to have hesitated at the risk. I was a coward to throw my chance away. And now it's too late. I'm almost an old woman and life has given me nothing. By my own fault. Oh, I know all about those years of degeneration, but even they were life; she *lived* and I've existed; when I look back on her life with its glory and its shame I know it was worth it. In my respectability, in my security, I envy her.'

'Even when you think of her pitiful, shameful end?'

'Even then. Do you remember what Elizabeth said about Mary Stuart? "The Queen of Scots hath a bonny bairn and I am but a barren stock." I look back on *my* life and see nothing but the waste of a great opportunity. At the Day of Judgement, if there is one, it would not be so strange if Charmian found more mercy than I. Oh, the bitterness of those words: too late!'

A sob broke from her and he knew she was weeping. He was deeply moved, but he was silent for he knew no words of consolation. What was there for him to say that would give her back the lost years? She turned to him suddenly and held out her hand.

'Good night. I'm sorry to have made a nuisance of myself. I won't see you in the morning. Goodbye.'

Her voice was strangled with her tears. She touched his hand and walked towards the house. When she came to the verandah the light fell on her and she climbed the steps, a large heavy woman in her ample draperies, with the weariness of one who has lost hope.

Next day, on his return to Penang, Convers heard that the line was repaired and in the evening he started for Bangkok. During the journey he thought much of Blanche and Charmian. He was a man of intelligence and he had some knowledge of the world. He smiled when he thought of himself, whom Blanche had looked upon as an absurd and callow youth, now giving her good advice. During a halt of the train he wrote a letter to her. He reminded her how ephemeral was the glory of the stage and how heart-rending its disappointments. He tried to make her see that there was beauty also in the normal life of ordinary people. Was it not Marcus Aurelius who had said that our life was what our thoughts made it? He said a number of wise and sensible things and he ended up with these words:

> *My dear, don't think me unsympathetic when I tell you that regret is meaningless. You couldn't have done anything but what you did. You think you could have acted differently because you've forgotten what sort of a woman you were then. Let's come down to brass tacks: now, twenty-five years later, you wished you had consented when some man wanted to become your lover, you've forgotten that then the mere thought of it filled you with physical repulsion.*

It wasn't only your mind that kept you pure, it was your nerves. The virtuous woman deceives herself when she thinks she could have been a light one if she had wished. They say every woman is a rake at heart. Nonsense. You resisted the temptations to which poor Charmian succumbed not because you were any better than she, don't think that for a minute; you resisted because there was no temptation. Only a harlot can be a harlot.

He posted the letter at a wayside station. The reply reached him a few days later. It was from Andrew MacArdle. It ran as follows:

Your letter came too late. Blanche killed herself last night.

WARTIME ARTICLES
IN
AMERICA

IN THE BUS

You never would have thought there was a war on. It was Saturday morning and the streets were crowded. The sky was blue and a pleasant touch of spring in the air made you feel that it was good to be alive.

There was a bus stop at the hospital and the bus pulled up. Two women were waiting to get in, working women; but they had put on their best clothes to go to the hospital; one was middle-aged, but the other was just a girl and she could not have been more than eighteen. She wore salmon-coloured rayon stockings and high-heeled patent leather shoes and a red hat. The bus was very full and they had to hang on to a strap. A man in a cap, with a handkerchief round his neck, saw that the girl was crying. He got up.

'Here, you'd better sit down,' he said.

The girl did not seem to notice and the elderly woman nudged her.

'The gentleman says, sit down in his seat, dear.'

The girl sat with her head thrown back, her mouth slightly open, and the tears ran down her cheeks.

'In trouble?' said the man to the older woman.

'It's her husband. He was only just twenty, poor fellow.'

The other people in the bus looked at the girl with curiosity.

'He was working on a trawler. A German plane came down and bombed them. But they never hit her. Then they come down low and machine-gunned them and Bert was wounded. She's been at the hospital all night, sitting with him, and she's tired out, poor thing. He died this morning.'

You'd have thought that the girl didn't hear a word of what was said. Her eyes were blank.

'They'd been courtin' for two years and they'd only been married twelve days. They was very much in love.'

No one in the bus said anything. There didn't seem to be anything to say.

Allied Relief Ball Souvenir Program, Hotel Astor, New York, 1940.

READING UNDER BOMBING

I am going to tell you about some books we are reading in England today, the sort of books I myself find agreeable to read just now, and the sort of books I hear of other people reading. I should explain first of all that I don't come here as a critic, which I'm not, nor as an author, which I am, but as an ordinary member of the public. I claim no more authority to speak on this subject than if I were a bus conductor or a Cabinet Minister.

Reading should be a pleasure. You are the final judge of the value to you of the book you are reading. No matter what the learned say about it, however much they praise it, if it doesn't interest *you*, if it doesn't please *you*, it's no business of yours. Of course, the great masterpieces of our literature, the books that enlarge our spirit and enrich our personality, afford entertainment, too, but I don't know how you feel about it. I find they want a detachment of mind and an aloofness which are difficult to secure in these distressful and momentous times.

I am made of weaker stuff. In these grim days I am content with the kind of reading which the severe contemptuously describe as escapist. To tell you the truth, I don't see why they should be so severe or so contemptuous. We have most of us put in a hard day's work at some kind of war work, and I don't see why we should be grudged a little relaxation at the end of it. If we were better men and our characters nobler, it may be that, however tired, however anxious, we should prefer *Paradise Lost* to P.G. Wodehouse; but there it is, we have to take ourselves as we are.

Since the beginning of the war I have spent two or three periods of great distress. I found no better way to get through the weary, bitter hours than to read detective stories. The writers of detective stories do not hold a very high place in the world of letters, and when you meet them they are apt to be rather apologetic about themselves.

How wrong they are to be so modest! They are benefactors of the human race. And don't let us pretend that they are read only by the lowbrows. Everyone reads them. The archbishop in his palace, the don in his college rooms, the financial magnate and the Secretary of State. They offer relaxation from toil and relief from anxiety. But they deserve their success for other reasons besides. They tell a story swiftly, they don't waste time on irrelevant detail, and they carry you on from page to page with the desire to know what is going to happen next. These are the essential qualities of a good novel, and it is because the authors of novels of a more ambitious character often neglect them that their books, notwithstanding their other merits, too frequently remain something of a labour to read.

Of course, no one can read nothing but detective stories. As I write these words I am conscious that they're not true. I know readers, like chain smokers who light one cigarette on the stub of another, who no sooner have finished one detective story than they begin a new one. I can't. I want a rest in between and so I'm going to tell you what sort of reading I've found very pleasant in wartime.

Before doing that, in case you should think I'm saying too much about my own likes and dislikes, I'll tell you what I've discovered by questioning other people. I find that they're inclined to go back to the leisurely novels of the nineteenth century, not so much the important ones like those of Dickens and Thackeray, though Trollope seems much in favour, but the lesser ones. They are reading Ouida again, and, what is very surprising to me, the works of Charlotte Yonge. I may remind you that she was a very popular writer in her day and her most celebrated book was *The Heir of Redcliffe*. In case you are tempted to read any others, I will mention the names of two more, *The Trial* and *The Daisy Chain*. I am not quite sure why, after the neglect of so many years, Miss Yonge is now finding new readers. She was a deeply religious lady and she wrote with a high moral purpose. But I do not think it is for this reason that people are beginning to read her again. I think it is because they find in her quiet novels the picture of a peaceful, secure, and easy-going life which, at this distance, looks as if it had been very pleasant to lead. The England she described is gone, never to return.

Another novelist who had some of the qualities that attract readers of the present day to Miss Yonge was Mrs Oliphant. She wrote one book, *The Beleagured City*, which, though not at all in her usual style, is a remarkable performance. It must be very nearly forgotten now, but in its way it is wonderfully good. I think you would be glad to read it.

Now, to my own wartime reading. I have found nothing so satisfactory as memoirs. They, too, take one out of oneself into a different world. Though English literature isn't as rich as French in works of this sort, we have at least some admirable writers of memoirs, and though they may not be so romantic or so picturesque as the French, because they tell us of our own people and portray a world our forefathers lived in, they have a significance to us that gives them a compensating interest.

THE
CULTURE
THAT
IS TO COME

Our culture depends upon our freedom. So far as the arts are concerned, history shows that nothing is produced by a nation that is enslaved. I do not know if any of you have been in Russia since the government was captured by the Bolsheviks, or in Germany since the Nazis gained control. If you have, you can hardly have failed to notice to what a lamentable state of decay the arts have fallen. The plays they produce are so poor that they are obliged to fall back on translations; their novels are worthless, their painting, their music, are negligible.

For the artist can only produce if he is free. He can only produce what is of value to the world if he can develop his personality to the utmost of his capacity; and he can only do that if he is allowed to think and to say what he likes within the broad limits which have been imposed by democracy. The cardinal principle of democracy is that the nation should be governed not for the benefit of the state, but for the benefit of the individuals that compose it. And so if you think that English culture, which is your culture also, should be preserved, you must wish with all your hearts that Britain should emerge victorious from this hateful war.

There is one great difference between America and Britain which is not always present to people's minds. We in Britain are a homogeneous nation. The Celts, the Anglo-Saxons, the Danes, the Normans have long since coalesced into one people. I don't suppose you could find one single inhabitant of my little island whose blood was unmixed. You on the contrary in this country have vast numbers of alien races who are in process of being assimilated. I was surprised the other day when I was in California to be told that in Los Angeles there are fifty thousand Russians. There is also a great colony of Mexicans. In other parts of the country you have dense conglomerations of Poles, Swedes, Germans, Italians, and so forth.

We in England, because we are a homogeneous people, must submit to limitations. I don't suppose we shall ever be a nation of painters or musicians. But as you assimilate these various peoples with their various gifts, it seems almost inevitable that there should arise up among them composers who will be as fertile and stimulating as the great Germans, and painters who will hold their own with the great Frenchmen. It is an exciting prospect. With your huge population, with your vast territory, your wealth and illimitable resources, it is inevitable that you should assume the leadership of the free world of the future. It is, of course, a terrible responsibility, and I can understand that many must quail at the prospect of assuming it; but it will be forced upon you whether you wish it or not, by the force of circumstances. It will be a great glory if you can add to this, leadership of the world's culture.

And remember this: culture is not just an ornament or a decoration. It is not the icing on the cake or the frill on a skirt. If it were, it would not be very important. Culture is the expression of a nation's character, and at the same time it is the powerful instrument to mould its character. Culture does not consist in having read certain books, in taking pleasure in listening to music or looking at paintings. If it did, it would be no more valuable than playing bowls or drinking a glass of beer. The end of culture is right living. The final test of a work of art is its moral value. Our culture is a statement in the terms of art of our ideals.

And what are our ideals? I am trying to think of them as objectively as I can. The values that we cherish are these: freedom – freedom of speech, freedom of opinion, freedom of worship – tolerance, compassion for the under-dog and mercy for the beaten foe, kindliness, a square deal to all men, decency in behaviour, truth and uprightness. Those are your ideals too. They assert the prime importance of the individual, and that I may remind you is not only the basic principle of democracy but also of the Christian faith. They are not the ideals of the totalitarian countries. *They* claim that the individual is of no account, and that his only value is in his service to the omnipotent state.

We in England are fighting not only for our security, to preserve our homes from destruction, and our children from death; we are fighting for our right to be free, our right to live according to our standards of good, and our right to speak our minds without constraint. Our culture tells us that it is the exercise of those rights which gives man his worth and life its meaning. And because these rights are yours too, because your culture is our culture, because your ideals are our ideals, we are fighting for you as well as for ourselves. And because we are fighting for these great values, we are convinced that with your help we shall prevail.

THE
NOBLEST ACT

She smiled at her own silliness. She hadn't done such a thing since she was a girl at school; then too she had crossed off the dates on a calendar, day after day, as the holidays drew nearer.

And now she put the calendar back on her desk; every day since the beginning of the month she had crossed off a date and now there were only thirteen to go, and then they would be going home. Home to England, and for good and all this time, after thirty years in the Malay States. She was so terribly homesick. She longed for the grey skies of England and the harsh winds of the moors and the bluster of the North Sea. They got leave only every five years, she and her husband, Dr Farley, and the few months in England were pitifully short. She longed for her children. Because children grow sickly in the East, they had left them at home when the eldest was only nine; they were grown up now and almost strangers to her.

And then there was her own health. She hadn't wanted to bother her husband about it – he had enough sick people on his hands without her – so she had taken advantage of a visit to Singapore to see a doctor there. He had told her there was nothing seriously the matter with her; it was only that she was worn out by all those years in the tropics; she had come to the end of her tether and must go home. The air of her native Yorkshire would soon put her to rights. 'You're going soon, aren't you?' he asked.

'In a couple of months,' she smiled.

'That's good. I don't mind telling you that another year in this climate would just about finish you. But go to England and lead a quiet life and you're good for another twenty years.'

Only thirteen days more.

Jim was late for dinner. She hoped it was only an interminable rubber at the club that was keeping him and not some case to which he had been suddenly called. She made up her mind to wait until nine. But just then she heard his car drive up. He came up the steps on to the veranda – a big, bluff, handsome man with clear blue eyes and a thatch of curling grey hair.

This Week, 4 January 1942.

He had immense vitality, and patients always said that he had only to come into the sickroom to make them feel better. It was remarkable that after so many years of hard work in that trying climate he should have kept his strength and his high spirits. 'I'm sorry I'm late, dear,' he said. 'Meadows, the Colonial Secretary, rang up from Singapore and insisted on talking to me.'

'Oh, what did he want?' she asked casually. Dr Farley laughed.

'He wanted me to do something that I've got no intention of doing.'

'What was that?'

'Well, you see, the war's upset things in the Medical Service. The chap that was going to replace me here can't come and they want me to stay on. Of course I told Meadows to go to blazes.'

Mrs Farley went even paler than she generally was. Something seemed to catch her by the throat so that it was difficult to speak. 'But who'll look after the people here when you're gone?'

'That's their lookout. They'll have to do without a doctor till the war's over.'

'But isn't it your duty to stay?'

'I'm fed to the teeth--doing my duty.'

There were tears in her eyes, but she forced a smile to her lips.

'I should have thought you were a bit too old to change the habit of a lifetime.'

He looked at her tenderly.

'My dear, it's you I'm thinking of. D'you think I don't know how you've been counting the days before we go? Meadows said you could go without me.' Dr Farley chuckled. '"You don't know my wife," I said to him. "She wouldn't leave me for anything in the world. Besides, I can't do without the old girl."'

Just for a moment Mrs Farley couldn't speak. She didn't want him to see that her hands were trembling. This was death for her. She gave a little chuckle.

'Of course I won't leave you, you old stupid, and of course you must stay.'

His face lit up. He'd hated the thought of going when he was needed so badly. She might have known it. But he looked at her doubtfully.

'You want to go home so much.'

'Not so much as all that. I've felt so useless since the war started. It's nice to think we can do our bit.'

He took her in his arms and kissed her.

'You're tops, Katie.'

'Hurry up and get ready for dinner, or it'll be ruined.'

He pounded heavily into his bedroom. Mrs Farley, so thin, so wan, so frail, stood where he had left her. The worn face was puckered with the effort she made not to cry. She would never see her children and her home again. The doctor in Singapore had given her a year; well, doctors were often mistaken. Anyhow, it didn't matter: Jim couldn't leave these people without anyone to look after them.

She went over to the desk and tore out of the calendar the sheet on which she had crossed off the first fourteen days of the month. That was that.

WHY D'YOU DISLIKE US?

I am going to deal in generalizations, and generalizations need to be qualified. They do not tell the whole truth and you can always find exceptions to any broad statement. But I do not think any Englishman can remain for long in the United States without discovering that his fellow countrymen are not regarded, on the whole, with warm affection. In these days, linked as the two peoples are by a common purpose, it seems to me worth while to examine this feeling and, if possible, to explain it.

How far this dislike obtains in the masses of the population it is hard to say. I should think that they are thrown so little in contact with the English that they are no more antagonistic to them than they are to other foreigners. It is natural to human nature to dislike the foreigner. His peculiar ways excite your ridicule, and his strangeness makes you uneasy. There is nothing odd about that. But there are certain sections in which the feeling of which I speak is prevalent, though even here there are, of course, a great many who, for one reason or another, like the English; and even among those who do not, the aversion is general rather than particular, and I think it would be hard to find an Anglophobe so rabid that he would not admit to liking at least some Englishmen. But I do not think I exaggerate when I say that among the rich people who have apartments in Park Avenue and country houses on Long Island or in Connecticut, among the businessmen and manufacturers of the Middle West, among the politicians and civil servants in Washington, and even among the men of letters spread up and down the country, the general attitude toward the English is one of dislike.

It has seemed to me curious that so many men of letters should have this antagonism toward the English, since, after all, they more than others profit by the heritage of English culture and English literature, which is common alike to Americans and English, and they use the same language to express themselves; so that you would have thought that, if anywhere, you would find among them a certain warmth of feeling for the country which has given them so large a part of their stock-in-trade. I have reason to believe that there are Englishmen whom H.L. Mencken does not positively detest, but I do not think he would deny that, on the whole, his regard for them is cool.

Saturday Evening Post, 11 April 1942.

Edmund Wilson is, I believe, the most acute critic now writing in America, but when you read between the lines of his intelligent books you can hardly fail to notice his general attitude of exasperated contempt for the English. And if, as I do, you turn every week to Clifton Fadiman's lively columns in *The New Yorker*, you will find that he seldom misses an opportunity to express his impatience with the English ways and our English opinions. That is his right; and the only point I want to make is that when he writes of the Bavarians or the Austrians, for instance, his sympathy leads him to to so with an indulgence he does not show to the English. Many people read Louis Bromfield's pamphlet in which, having cast the dust of a decadent Europe from his feet to settle in Ohio, he told the world at large how low was his opinion of the English. Since writers follow a profession that conduces to sound judgment, impartiality, tolerance and catholicity, their views naturally deserve consideration.

Now, since the war that they are waging in common against the Fascist powers has brought the people of America and the people of Britain into a closer connection than has ever existed between them before, and since it looks as though in future, if the world is once more to be a place in which human beings can live in well-being and freedom, this connection must become closer still, it seems to me important to discover why the English are disliked in this country. I want, in this article, to examine the defects which excite this bitterness of feeling and to consider what justification there is for the charges that are brought against the English. I will try to be honest and impartial. I will not try to excuse what is inexcusable, but I will try to explain how certain failings that irritate others have arisen among the English, in the hope that the Americans will understand them better, and so feel more kindly toward them.

I must begin by saying that nothing has come upon the English as a greater surprise than to realize that they are disliked. They have looked upon themselves as kindly and easy-going people, and it has been a real shock to them to learn how very different they were considered by others. Let me take the instance of Louis Bromfield. No one could have been more popular in England than he. He was a welcome guest in the houses not only of the great but in those of all kinds of people. He was held in affection because he was friendly, gay, voluble and amusing, so that it came as a blow when it was discovered that he held the English in profound disdain.

They sought rather helplessly for reasons to explain his dislike for people who liked him so much, and could only suggest – what was doubtless false – that he had had some unpleasant personal experience that had embittered him toward the whole nation. It is true that a trifling incident may often affect a person's general attitude. I know of an American woman of wealth and station who conceived a mortal antipathy to the English because when she was staying for a week in a great country house she was presented with a bill for her laundry. For my part, I think it deplorable to ask your guests to pay for their own laundry, but it appears to be a common English practice and you must accept it just as you must accept the equally reprehensible practice of slipping fifty francs into the butler's hand when you have dined in a French house. I have heard the Anglophobia of a very distinguished American newspaper proprietor attributed to the fact that his mother, affronted because her husband's situation in London did not secure her the social recognition she thought was her right, conceived an animosity toward the English which she imparted to her son.

I merely give these instances to show the sort of explanations the English give to account for feelings that honestly seem to them inexplicable. It does not occur to them to ask themselves whether Americans dislike them because in fact they merit it. So far as I know, the principal charges brought against the English are the following: self-complacency, superciliousness, stinginess, bad manners, inhospitableness, snobbishness and lack of humour.

No Englishman can travel in this country without hearing the story about his fellow countryman who asked a Californian what they did with all the fruit that they grew in that fertile state. 'We eat what we can and what we can't we can,' was the reply; but when he repeated it, he said, 'We eat what we can and what we can't we tin.' In the thirty years I have been coming to America I must have heard it at least four hundred times as an example of the English inability to see a joke. I bear it. I think it hard to assert that a nation that has produced Falstaff, Mr Shandy, Mr Micawber and Sam Weller is devoid of a sense of humour.

My own impression is that the English have a sense of humour as keen as that of the Americans, but it happens to be different. As a rough generalization, I would hazard the opinion that American humour depends on exaggeration, while English humour depends on irony. But it would be foolish to suppose that Americans dislike us because they are persuaded that we have no sense of humour; that only makes them regard us with good-natured scorn; they accuse us of more serious defects than this, and with them I will now deal.

First there is the charge of stinginess. It is well founded. I know of a distinguished English novelist who came to the United States on a lecture tour and in the six months he spent here, since he stayed with friends wherever he went and his railway fares were paid for him by the lecture agency, he is currently reported to have spent seventeen cents. How he spent them is a pretty story. He was walking down Fifth Avenue with two friends, both men of letters, when they passed a drugstore. He said he wanted to go in, and asked them to wait outside. They thought he meant to buy toothpaste or bicarbonate. In a few minutes he came out wiping his mouth and said, 'I just went in to get an ice-cream soda.'

It is true that when the English come over here, generally to make money – for the State Department, to my own knowledge, does not look with favour on aliens coming to this country solely for pleasure, thinking, perhaps, that with such an object in view they will corrupt the virtue of citizens – they count every penny they spend, and spend as little as they can. It is a pity. I wish they were more lavish. I do not seek to excuse their parsimony, but in extenuation I should like to offer an explanation. The earnings of the English have always been much smaller than those of the Americans, and when they come to the United States they find everything alarmingly expensive. It seems to them that they have to pay a dollar for what they could get for a shilling in England, and they button up their pockets; when their American hosts are so willing to pay up for them, they let them do it with the more alacrity since they appear so well able to afford it.

The English are not so close-fisted as the French; in France, indeed, they have always had the reputation of being reckless spenders, but it would be foolish to deny that compared with the Americans they are mean. They have had it dinned into their ears for generations, that if you take care of the pence, the pounds will take care of themselves, and if they have acquired wealth, it has more often been by prudence and economy than by rapid acquisition through a clever invention or a fortunate deal. Until the depression of 1929, Americans, on the whole, made money easily, and, having a natural inclination to do things in the large way, they were impatient of small economies. In England the summer is uncertain, so that when we have a fine day we try to make the most of it, but in the American summer one fine day follows another, so that there is no particular need to take advantage of any one of them. So it is with money in England and America.

Now let us discuss another matter. Americans are often, and very justly, hurt because when English people come to America they have entertained them largely and have put themselves out to make their sojourn pleasant, but when they, in their turn, go to England, little or nothing is done for them. The English are much to blame for this and I will not try to excuse them. It should be their pleasure, as in gratitude it is certainly their duty, to make the stay of visiting Americans in England as agreeable as the stay of visiting English is made in America. One cause of their remissness in this respect is, strange as it may seem, their modesty; they know they cannot offer entertainment as splendid as they have received, and, honestly fearful that the little they can do will seem insufficient, are inclined to do nothing.

They are creatures of settled habits and they find it difficult to effect the disturbance which is caused by taking a newcomer into their midst. They are apt, especially in a vast city like London, to live in a small circle of intimate friends, and when acquaintances they have made in America descend upon them they are harassed by the fear that they will not fit in. The American who settles in London leads for some time a very lonely existence [and] is likely enough, if he goes away then, to take with him a very captious impression of British good will; but it is only fair to add that when he has once made his way into English life he is there for keeps. The English don't very much like strangers, they are uneasy with them, but when an American has made friends in England, they are his friends forever. He will find them faithful, devoted and cordial; and then he certainly will not be able to complain of any lack of hospitality. He will not find himself the guest of honour at a dinner of twenty people, for parties of that kind are not, certainly since the last war, in the English habit, but he will be asked to take pot-luck, he will be welcome to drop in whenever he has nothing better to do, and he will be asked to stay in the country as often as he likes to go. He will become one of the family.

Now, the Americans like strangers. They are curious to see what sort of odd creatures they are; they like to give parties and the visiting fireman is a welcome excuse; but they grow tired of the stranger very quickly – much more quickly than we do in England when we have got over our first shyness toward him – and the Englishman visiting this country must often have been surprised, when he has been received with such warmheartedness that he thought he had made new friends, to realize that, having seen him once and made much of him, his hosts of the evening have had enough of him. The Americans like new people, and when their newness has worn off they are not greatly interested in them. I have known plenty of Englishmen who have come over to this country for the first time and have been so generously entertained and have so much enjoyed themselves that when they got back to England their only idea was to return to America as soon as they could. But I have always said to them, 'Remember, they won't like you nearly so much the second time as they liked you the first'; and have besought them to wait till they were forgotten, or had something in themselves fresh to offer, so that they could come again with the advantage of novelty.

For my own part, the first time I came to America, to which I came as a suddenly successful dramatist, anxious not to outstay my welcome I made up my mind that the first day on which nobody had asked me to lunch or dinner I would take my passage home. This happened six weeks to a day after my arrival in New York and I had no sooner swallowed my breakfast than I hied me to the Cunard office and booked a stateroom on the next ship out. I have since thought that I did very well to last six weeks.

Manners. It is not only in America that the English are accused of rudeness; it is true that they haven't the florid manner of the French, for example, or the stiff politeness of the Germans. But there are the good manners of the heart and what I may call the good manners of the finger-tips. The English, I think, are a good-natured, amiable people, as anyone can see for himself if he mixes with the crowd on a public holiday, and I do not believe that they are more deficient than other nations in this politeness of the heart.

The politeness of the finger-tips is different in different countries and it is unreasonable to find rudeness in what is only different usage. It is evidently desirable that a stranger should make himself acquainted with the habits of politeness of the country he is visiting, and adopt them, but I don't think we need to be too hard on him if he errs from ignorance.

When it comes to the English and the Americans, slight dissimilarities in custom make an Englishman seem rude when he has no desire to be. For example, in England we do not use first names as commonly as you use them in America; when we know Brown, we should think it very stiff and chilling to call him 'Mr Brown' and unwarrantably familiar to call him 'Jack'. It took me a long time to discover that in this country I could call him by his first name when I had seen him two or three times, without his thinking me impertinent, but that, if I called him 'Brown' instead of 'Mr Brown', he would think me patronizing. Differences of language may likewise give an appearance of rudeness where none is intended. Let me take an instance on the English side. You commonly use 'want' where we use 'will'. The other day in the country I heard a woman say to her small son, 'D'you want to go down to the garage and have the car sent up?' Well, he had made a number-plate out of a piece of pasteboard, which he had attached to the back of his bicycle, and was pursuing desperate gangsters in the high-powered car of his imagination. He didn't 'want' to do what she asked him, but he knew that 'do you want' meant 'will you', and dutifully went off on the errand. Long as I have been in America, it gives me something of a start when someone says to me, 'D'you want to dine with me tomorrow?' It gives me the impression that my host doesn't want me, but is prepared to put up with me if I am going to make a point of it. But I think I should be very silly to take offence.

English manners are more casual than American manners. The English notion is that the less fuss you make the better, and that you should leave people alone. There is a story I was told in my youth of the late Duchess of Cleveland, the mother of Lord Rosebery, who was sometime prime minister; she was an old woman who walked with a stick and she lived at Battle Abbey. One day she got out of her chair to ring the bell, and a young man who was staying in the house jumped up to ring it for her, whereupon she gave him a smart rap with her stick and said severely, 'Officiousness, sir, is not politeness.' Americans often complain because when they go to a party in England, or to spend a weekend in a big house in the country, they are sometimes introduced to nobody. That is an English custom which I, who live in England but little and so may find myself in a gathering where I know hardly anyone, do not like; but it would be a mistake to look upon it as rude, since the idea at the back of it is the flattering one that you are sufficiently familiar with the great world to know everybody, and therefore introductions are unnecessary.

There are many small politenesses which Americans practise and which add grace to social intercourse, but which the English do not know. They have not the charming habit of sending flowers to their friends or, when they are crossing the ocean, giving them books, fruit and candy. They do not often trouble to see them off or to meet them when they arrive. This is perhaps because England is a small country and travel is not a formidable business, and also because, having been for so many generations inveterate travellers, they see no particular reason to make a to-do because someone is starting on a journey.

The Americans are naturally more cordial than the English. The English suffer greatly from the abominable affliction of shyness, and this makes them stiff in social intercourse and makes them appear rude when, in fact, they are only self-conscious. They suspect cordiality. They look askance at the man who is a good mixer and slaps them on the back. To call a man 'a hearty' is a term of depreciation. There is a house in London I often lunch at when I am there, where the hostess, a late riser, seldom comes downstairs before her guests are assembled. When you are shown into a gathering of perhaps seven or eight people, you are met with glances of cold hostility, and you seem to read in those suspicious eyes the question: 'How the devil did this fellow get here?' No one will speak to you unless you address him, but if you do, he will answer with amiability. It is nothing really but social awkwardness.

The English casualness, I am prepared to admit, is often carried so far as to result in an offensive lack of courtesy. Let me give you an example. Not very long ago a manager, being about to produce a play in Washington that he thought would interest the English, communicated his wish to the responsible person to send seats for the first night to such members of the staff of the British embassy as would care to come. He was somewhat surprised to be given a list of forty, but sent them all telegrams; ten accepted, and to each he sent a couple of seats. Only two of them sent him a word of thanks. I was surprised when he told me, since persons connected with diplomacy, in all countries, though apt to look upon themselves as a class apart, and so to be somewhat deficient in the politeness of the heart, are careful, as a rule, to practise what I have called the politeness of the finger-tips. I can only hope that the recipients of my friend's bounty were so busy with their onerous duties that they simply hadn't the time to drop him a brief note of thanks, but I have an uneasy feeling that they thought they did him so great an honour in accepting his hospitality that they felt thanks were unnecessary.

This brings me naturally to the self-complacency which more than anything else irritates the Americans with the English, and for a reason which I think few English people realize. Because the Americans are boastful, they have thought them arrogant; and they have not seen that this boastfulness was merely a defensive armour put on to conceal a very real diffidence. I see behind the façade of assurance a sort of spiritual malaise, as though for all their brave words they were distracted by hesitations they could not overcome. They are very willing to put the best foot forward, but they're not at all sure which is the right foot to put. They seem to me sometimes like men wandering in a trackless desert who tell one another they know the way, and yet in their heart of hearts fear they are lost.

Is it very surprising that for a period the English were self-complacent? They had a long and, with the exception of some unfortunate incidents, a glorious history behind them, and a literature no less glorious; they were the richest and most powerful nation in the world; they had a stable and honest government, and they led in the field of sport. It would have been becoming if they had accepted all this with modesty; I do not think they were overbearing in these fortunate circumstances, but they were undoubtedly pleased with themselves. But all this is changed. The first blow came when other peoples adopted the sports in which the English had excelled and their supremacy was wrested from them. It was a shock to them to find that others could beat them at swimming and sailing and running, at tennis and golf and polo; but I don't think it can be denied that they accepted their defeat in what is known as a sporting spirit.

Not long ago Winston Churchill stated publicly that the United States is now the most powerful nation in the world, and no one in England, so far as I know, uttered a word of protest. The English have seen the wealth of the world transferred from the shores of Albion to the coasts of America, and they have accepted the fact with the same good humour that they showed when Americans swept all before them at Wimbledon. There's not much self-complacency about the English now, but prejudices die hard and I know that it will be long before the people of America forget that the charge they bring against us, true once, is true no longer. I am sure we were insufferably patronizing. It showed want of tact – never a striking characteristic of the English – and want of manners. We belong to an old nation, of long-settled ways, and it was not unnatural that when we came to visit this new country and found its habits different from ours, we, thinking our own much better, were unable to conceal our disapproval. It is natural to think that what we are used to is best; that is a failing of the human race, and since the Americans belong to it, too, it may be supposed that even they are not entirely immune from it. There is no inclination now in England to patronize the Americans.

In the early editions of his entertaining book on the American language, H.L. Mencken prophesied that the English spoken in America and the English spoken in England would in a few generations so diverge that the inhabitants of one country would cease to understand the speech of the inhabitants of the other. He has changed his mind now, for a very unlikely thing has happened; English has become Americanized, and Mencken in his witty way said to me that he was thinking of sending a body of Harvard students over to England to collect Anglicisms before they died out. But it is not only the English language that has been Americanized; English life has been too. We have adopted the cocktail, jazz and the safety razor, the cinema and the neon light; the hire-purchase system, the multiple store and the skyscraper; and, in fact, a hundred things that are entirely and essentially American. There is surely no trace of patronage in the attitude that can enthusiastically adopt so many devices that add to the convenience and pleasure of life. The most influential poet in England today is an American, and the American novel, the American short story have had a vitalizing effect on our English fiction. The English of today are only too glad to learn what they can from America, and it is unreasonable to blame them because they reject what they do not find suited to their own civilization.

Finally I come to this matter of class distinction, with its attendant snobbery, the prevalence of which in England disturbs so many people who are not otherwise unsympathetic to the English. If Americans are under the impression that there are no class distinctions in America, they deceive themselves. The foreigner has only to read *Babbitt* and go to the picture called *Andy Hardy's Private Secretary* to see that class distinctions exist as much here as anywhere else. The Americans have a natural geniality, so that, for example, the bank president, getting into conversation with the travelling salesman in the club car of a train, will talk to him on terms of perfect equality, but I am not aware that he will think of asking him to visit him at his home on Long Island. No one who has ever been to Santa Barbara or Charleston can imagine that the wife of the travelling salesman, charming and pretty as she may be, will be received by the old-established inhabitants of those delightful communities with shouts of acclamation.

I was once invited to lunch with a woman who, I was told, had twenty million dollars and, believe me, I have never seen a duke in England treated with such deference as she was by her guests. You would have thought that every word that dropped from her opulent lips was a hundred-dollar bill that we would be allowed to take away with us.

In any ordered civilization there will be class distinctions, and it is illusory to imagine that they can be altogether abolished. Class distinctions depend on power. In England, during the eighteenth century, power was in the hands of the territorial magnates and they were, for the most part, men of rank. It was not till the nineteenth century that the industrialization of the country introduced a new class which to a great extent wrested power from the great landholders. It remains to be seen what the effect on class distinctions will be when, as seems likely to happen, power comes into the hands of the wage-earners. My own belief is that they will still prevail.

It is a mistake to imagine that they exist only among the well-to-do. In England the wife of the skilled artisan will refuse to consort with the wife of a common labourer; and I have myself seen in Bermondsey, one of the poorest parts of London, the very nice and pretty daughter of some friends of mine coldly received by the family of the young printer she married, because they lived in what they thought a better street than that in which her family lived, though to my eyes there was nothing to choose between those two mean and sordid slums. Nor is this state of things peculiar to England. I could name a town in a Western state, a flourishing lumber town, only sixteen years old and beautifully laid out, where class distinctions are so great that the dwellers in one block will not play bridge with the dwellers in another. The men in one go to work in a collar and the men in the other do not.

Snobbishness is an odious vice, and though it is a defect not confined to the English people, it is more marked among them than any other. But I think it is evident that the war will at least attentuate this national failing of ours. For one thing, we shall all be very poor, and poverty is a great leveller. The hardships, the privations, the dangers we have endured have brought the various classes together. Here is a little anecdote that seems to me significant.

A friend of mine, bombed out of her London house, was staying as a paying guest in the country, and one afternoon she was having tea with her hostess, a duchess, and a Colonel Blimp and his wife. Conversation was a bit flat when suddenly a van flashed past the drawing-room window. They all stopped talking and crept up to the window. She couldn't think what had happened.

Then the duchess murmured, 'It's the butcher.'

And the colonel, putting his monocle to his eye, said, 'By gad, ma'am, you're right; it is the butcher.'

The butler came in and said, 'The butcher, your grace.'

'Show him in,' said the duchess; and in he came, a fat, red-faced man, carrying a fine piece of beef on a platter.

'Meat's a bit easier this week, your grace,' he said, 'and I've brought you a nice tender joint.'

They admired it and patted it, and the duchess asked him how his wife was, and then she said, 'Why don't you sit down and have a cup of tea with us?'

So they all sat down and had a grand time. And this was not cupboard love, but sincere friendliness.

The great breeding-ground of snobbery in England has been that institution which you know as a private school and we as a public school. But parents can no longer afford to keep their boys at establishments of this character. The public schools of England are faced with ruin, and, for the most part, will be unable to subsist unless they receive aid from the state. It is inconceivable that the state will consent to grant them subsidies if they are to be maintained for the exclusive use of the privileged classes. They must become what they were originally meant to be – places where rich and poor can receive the same education. It seems unlikely that when the squire's son and the baker's son, the banker's son and the truck driver's son work and play together during the formative years of their youth the snobbishness which has been one of the ugliest features of our English civilization can endure.

Actually now, when thousands upon thousands of young men of education, means and family are serving in the ranks and discovering that young men who have not had their advantages are every bit as good as they are, the process is going on. And what is no less important, the baker's son and the truck driver's son are finding out, to their surprise, that the squire's son and the banker's son, whom they looked upon before with suspicion and mistrust, are men very like themselves.

I have spoken only of the defects of the English and not of their merits, for to do so was not the object of my article; and in any case I have a feeling – due, you may say, to my British self-complacency – that they can be left to speak for themselves. All I have tried to do is to reason with you on the particular characteristics that make you dislike us, and sometimes hate us, in the hope that by understanding us better you may regard our faults with more indulgence.

There must always be misunderstandings between the English and the Americans, but they can be mitigated by good sense and good will. The readers of *The Saturday Evening Post* will know that the British government, anxious that the young airmen who have come to be trained here should make as good an impression as possible on the people with whom they are brought into contact, issued a paper in which they were told what to do and what not to do.

For my part, I think it would be to the purpose if a similar document were handed to every British subject who is about to visit this country, and I wish I were asked to write it. I should begin by saying, 'You cannot hope to get along in America unless you like the Americans.' And I should add, 'They are not hard to like.'

To
KNOW ABOUT ENGLAND
AND THE
ENGLISH

The only way to get to know a country is to go and live in it, but if you can't do that, you can get some kind of notion of it by reading the right books; and by the right books I don't mean only books of information: the novelist and the poet can tell you things about a country and its people that you will never learn from the erudite works of the historian or the social economist. Nevertheless, you cannot expect to know much about a country and its people unless you know something of their history, and so to anyone who wants to know about England and the English I would suggest that he should read first Trevelyan's *Shortened History of England* (Longmans). It has the merit of being very readable. Another admirable work of information is Maitland's *Constitutional History* (Macmillan). This sounds dull, but it isn't: it is solid, of course, but it is fascinating; and it shows you very well how it has come about that the English differ from the other peoples of Europe. A third work is Arthur Bryant's *Pageant of England: 1840–1940* (Harper). This gives a vivid picture of the period it deals with and is as easy to read as a novel. That would end my list of purely instructive works and though all are interesting I would not recommend any inquiring reader to read them one after the other. I would recommend him rather to intersperse them with lighter reading.

And I should like him to get some notion of what England was like before the war, and I have racked my brains to think of a novel, or even a series of novels, that would give such a picture of life in England as Trollope gave in his time and as Galsworthy, with less vigour and less talent, gave a couple of generations later. Alas, there is no such novel, and the only books I can think of that might give a stranger some inkling of how we lived and what sort of folk we were during the first thirty or forty years of this century are Siegfried

Sassoon's charming *Memoirs of a Fox-hunting Man* (Doubleday), E.M. Delafield's *Diary of a Provincial Lady* (Grosset), and J.B. Priestley's *English Journey* (Harper).

As a gay and bitter commentary on them I would suggest Low's *A Cartoon History of Our Times* (Simon & Schuster).

But when you want to find out about a country it is well to hear what foreigners have to say about it. Paul Cohen-Portheim, a Dutchman, has in *England the Unknown Isle* (Dutton) written an amusing and sympathetic book about us. It makes fun of us, but you can hardly read his book without discovering that notwithstanding our absurdities he likes us. Margaret Halsey's *With Malice Towards Some* (Simon & Schuster) is just as amusing, but it could hardly be described as sympathetic; her naïve assumption that manners and customs which are not those of her own home town are *ipso facto* ridiculous is one that we are all apt to make and such a book is useful to put one on one's guard against this common failing; but hers is well worth reading not only on that account, but also because it is well to know both sides of a story, and for its author's sprightly humour and acid observation.

We are at war, and you want to know how the people of England are conducting life, for life goes on: babies are born, young people marry, the old still die in their beds. Well, there are several books that will tell you this. There is Phyllis Bottome's *London Pride* (Little, Brown), there is Margaret Kennedy's *Where Stands a Winged Sentry* (Yale), there is Margery Allingham's *The Oaken Heart* (Doubleday). And for a vivid picture of the bombing of London there is John Strachey's *Digging for Mrs Miller* (Random House). Jan Struther's pleasant *Mrs Miniver* (Harcourt, Grosset, Pocket Books) has been so widely read in this country that it is hardly necessary to mention it.

I have only one book more to mention. History will have much to say of Winston Churchill, but we shall all be dead before all the facts with which he has been concerned are known. Meanwhile it is worth while to learn what one can of this remarkable and perhaps great man. Philip Guedalla has written in *Mr Churchill: A Portrait* (Reynal & Hitchcock) a work marked by his usual liveliness which will tell you all there is at present to tell about him, and also a good deal about England and the English, for it is because Winston Churchill has the typical characteristics of the English in a pre-eminent degree that the English people have given him their confidence and freely accepted his leadership in this most momentous period of their long history.

MORALE MADE IN AMERICA

I suppose everyone knows now that one of the causes of the French defeat, and not the least important either, was the collapse of morale in the French troops. During the first winter of the war, I spent a short period with the army of Alsace, and wherever I went saw soldiers wandering aimlessly about the streets or playing interminable games of cards in sordid bars. I talked to some of them; I talked to their officers; I heard the same story. They were bored to death; they were lonely. They were homesick; they were ripe to listen to Communist propaganda from within and to German propaganda from without.

I asked whether games could not be arranged for them to play, and was told that the French soldier did not care to play games. Now and then a travelling company of actors gave a performance, but so far as I could hear, that was the only entertainment provided for them. It may be that now and then a lecturer came from Paris and delivered a discourse; I have heard of it. But for the most part, the men were left to rot in idleness. I was so shocked by this that when I went to England and saw the Commander-in-Chief, the first thing I asked him was what was being done in England for the entertainment of the troops.

I heard a very different story. From the very beginning of the war, steps had been taken to keep the men occupied and amused. They were given the opportunity to study any subject that interested them. They were encouraged to play games. (The British soldier needs little encouragement to do this. Give him a football, and he knows what to do with it.) Theatrical performances, concerts, lectures give him diversion according to his taste. I visited the establishments of the Y.M.C.A. I heard the performances of concert-parties during the lunch-hour at factories, for the authorities very sensibly judged that it was no less worth while to maintain the morale of the workers than to maintain that of the soldiers and sailors. The result of all this effort was manifest. All who were competent to judge agreed that British morale, both in the armed forces and among the workers, was grand.

Convinced as I am of the importance of morale, I jumped at the opportunity, when it was given me, to see something of the work done to build it up in this country by the U.S.O. I do not wish to pretend to a greater knowledge than I have. I know only what the U.S.O. is doing in South Carolina, but I think it safe to assume that its activities are the same in the other States of the Union in which it operates. What I saw I propose now to tell the reader. The United Service Organizations were constituted to offer social and spiritual recreation to the huge numbers of young men enrolling in the forces, and to the young men and women who had to leave their homes to work in the new industrial plants. This service was to be rendered through the united action of six welfare agencies, Catholic, Jew and Protestant. The public was asked to contribute money; it contributed something over thirteen million dollars; the Government promised legislation to pay for the construction of more than two hundred new buildings to be leased to the U.S.O. When it could find buildings suitable to its purposes, the U.S.O. rented them. At the time of writing, it is operating 395 clubs. They are located near Army camps and Naval posts. I have seen some of the new buildings. They are convenient and good to look at. They and the older buildings, duly made over, are well, tastefully and comfortably furnished.

A successful attempt has been made to make them cosy and homelike. Here men can come to read and write letters, to play games, to play the piano or the phonograph, to see movies, listen to concerts, and on Wednesday and Saturday to dance. They have proved an inestimable boon. One soldier told me that for six months he'd walked up and down the streets, and never once did anybody give him a friendly word. 'People seemed afraid of uniforms,' he said. They are lonesome, many of these men who have never before been away from their farms, or left the small towns in which they were born and bred. They are so terribly homesick. They hanker for their mothers and their girls. It is a great solace when they can find women not too young, or friendly men, to whom they can tell their troubles and who will give them wise counsel in their distress.

One boy had been married four years, and at last to his joy his wife became pregnant. When he was ordered to Charleston, so that she might be with him to the end, they decided to drive there from their home in a Midwestern State. But the springs of the old jalopy were none too good, and the going was rough. The young woman was taken ill, and in fear of a premature birth, he took her to the hospital in a town they were passing through.

He was obliged to leave her in a strange place, among strangers, alone. On arriving in Charleston, he learned that he was to embark next day for he knew not where; he could not hope to hear how his wife fared; he could not hope to know when his baby was born. He told his anxiety to a woman at the club who had gained his confidence, and she suggested that he should write to his wife and tell her all he felt. Well, he wasn't much as to writing letters, and he started three or four times and tore up what he had written. At last he got into the swing and wrote and wrote and wrote more. When he had finished, he turned to the kindly woman whose advice he had followed. 'I feel better now,' he said. 'Yes,' she answered, 'I thought you would – and your wife'll feel better when she reads it.' I don't know why the actions of that unlettered boy pouring out his soul on page after page seems to me so pathetic.

I went to a dance at the clubhouse of the U.S.O. in Charleston. There must have been nine hundred people there, but too few girls, so that many of the men had to content themselves with looking on, and when a man got a partner, the chances were that after a few steps someone would cut in on him. But I think everyone enjoyed himself. I have never seen a better-behaved crowd. Military police wandered about, but there was nothing for them to do. Soldiers and sailors were very trim and smart in their well-fitting uniforms. They looked clean, healthy, keen and intelligent. I thought that if I were an American, I should feel immensely proud that my country produced such fine, decent young men: being English, I was glad to think that we in Britain had such allies.

Refreshments for these dances are provided by one or other of the numerous societies of Charleston or by generous individuals; but there is a snack bar in the basement where those who want more substantial fare can get it. In the interval it was crowded. It was a gay and vivacious throng. When the dance was over, the ping-pong tables were cleared away from the basement and cots set up, so that such as cared to spend the night could sleep in clean linen and comfort. The charge for the bed is a quarter, and for towel and soap and a shower next morning five cents. At one period during the evening I went into a large room where men were chatting and reading, and there was a group round a piano at which a soldier was playing Schumann. 'Gosh,' said one man, 'it does me good to hear good music again.'

Of course the success of the U.S.O. clubs must depend largely on the quality of the men and women who operate them. A direction that is harsh, puritanical and domineering defeats the organization's aims. I was glad to discover in the establishments I visited that the persons in charge were lenient, broad-minded and tolerant. They realized that these were young men they had to cope with, and when they broke the reasonable rules made for their own good, dealt with them with sympathy and good sense. Several stories were told me to prove how successfully the method worked. These soldiers and sailors were not the men to turn a deaf ear to an appeal to their good sense and good nature.

With the outbreak of war large numbers of troops were placed in small units on guard duty, and they could no longer take advantage of the U.S.O. clubs. A special mobile division was established. There are five truck units now, operating on the Eastern seaboard. The truck I saw travels incessantly up and down the coast of South Carolina, on a tour of three hundred miles, bringing to lonely groups movies, books and what-not, and what is no less valuable, the assurance that people are thinking about them and caring for them.

I have not room to mention all the activities of the U.S.O., but there is one of which I must say a few final words, for it is of peculiar interest and importance.

This is the work that is being done to serve the large numbers of young men and young women in the new industrial plants. I visited the headquarters of one such agency in South Carolina. Its head is a lively, competent and active woman in the thirties. She could find no accommodation in the overcrowded town, and was forced to establish herself in the two tiny dressing-rooms for the players at a baseball field. She has to deal with eighteen hundred families in the settlements that have been run up to accommodate the huge influx of population, and with a group besides of five hundred trailers in which dwell no less than eighteen hundred persons. They come from all parts of the Union; at one party in her own small quarters there were thirty-eight women from sixteen different States. They are lonely in their unaccustomed surroundings, these people brought here from far and near. They are ill at ease and shy. This woman, this grand woman, gets them together at parties in the high-school auditorium; and they come, men, women and children – for the women can't come unless they bring their children – and get acquainted. To break the ice, she gets them to play games, to sing and to dance folk-dances. Anyone can come into her tiny offices (they are her sleeping-quarters too) from early morning when she opens them, to nine-thirty at night; anyone can come for friendly advice, for information or just for a chat.

One day fifteen British sailors from an aircraft carrier looked in on her, and she gave them an English tea. One day three soldiers came along and found her washing up. They set to and did it for her. 'When I get back home,' said one of them, 'my wife'll say to me: "Why, Chico, wherever did you learn to wash dishes like that?" And I'll say: "It's wonderful, the things you learn in the Army."' And one day a defence-worker from Florida brought his wife and said he'd heard she was doing fine work, and he and his wife would like to help. She hesitated to accept his offer. 'You've got your job already,' she said. 'I imagine that keeps you busy.' 'To win this war,' he answered, 'everybody's got to take an outside job as well as his own.' And as he left, having arranged to come in with his wife and work wherever he was needed, he took some money out of his wallet. 'Here's two bucks for you,' he said, 'and if you want more, there's more where that came from.'

That's the spirit, gentlemen. Let us be proud that we have among us English-speaking people so many men and women of good will and good heart.

VIRTUE

The virtue I want to write about is the ordinary virtue of decent people: integrity, loyalty, unselfishness and common sense; but why I have chosen so austere a subject will I hope appear in due course. I do not wish to preach. I have no dogmatic statements to make. I am only going to put down certain reflections that have occurred to me during the last year or two, and it is for the reader to judge if they are of any value.

These reflections have been borne in upon me by the tragic and unexpected fall of France. That is a catastrophe from which we are all suffering now. Except for this catastrophe, the war might well be over, and in all probability the United States would never have been drawn into it. The civilized world was shocked by it, and a great deal has been written to explain it.

The defeat of the French has been ascribed to the antagonism of the General Staff to the régime of the Third Republic, which made them willing to see it swept away even at the cost of the ruin of their country. It has been ascribed to the fact that the French generals, in their sloth and conceit and notwithstanding abundant warning, sought to fight this war with the methods of the last. It has been ascribed to the treachery of politicians. It has been ascribed to the fear of bolshevism that haunted the possessing classes, and led them to suppose that they might well be better off under German rule than under the communism which they thought was the only alternative. And it has been ascribed to the ill-will of the working classes, who thought the employers were taking advantage of the war to deprive them of the reforms that had been instituted under a socialist government, and so obstructed the war effort with strikes and sabotage.

All these were contributory causes to the French defeat; but my own opinion is that they were symptoms and effects of a far more fundamental cause, and that is the general lack of morality in France. And I must remind you that I do not mean sexual morality. There is no foundation for the notion common in Anglo-Saxon countries that the French had lower standards of sexual morality than other nations. I am speaking of morality in general.

One must be careful of generalizations; and before I proceed, I want to state that of course there were a great many Frenchmen, thousands and thousands of them, who were honourable, disinterested and patriotic. There were not enough. Too many politicians were unscrupulous; too many newspapers were venal; too many employers were grasping and tyrannical; too many working people were dishonest and avaricious. France was defeated from within before ever she was defeated on the field of battle. I do not make these statements in any spirit of self-righteousness. We can only regret that a great country has been brought to destruction. We all owe much to its civilization, and we should not allow ourselves to forget that at this very moment Frenchmen and Frenchwomen are risking their liberty and their lives to combat the invader by every means in their power. But we have ourselves to think of, and we should be very stupid if we did not take warning from the fate of France.

Democracy today is on its trial. The time is past when one could accept it without misgiving as the most desirable form of government. Many people are attracted by the ideology of totalitarianism, and on the face of it there is much that is appealing. Plato's *Republic* is the first systematic exposition of the theory that has come down to us, and I think few can have read that great book without being fascinated by the reasonableness of many of its conceptions.

It seems sensible, for instance, that the members of the community should be divided into classes to perform the duties for which they are best fitted. In Plato's ideal commonwealth, a class of workers was to provide for the material needs of the population; a class of guardians was to defend the state from invasion; and a class of rulers, rigorously trained, was to administer its affairs. Italian fascism has taken over this valuable notion that the business of the country should be conducted by experts chosen for their particular knowledge rather than by politicians elected by popular vote for reasons that might very well have nothing to do with their ability to perform specialized tasks efficiently.

We all know that in the democracies there are far too many square pegs in round holes. In return for the surrender of their liberties, totalitarianism has offered the people security of employment and well-being. The plan might have worked if the men who thus assumed authority over their fellow-creatures had been very wise and very virtuous. But it hasn't worked. From all accounts we have of life in the totalitarian countries, it appears that the condition of the people is worse than it ever was before.

The welfare of the people has been sacrificed to the aggrandizement and enrichment of the ruling class. The ruling class has been able to maintain its power only by force and, to deal with the prevailing discontent, has been obliged to introduce police control of unparalleled severity. Because it cannot permit criticism, freedom of speech and freedom of the press have been abolished. The arts, which add grace and meaning to life, have languished because it appears that the artist can produce only in freedom. The system is condemned because despotism cannot be benevolent. The despot is human, and power corrupts, while absolute power corrupts absolutely.

A state exists not only for the sake of life, but for the sake of a good life, and the events of the last twenty years seem to show that the good life is more nearly achieved in the democratic than in the totalitarian states. We have all of late heard many criticisms of democracy, and some of them are justified. Among the most important of the charges brought against it are that it is slow and irresolute, inefficient and extravagant; but with all its advantages, it looks as though the human race were incapable of formulating any scheme of government that better serves the purpose of the good life. And it is within our power, if not to put an end to its disadvantages, for they may be inherent in it, at least to mitigate their harmfulness.

I am a writer by profession, and I discovered long ago that writing was a whole-time job. People are wrong who suppose that you pound a typewriter for a certain number of hours a day and that is the end of it. I have been told by business men that when they left their office in the evening, they put their work completely out of their minds and did not think of it again till they went back to their office next morning. That may be possible for a business man; it isn't possible for a writer. For a writer is not made by one or two books; he is made by a body of work, and he can only produce that if he deliberately takes steps to develop his personality, enlarge his experience and increase his knowledge. He must read widely and wisely; he must meet all sorts and conditions of men to gain an intimate knowledge of human nature; and he must put himself in the way of experiencing the ordinary vicissitudes of life which will be the material of his work.

It seemed to me that the whole day was not long enough for me to do what I had to do. We live in an age of specialism, and I was a specialist. When I was sick, I did not try to cure myself: I consulted a doctor; when something went wrong with my car, I did not try to put it right: I took it round to a garage. And so it seemed to me reasonable that like the cobbler I should stick to my last and leave the government of my country to those whose business it was to attend to it.

Events have shown me that I was completely wrong. I know now that no one can afford to stand aside from the political life of his time, for his freedom depends on it, and without freedom the good life is impossible. Our democracy is representative. That I may remind you is a form of government in which the citizens elect representatives, who then exercise the functions of government.

Democracy can survive only if our representatives are competent, disinterested and honest. It is their business to place the interests of the community above those of any single class, and the interests of the country above those of any section of it. But is it likely that we shall choose representatives who are competent and honest unless we are honest and competent ourselves? Shall we choose men who are disinterested if we ourselves are interested?

I put it to you that, in the final analysis, democracy depends on the virtue of the individual. We shall not fulfil our political obligation unless we have integrity; and if we do not fulfil our political obligation, democracy is doomed.

But we have not finished with it when we have chosen representatives who will carry out the policies that we consider right. For today democracy is exposed to twin dangers that demand from us wariness and discernment. One is the excessive power it accords to oratory. Leaders are apt to have acquired their predominance because they have the knack of stringing together striking phrases, or because they possess a voice of unusual persuasiveness. It is a happy accident that the President of the United States and the Prime Minister of Great Britain combine with these gifts resolution and ability; but it is only an accident. The gift of oratory is not necessarily accompanied by wisdom or foresight.

The second danger is the influence exercised on opinion by the press and the radio. It is well to remember that these mighty instruments of propaganda may be controlled by groups that have not always the best interests of the country at heart. It is therefore now more than ever our political obligation to inform ourselves on the problems that confront our government and come to a considered and unbiased decision upon them. Abraham Lincoln long ago put the matter in a nutshell. 'While the people retain their virtue and vigilance,' he said, 'no administration by any extreme of wickedness or folly can seriously injure the government.'

When the importance of political obligation was at last borne in upon me, being a very ignorant person, I looked about for books that could instruct me on the subject. But I could find nothing to my purpose.

T.H. Green, who was a philosopher of distinction in his day, delivered a series of lectures on it; but when I read them, I found that they were concerned more with the rights of the state than with the duties of the citizen. And it was with the duties of the citizen that *I* was concerned. I was obliged to look elsewhere; and knowing that in American universities there are courses on pretty nearly every subject under the sun, I inquired of my friends whether there were any on political obligation from which I could learn something. They seemed bewildered, but were good enough to make enquiries, and sometime later told me that there were at this university and that courses on political science and they presumed that that included political obligation, but that it was not a required subject and so it was difficult to find anyone who knew anything about it.

I wish it were a required subject, for I cannot imagine one that is more important. Is English more important? It is well that we should learn to speak and write our native language with correctness, but I wonder if it will matter very much how we write and speak it if we lose our freedom; and I put it to you that we may very well lose it unless we know our political obligation and fulfil it.

When I heard my friends in France lamenting the corruption of politics in their country, I asked them why didn't themselves run for political office. They shook their heads and said it was such a dirty business that they could not hope to make any headway in it or to wield any influence. It was hard for me to understand how they could expect to have an honest government if honest men refused to take part in it.

In England our attitude has been different. Politics has been a career that has always attracted young men of ability and high purpose. It is not a career that has brought wealth, but it has brought consideration, and sometimes fame. Our governments have often made lamentable mistakes, but certainly for the last hundred and fifty years they have been honest. Our politicians, though sometimes foolish and misguided, for they are but human, have been men of integrity, with the welfare of the country at heart. In a democratic state there can be no higher goal for the citizen's ambition than success in a political career. It is his political obligation, so far as lies in his power, to take part in the administration of his country; for in a democratic state the well-being of the community is the pressing business of the individual.

I should like you to read once more those words of Abraham Lincoln that I have quoted. They are the gist of all my story. But virtue as we know is difficult to achieve. I once asked a Russian psychologist, who was also a doctor of medicine and so had a practical as well as a theoretical knowledge of human nature, what he thought were the chief defects of human beings. 'I can tell you the worst three,' he said, 'selfishness, selfishness and selfishness.' Well, that is comprehensible. Each one of us looks upon himself as an end, and it is natural for him to put his own interest first and foremost. So I have asked myself how it may be possible to induce men, thus constituted, to subordinate their private concerns to the common good and to practise those humble virtues which come so hardly to most of us and without which, as I think the example of France shows, democracy must perish.

The *Pensées* of Pascal is a book more often quoted from than read. It was he who said that if the nose of Cleopatra had been shorter, the history of the world had been different. The *Pensées* consists of a collection of notes that Pascal made for a book he did not live to write, and many of the sayings in it have become famous. I was reading it a little while ago, and I was struck by a passage that seems pertinent to my present inquiry. He says in brief that the beliefs that men accept with their reason will only have an enduring effect on conduct if they are in due course accepted from habit. That seems to me true. We are all prepared to admit the value of uprightness and self-sacrifice, but that is not enough to weigh against the powerful motive of self-interest; we can only practise these virtues if they have become habits so ingrained in us that to practise them is instinctive. If they are as important as I think, it is worthwhile to consider how they can be made as much a matter of habit as to wash one's teeth night and morning.

Now that religion has largely lost influence over the behaviour of men, it looks as though the habit of virtue could only be acquired by education, first in the family and then in the schools and colleges. The virtue of the Nazis and the Fascists is not our virtue, but from the beginning they saw the value of this and so took care to instil their principles into the youths of their respective countries, from childhood to adolescence and from adolescence to maturity, till they had shaped them into the willing instruments of their purposes. We might well take this leaf out of their books. If there is any truth in this notion of mine, then the future of our civilization rests in the hands of parents and teachers.

It is not my business to exhort anyone to virtue; nor am I the proper person to do so. All I would suggest is that unless you yourselves and those who must learn from you – your children if you are parents, your pupils if you are teachers – are prepared to sacrifice your private interest to the common good, and to practise that elementary morality that will alone enable you to fulfil your political obligation, you stand gravely in danger of losing your freedom as France has lost hers. For the price of freedom is vigilance and virtue.

READING
AND WRITING
AND YOU

A little while before I left England I was asked to speak over the air about the books that people were reading during the war, and in order to provide myself with the necessary information I went to various bookstores and consulted the librarians of public libraries. I discovered first that there was an enormous demand for detective stories. This did not surprise me, for some time before, after the fall of France, I had come from the Riviera to Liverpool in a collier with five hundred other refugees – an experience recounted in the pages of this magazine.

We had neither lifeboats nor rafts on board sufficient for that great number of people and if we were torpedoed it was inevitable that nearly all of us would be drowned. As the sun rose each day we could never be sure that we should live to see it set. We were living an adventure more exciting to us individually and infinitely more probable than any of the detective stories we eagerly devoured; and yet we devoured them eagerly.

At the time I was asked to make this broadcast,[1] London was being bombed every night from sundown to sunrise. Few days passed without the mournful wail of the siren that announced a raid. People found it took their minds off the dangers they were running to follow their favourite detective in his inevitable elucidation of a complicated mystery.

Believe me, few writers have done more during the last two or three years to bring solace and forgetfulness to their sorely harassed fellow creatures than the writers of murder stories. They receive little honour among men and their pecuniary reward is small. Let us at least offer them the inexpensive tribute of our heart-felt gratitude.

But what really surprised me, when I went about making my inquiries, was to learn that many readers were turning again to those huge unwieldy novels

---

Redbook, June 1943.

[1] 'Reading Under Bombing', p. 175.

written during the Victorian era to satisfy the taste of a public that had abundant leisure and had not yet learned the delight of the movies and the charms of the radio. I am not speaking now of Charles Dickens; he has always been read; nor of Thackeray. Anthony Trollope, after being neglected for many years, some time ago regained his hold on the public, and I learned now that the vogue for his works, which had somewhat dwindled, had suddenly revived and people were reading not only the Barchester series on which his fame rests, but also his political novels. But that is not all. Novels by other authors, celebrated in their day but long forgotten, which for thirty years had lain undisturbed on dusty shelves, suddenly began to be asked for.

Until lately there cannot have been many persons still alive who had read the works of Charlotte M. Yonge. Yet she was one of the most popular writers of her time. She wrote historical romances, but her great success was with novels of an improving character about the fairly well-to-do country people of England. I have read her best-known book, *The Heir of Redclyffe*, but I was frightened off by the title of her next most famous work. It was called *The Daisy Chain*; I felt I couldn't face it.

Mrs Henry Wood is perhaps better remembered, for out of her most celebrated novel, *East Lynne*, a play was made which held the boards for many years both in England and America. I should guess that more than enough tears have been shed over the sorrows of its heroine to float a battleship. But Mrs Wood wrote a great number of other books. She was more melodramatic than Miss Yonge and she was not averse to dealing with the dangerous subject of adultery, a subject from which the chaste and evangelical Charlotte would have turned with horror; but in her novels, as in Miss Yonge's, in the end virtue invariably triumphed over vice. Our Victorian ancestors may not have been themselves models of propriety, but not for a moment did they allow this to go unpunished in fiction.

The reason for the vogue of these books is clear. They described a world of leisure, ease and comfort. There was security in the land. Peace seemed assured for generations. The country was prosperous and taxes were negligible. Most people were content with that sphere of life in which they were told a merciful Providence had been pleased to place them. It is true that there were grave social evils under the surface, but the novelists for the most part turned their eyes away from them, and their readers certainly didn't want to read about them. On the whole it was a pleasant world to live in. It is very natural that in these tragic days of war people should turn back to it with nostalgia.

When finally I made my broadcast I suggested to my listeners that they might find the same sort of satisfaction as they did in these novels of the Victorian era in the journals, biographies and memoirs in which our English-speaking literature is rich. For besides Boswell's immortal biography of Dr Johnson, there is his *Tour in the Hebrides*. There is Fanny Burney's delightful diary, and as we know she was one of Dr Johnson's favourite girls. There are Hervey's scandalous and amusing memoirs of the Court of George II. There is Benjamin Franklin's delicious autobiography, and there are the Greville memoirs.

All these are good books to take your mind off your troubles. It is escape literature, of course, and the critics are apt to be a trifle scornful about that.

I think they are ill-advised. After all, you and I are not critics. We are plain citizens, we have to read a certain number of books for instruction, and as good citizens it is evidently necessary that we should acquaint ourselves with the problems that confront us at the present time, but there is no reason that I can see why when we have done our day's work we should not amuse ourselves as we like; and I as an assiduous reader know no better way of amusing myself than to read an interesting and intelligent book.

It is an unfortunate delusion which many people suffer from, that if a book is entertaining it is perhaps waste of time to read it. That is not so. Reading should be enjoyable and, if you start a book and find you do not enjoy it, my advice to you is to drop it, even if all the critics in the land assure you that it is a masterpiece. And don't forget that escape literature may be very good literature. One of the greatest books that has been produced in this country is *Huckleberry Finn*, and if that isn't escape literature I can't imagine what it is.

One of the most hopeful events of the last few years has been the production in ever-increasing quantities of low-priced books of high quality. Several publishers have contributed to this good work and I am proud to think my own publishers have taken a prominent part in the diffusion of books of all kinds, books of information and books for recreation, at prices that put them within the reach of even the smallest income. We can only be truly civilized if we are well-read. By reading we become more tolerant, more broad-minded and more sympathetic. It is not often in this world that we can combine pleasure and profit, but that is just what we can do by reading wisely and well.

This war has put us authors on the spot. We want to make the best use we can of such gifts as nature has provided us with, and when war broke out we asked ourselves how best we could serve the common cause. It was all very well for the young; they joined up or were drafted; but for the rest of us it was more difficult to decide how to cope with the situation. Even if we had had the detachment to go on writing our poems, plays or stories, we could not but ask ourselves if we were justified in doing so. When the future of the world depends on the result of this struggle, when not only freedom of nations is at stake, but all the things that give man his dignity and life its value, can we square it with our conscience to sit back and let others fight for us while we scribble on our writing-pads or pound our typewriters?

Many of us who had been engaged in the last war offered our services and were mortified to be told that we were too old to be of use. We found that there was nothing better for us to do than to engage in some form of propaganda. The result has been a spate of mediocre poems, indifferent plays and poor novels. To write a good novel or a good play needs just that same emotion recollected in time of tranquillity as Wordsworth claimed was needed to write a good poem. When we authors try to make our fiction instruments of propaganda, we produce something that is neither fish, fowl nor good red herring. And we didn't know what to do about it.

But the course of events has made our way clear to us. I think we have a useful and even an important function to fulfil. First we have to win the war, and then we have to make the world a good and decent place to live in. Everyone will surely agree with me that it is impossible for these two objects to be attained unless the people of America and the people of Great Britain and the Dominions hold together. We know that the powers of the Axis are using every means at their disposal to sow dissension between us. That is the obvious thing for them to do, since they are well aware that so long as we remain united their defeat is inevitable.

We are different peoples and our interests cannot always coincide. We British are a homogeneous people, for there has been no great introduction of foreign blood into our island since the Norman Conquest; the opportunities offered by a free and developing country have attracted to the United States during the last hundred years vast numbers of immigrants from all parts of Europe and they have brought with them their manifold diversities. I am not surprised that misunderstandings should arise between us; I am only surprised that they do not arise more often.

Fortunately we have the inestimable advantage of a common language and we share the same great heritage of a common culture and a common literature. And fortunately we have the same standards of honesty, uprightness, truth and loyalty. We must remain united not only to win this war, but to win a lasting peace, and we can best remain united if we come to know one another.

The ignorance that obtains in Britain about America is only equalled by the ignorance that obtains in America about Britain. The average Englishman's idea of America is a fantastic construction that he has fashioned from what he has seen at the movies and read in detective stories and gangster novels. The average American still looks upon Britain as a feudal, self-complacent, laggard country riddled with class distinctions. It is nothing of the kind. This is not the place for me to enlarge upon the efficiency of our factories, the activity and farsightedness of our social services and the extension of democratic feeling which was evident long before the war but which the war has greatly emphasized. The point I want to make is that nothing is more necessary than that we should learn the truth about one another, and that is where we authors can be of service.

If American and English writers will write sincerely and honestly of their own world and their own people so that readers on one side of the Atlantic can get a faithful picture of the sort of life that is led on the other side of it and what sort of people they are who live it, they will do a great deal to help us to understand and so to sympathize with one another; and we shall learn that the differences that divide us are superficial and that at heart we are very much the same sort of people.

A little while ago I was asked by the Office of War Information to prepare a list of books[1] that Americans could read to give them some idea of what England and the English were like now. I do not know if a similar list has been made of American books for English people to read, but I am sure it would be very welcome and very useful. I have a firm belief that the more we know of one another the more we shall like one another, for the fact is, we are very likeable people. Thousands upon thousands of American soldiers have gone over to England and won all hearts by their geniality, their high spirits and their good nature. Sailors have come in their battered ships to these shores, often to spend weeks or months while their ships were being made ready to go

---

[1] The list of books accompanying this article is given in Appendix II.

to sea again; young airmen have come from Britain and the Dominions to train in various parts of this country; sailors and airmen have won the friendship of all who came in contact with them. Familiarity breeds contempt only for the contemptible; where there is honour and good will, it breeds respect and fellow-feeling.

There is no need for us writers to write propaganda. All we need do is to write our best, for so can we best increase the understanding and so cement the friendship between our two great nations. Americans are a kindly, generous-hearted and merciful people. We British are shy and reserved; we do not make friends easily, but when we do we are faithful friends. When you come to know us as I should like you to know us, I think that you will find that we too are a kindly, generous-hearted and merciful people. We too hold these truths to be self-evident: that all men are created equal, that they are endowed by their Creator with certain inalienable rights; that among these are life, liberty and the pursuit of happiness. These great and solemn words are the Magna Carta of Democracy. We accept them as whole-heartedly and as unreservedly as you.

WE HAVE
A
COMMON HERITAGE

In the early editions of his book, *The American Language*, Mr H.L. Mencken stated his belief that the language spoken in Britain and the language spoken in America would in course of time so diverge that the inhabitants of one country would no longer be able to understand the speech of the inhabitants of the other. He foresaw that the two languages would eventually be as different as Italian and Spanish, which are both derived from Latin. He has changed his mind now. For a strange and unexpected thing has happened. English has become Americanized.

Mr Mencken is one of the best conversationalists now alive and the wittiest of men. He told me when last I saw him that he was thinking of sending a body of Harvard students to England to collect Anglicisms before they die out. Americans have often told me how surprised they have been to hear in England locutions that they had always thought typically American, and how much more surprised to find them not only used currently in conversation, but in the written language as well.

Sometimes, of course, what people in this country look upon as Americanisms aren't anything of the kind. For instance, Mencken says somewhere in his book that if you stop a man on the street in England to ask him the way he'll say 'round the next turning'. Whereas if you ask him the same thing in America he'll say 'round the next corner', I think he's wrong. I believe the difference there isn't between the American and the Englishman, but between the town-dweller and the countryman. I think an Englishman who habitually lives in the country would say 'round the next turning' and if he lives in a city would say 'round the next corner'.

But there are numbers of strictly American words and phrases which a generation ago were unknown to the English people, and which have now been so commonly adopted that the people who use them have no notion that they are no longer speaking the English of their fathers. Sometimes, indeed, they use them in a way that causes surprise. When I was last in London I asked an elderly girl-friend to lunch with me and she answered: 'O.K. by me, baby.' You could have knocked me down with a feather. This change in the language spoken in England is due partly to the radio, but chiefly to the movies. The colloquialisms the British public heard in them struck them as a charming novelty; they found them gay, vivid and amusing; and adopted them eagerly.

Purists complain that the English language is being debased. I think they are wrong to do so. English is a hodge-podge of different languages – Anglo-Saxon, Danish, Latin, French. It has always been hospitable to importations from abroad.

I wonder if you have ever stopped to ask yourselves why it is that we English-speaking people alone have such words as beef, mutton and veal for the dead beasts that when alive we know as the ox, the sheep and the calf. The explanation is simple. After the Norman Conquest the Saxon serfs continued to call the animals they tended in the fields by their Saxon names, but when they had slaughtered them for the tables of the Norman lords they called them by the French names their masters had used when ordering them: *boeuf, mouton, veau*. And so it came about that the living animal was known as an ox, a sheep or a calf, and when transformed into meat as beef, mutton or veal.

These importations have enormously enriched the language, to what extent we can see by comparing a French dictionary of synonyms with that work indispensable to every author, Roget's *Thesaurus*. The French book is a slender, loosely-printed volume of three hundred pages. Roget is a fat book of nearly a thousand pages, printed in double columns!

The language doesn't retain all these importations. It tries them, and if they suit the needs of the time, if their novelty or picturesqueness appeal to the public taste, it adopts them; and if they fill a need they become a permanent part of the language; if their utility is only temporary, if a newer word replaces them, they are dropped. No one can have failed to notice how many slang words and phrases have overrun the country only to be thrown into the discard in a year or two when everyone has grown sick of them. Some, however, remain and become incorporated in the language. Sober writers begin to use them and they become part of the language of literature.

Let me give two trifling instances. When I was young it was slangy to talk of a bus. People used to say 'omnibus', and when 'bus' was brought into common use, writers for long put an apostrophe in front of it to show that they were using an abbreviation. Now they boldly write 'bus' and, when they write it in the plural, some go so far as to write 'busses'. It will doubtless in due course be thought pedantic to do otherwise. I happened when I was hardly more than a boy to be staying with a writer well known in those days and being thirsty one day asked for the wherewithal to quench my thirst. When I got home again I received a letter from my host saying that he had heard me to his dismay asking for a drink. He added that he had never heard me vulgar before, and thought I ought to know that it was shocking to ask for 'a drink' when a gentleman would naturally ask for 'something to drink'. Well, to speak of a drink has long since ceased to be a vulgarism, and the word is at home in the writing of the most scrupulous authors.

For my part, I welcome the Americanization of the English language. For one thing, whether one likes it or not, the future must inevitably draw the English-speaking peoples into closer contact than ever. And it is desirable that we should understand one another with ease. English will not be defiled if we in Britain call a good chap a 'regular guy'. Americans have given a new vitality to the language. They have made it more actual and more precise, and, to the English at least, the innumerable words and expressions that we have borrowed have a colour and a vividness which is fresh and pleasing.

Good writing is a stylization of the common speech of the people. To my mind, the two great masters of prose that America has produced are Hawthorne and Herman Melville. Melville learned to write from his study of the great English stylists of the seventeenth century, and at his magnificent best he has a splendour, a majestic, resonant eloquence, that no modern writer has surpassed. Hawthorne, as we know, was deeply read in the English authors of the eighteenth century, and his almost perfect prose has their clarity, their distinction and their elegance.

They wrote for their time and we must write for ours. American writers have at last – and wisely – shaken off their subservience to English models. The best writers today in this country have, to their great advantage, served their apprenticeship in journalism. It has taught them to go straight to the point, not to waste words, and to look for their material in the life about them. These are admirable things, and the influence of their novels has been very salutary to the English writers of fiction.

The faults of English writing have always been diffuseness, verbosity, and, in the novelists of my own generation, anaemia. This anaemia, however, strange as it may seem, we owe largely to an American writer, Henry James. His influence on English fiction was enormous. Henry James never came to grips with life. He was afraid of it, and knew it only as you might know what is going on in a busy street by looking out of an upstairs window. The problems that he examined with such scrupulous integrity were little social problems of no real significance. But such was his skill, such was his charm and such was the power of his personality that he led many of the better writers in England to turn their eyes away from the needs, passions and immortal longings of humanity to dwell on the trivial curiosities of sheltered gentlefolk. But if the subtle poison came from America, the healthy antidote has come from there too. The novels of Sinclair Lewis, Willa Cather, Hemingway, Steinbeck and others, have brought new life to English fiction.

The verbosity of the English language, which I have mentioned, is due, I believe, to our love of words for their own sake, apart from the meaning they convey. In the sixteenth century a great many Latinized words were brought into the language, and since the words were unfamiliar to the reader the old English words were given too. So, writers could speak of the stormy and tempestuous sea, or a roomy and ample garment.

I have a notion that this is one cause of the plethora of adjectives that is one of the defects of most English prose. One day Alfred de Musset went to see his friend George Sand, then a famous novelist, and as women will, she kept him waiting. To pass the time he took up one of her books and to amuse himself he crossed out all the superfluous adjectives he came across. History relates that, when the lady came in and saw how he was occupied, she did not receive him with her usual show of affection. There are few English writers whose prose would not be bettered by the same drastic process.

Of course we all know that American novelists have for some time been far from succinct, but I look upon this as a temporary aberration. I think that the natural instinct of the American people for speed and brevity is proved by the fact that, since the days of Washington Irving, they have produced a long line of short-story writers who can compare favourably with the greatest in the world, and that they know how to get an abundance of material into a little space is shown by such admirable books as *The Red Badge of Courage*, *Ethan Frome* and *Of Mice and Men*.

Not only is the English language the essential instrument of English-speaking culture; it is the bond that unites the people of this country, notwithstanding temporary disagreements and superficial differences, with all the other peoples on this earth who speak it.

When I last arrived in this country, I was asked to speak to a large audience on English culture. That seemed to indicate that there was an English culture distinct from an American culture. Is there? I don't believe it. My own impression is that, if we look at the matter reasonably, we can hardly fail to see that there isn't an American culture and an English culture, but one culture, one culture only, the culture of the English-speaking peoples. In its beginnings American literature was of course very much under the influence of English literature. That is natural enough, for a writer must form himself on models until, if he has originality enough, he can step out in his own way; and the models American writers chose were English ones because it was English they were writing.

I said that Melville and Hawthorne learned to write from their study of the English authors of the seventeenth and eighteenth centuries. They had no doubt English literature was as much America's heritage as England's. It took a long time for American writers to break away from the powerful influences that beset them, and their way was made harder for them by the lack of copyright laws. Publishers and magazine editors provided the public with English reading-matter because they didn't have to pay for it, and it was the devil's own job for American writers to get a hearing. It is a tribute to their strength and originality that, with such difficulties confronting them, they succeeded in the end in producing a body of work that smacked of the soil and could only have been written by Americans. Mark Twain and Walt Whitman are names of which any literature may be proud. This is obvious. What perhaps is not obvious is how greatly American writers in their turn have influenced English writers.

It is perhaps trite that I should state here that the culture with which I am now dealing is not culture in general, but only that part of it, that essential part, that is concerned with the arts. Now, it's no good fooling ourselves. Our English-speaking peoples have never greatly distinguished themselves in music or painting. Our achievements have been respectable, but except in the introduction of jazz we have shown no marked originality. The greatest music the world has known has been composed by the Germans. We have produced no composer who can be compared with Bach, Mozart, Beethoven or Wagner.

The same must be said of painting. Reynolds, Constable, Gainsborough, Turner were good painters, but they are small fry when you put them beside the great masters of Italy, Spain and France. During the last hundred years or so France has produced an astonishing number of great artists; the best we can say is that we have produced a few competent craftsmen.

There is one branch of art in which we have achieved distinction. That is architecture. In the Georgian era we in Britain learned to build for comfort, spaciousness, convenience and dignity. It is true that it was inspired by the Italian architecture connected with the name of Palladio, but we suited it to our needs and gave it a character of our own. America's beautiful Colonial architecture is derived from it. It has those same qualities of proportion, dignity, spaciousness and comfort. I can't think that it is an accident that we have cherished those particular things in our domestic architecture. I think we have aimed at them because we are home-loving people who like air and space, comfort rather than show, and freedom to lead our lives with decency.

But times have changed, and the immense increase of urban population in this country constrained American architects to solve the problem of housing vast numbers of people on a limited space. All the world admits that they have solved it brilliantly. The immense apartment houses, the vast office buildings, must serve as an example to England. English cities have been in part destroyed; a great deal of rebuilding will have to be done; the slums which have been a disgrace to our civilization will have to be cleared away; and our architects will profit by the experience Americans have acquired to rebuild finer and more commodious cities.

Our great achievement in the world of art, however, is not in architecture, still less in music or painting; it is in literature. Our novelists can hold their own in comparison with any that the other nations of Europe have produced. But Defoe and Fielding, Scott, Dickens and Thackeray, to mention but a few, are part of America's heritage, just as Melville and Mark Twain are part of Britain's. It seems to me that by portraying the world of their own time and showing us the people who inhabited it, they have clarified our native characteristics.

What are the qualities of these novels? At first sight it seems strange that, though so different and though they were written over so long a period, they should be so similar. They are robust, good-humoured, kindly, sometimes coarse; they show a love of sport and the open air and a passion for freedom. Aren't these the characteristics Americans know in themselves? They are certainly those that seem to me typical of my own countrymen. The Germans, the French, the Italians have other qualities, and doubtless admirable ones, but they are not just those.

Yet the crowning glory of our literature has, of course, been our poetry; and that is due, I suppose, in part to our natural bent, but also to the great riches of our language. I do not think it is a patriotic bias that makes me believe that no other country of the modern world has produced such a wealth of great poetry as my own. Italy has had Dante, Germany has had Goethe, but England has had Chaucer, Shakespeare, Milton, Keats, Wordsworth, Shelley and a dozen more.

When I went to the last Paris exposition and visited the collection of modern art, I was staggered at the strength, variety and power which the French painters of the last fifty years have displayed. When I turn over the pages of the *Oxford Book of English Verse* I am overwhelmed at the magnificence and beauty of our English poets. They are America's poets as much as England's, for it is in our common language they write and it is our common ideals and aspirations that give their verse its significance.

I have mentioned a number of English-born poets, and it may seem that in poetry the debt America owes England is heavy, but in the nineteenth century America did much to repay it. One may or may not admire Walt Whitman, and I will admit that he is an acquired taste, but what no one can deny is his immense influence on English poetry.

He broke up the formal patterns of English verse and gave the poets who came after him a welcome freedom. He showed that poetry could be found not only in the well-worn subjects of love and despair and death, not only in the song of the nightingale and in the glamour of the moon, but in the living life around us, in the farm, in the factory, in the railroad, in the manifold activities of men.

In writing of the America he knew, he discovered a new and fruitful world to the poets who came after him. Because of Whitman, we have little patience any more with the poets who try to tread in the footsteps of Shelley, Wordsworth and Tennyson. It is a fact to be pondered over that if we have a great poet now in England it is not an Englishman, but an American, T.S. Eliot, and it is in him that the young English poets have found their inspiration.

But my point in writing all this is not to draw a balance between the cultural debt America owes England and that which England owes America. What I have tried to indicate, superficially of course and perhaps tediously, is that owing to our common ancestry and our common language we cannot but have a common culture. And when we are fighting to maintain that, we are fighting, you Americans and we British, to maintain our common property.

WHAT READING CAN DO
FOR YOU

Reading should be a pleasure. Don't allow it to enter into your heads for a moment that pleasure is a bad thing, as those of you with Puritan ancestors may have an inclination to do. Pleasure is good and conduces to health. Of course there are certain pleasures that have evil consequences and these it is only common sense to avoid, but reading is certainly not one of them. Now if the only pleasure you can get out of reading is the reading of detective stories, you are right to read them and we all have cause to be grateful to the writers of them.

But I also hope that you are not frightened by those books which are commonly ranked as classics and think you will be bored by them. That, I'm afraid, is because so many people have been obliged to read some of them in school or college and so what should have been a pleasure has been turned into a task.

What makes a book a classic? Not the opinion of critics, schoolteachers or college professors. A book becomes a classic for one reason only, because succeeding generations of readers, plain people like you and me, have found it moving, human and interesting. Did the critics or the professors of literature make a classic of *Huckleberry Finn*? Not a bit of it. They dismissed it with a shrug of the shoulders because Mark Twain was a funny man. But his readers for the better part of a century now have found it true and touching and full of life and colour and fun. It is only of late years that the critics and the professors have discovered that *Huckleberry Finn* is one of the most important and significant works in American literature.

But this is only one book out of many that are as important and as readable if you will give them your attention and your sympathy. They can all be bought very cheaply, and after all, if you don't like them you can easily lay them down. For I have to insist upon this, however important a book is, and whatever reputation it may have, unless you find you can read it with enjoyment it can be of no possible use to you.

Life Story Magazine, August 1945.

I don't want to advertise my own wares, but I hope you will forgive me if I tell you that two or three years ago I brought out a little book called *Books and You* in which I spoke of a number of books which every educated person should read and why he should read them.

In this book I spoke chiefly of novels, poetry, biography and essays. I had no occasion to speak of history, but you know, history can be very good reading, if one has leisure to read it. Just now it's important that we all know something about the past of the countries whose present is so much our business.

It would be reasonable if you asked me what practical use it can be to you to read the sort of literature of which I've been speaking. The answer is this: It will give you a wider outlook, it will deepen your character and enlarge your personality. That can be of practical use to you now. The war is drawing to its end, and it looks as though the world of the near future will be a very different one from the world before the war. Believe me, you will cope with it more competently if you have used this period to acquire a wider vision, greater knowledge and a keener sympathy with your fellow men.

'ABOVE ALL, LOVE . . .'

Long ago Abraham Lincoln put the whole matter in a few simple words. 'While the people retain their vigilance and virtue,' he said, 'no administration by any extreme of wickedness or folly can seriously injure the government.' That puts an immense responsibility on the individual, for it means that in the end the welfare of the State depends on his uprightness. Democracy that is corrupt is doomed.

The child is father to the man, and it is in his home, by the example of his parents, that the child must learn the value of goodness, so that when he is a man it will be like an instinct in him and he will rather lay down his life than betray it. The future of this country, of any country, lies in the home, for it is there that the men and women who will create the future are fashioned.

But whereas young people have it dinned into their ears often enough that they owe their parents love and duty, I don't know that the parents often have it impressed upon them that they likewise owe their children something too. They owe them, above all, a love great enough to allow them to be themselves; and their duty is to permit them to develop their own personalities to the utmost of their capacities. That means that they must allow the ties of family to be loosened when they hamper rather than assist.

It requires a great deal of fortitude, tolerance, and self-sacrifice to allow children to go their own way whom you have been accustomed to guide. But can we any of us learn from the experience of others? My own belief is that we can only learn from our own.

The soundest insurance of democracy's future lies, perhaps even more than in the weapons it builds, in a sane and healthy family life given by its people to their children.

Rotarian, November 1952.

ON
PEOPLE
AND
PLACES

MY
SOUTH SEA ISLAND

I have always thought it must be the most delightful thing in the world to own an island; not Ireland, of course, or Borneo – that would really be too much of a good thing – but an island that you could walk round without hurrying yourself in a couple of hours; and now and then I have been offered one, if not for a song, at least for no more than I shall get for this article. But it was always at least a thousand miles from where I happened to be, and that seemed a considerable distance to go (especially as there was no means of getting there) in order to inspect an island which, after all, might not be exactly the sort of island I wanted. Besides, if I were not living on it, I should always be worried about it; I should awake in the night in London and wonder anxiously whether anyone had run away with it. You have to be so careful with portable property in the South Seas.

But in Tahiti I met a man who owned an island, and when I told him that I envied him he offered to lend it to me. There was something so casual about the suggestion, like a man in a railway carriage who asks you if you would like his *Punch*, that I accepted at once.

The island happened to be no more than a hundred miles away from anywhere else (that in the Pacific is cheek by jowl, no farther than Piccadilly-circus from Trafalgar-square), so that it was a wonderful chance to enjoy the satisfaction of proprietorship.

I found a small cutter with a gasolene engine to take me over; I had a native servant whose extraordinary incompetence was only equalled by his unfailing good nature, and I engaged a Chinese cook – for I thought this was an occasion to do things in style.

I bought a bag of rice, a quantity of tinned goods, a certain amount of whisky, and a great many bottles of soda, for the owner had warned me that there was no water on the island.

I set my foot on the beach. The island was mine for as long as I chose to inhabit it. The beach really had the silver whiteness that you read of in descriptions of the South Sea Islands, and when I walked along in the sunshine it was so dazzling that I could hardly bear to look at it. Here and there were the white shells of dead crabs and the skeletons of sea birds.

I walked up through the coconuts and came upon a grove of enormous, old, and leafy trees; they gave coolness and a grateful shade. It was among these that the tiny settlement was built. There was the headman's hut and another for the workmen, two more to store the copra, and a somewhat larger one, trim and clean, which the owner of the island used when he visited it and in which I was to dwell.

I unloaded my stores and bedding and proceeded to make myself at home. But I had not reckoned with the mosquitoes. There were swarms of them; I have never seen so many; and they were bold and fierce and pitiless. I rigged up a net in the verandah of my hut, and placed a table and a chair beneath it, but the mosquitoes were ingenious to enter, and I had to kill twenty at least before I could sit down in peace.

Here I took my frugal meals, but when a dish was hurriedly passed between the curtains a dozen mosquitoes dashed in and I had to kill them one by one before I could eat.

I set about exploring the island. It had evidently been raised from the sea at a comparatively recent date, and much of the interior was barren and almost swampy, so that I sank in as I walked. I suppose what was now dry land had not very long ago been a brackish lake. Beside the coconuts nothing much seemed to grow but rank grass and a shrub something like broom.

There were no animals on the island but rats, perhaps, and though throughout the Pacific you find everywhere the mynah bird, noisy and quarrelsome, to this lonely spot he had never found his way; and the wild fowl I saw were great black gulls with long beaks. They had a piercing, almost a human, whistle. I thought that in them abode, restless and menacing, the souls of dead seamen drowned at sea. They gave something sinister to the smiling, sunlit island.

But it was not till I had been on the island for several days that I discovered they were not the only sinister things there. I thought I had explored every inch of it, and I was surprised one evening to catch through the coconuts a glimpse of a little grass hut. I saw a moving shape, and I wondered if it was possible that anyone lived there.

I strolled towards the hut and I saw what was certainly a man, but as I approached he vanished. I supposed that I had startled him and he had slunk away among the brushwood. But I wondered why he had chosen this lonely dwelling, who he was, and how he lived.

The Polynesians are a friendly and a sociable race, and I was intrigued to find anyone in that tiny island who needed solitude so much that he must live away even from the half-dozen persons who formed the island's entire population. I puzzled my brains. It could not be a watchman, for among the coconuts there was nothing to watch and no danger to guard against.

When I returned to my own house I told the headman what I had seen and asked him who this solitary creature was; but he would not, or could not, understand me. It was not till I was once more in Papeete that I found out. I thanked the owner of the island for the loan of it and then I asked him who was the mysterious man who seemed so to shun the approach of his fellows.

'Oh, that's my leper,' he said. 'I thought he'd amuse you.'

'He tickled me to death,' I answered. *'But haven't you rather a peculiar sense of humour?'*

MRS
GEORGE STEEVENS;
DORIS ARTHUR-JONES

I suppose there are few people now who remember Mrs George Steevens. She was a woman of remarkable character. She was of a good Scotch family and was first married to a lowland laird of considerable wealth. During her youth, as a widow in comfortable circumstances, she cut something of a figure in the narrow circle of which society then consisted. Her sister was married to a chamberlain of the Duke of Cumberland and she was intimate with many exalted persons. But she was involved in the divorce proceedings which cost Sir Charles Dilke the premiership and the doors of Mayfair were henceforth closed to her. So different were the manners and customs of that day and this. She had been madly in love with that dull, but fascinating man, but it was at her house that he used to meet Mrs Crawford, and this fact, brought out in court, created a scandal greater than she, with all her courage, could face. She was shattered. For many years she lived in retirement, but at last, I forget how, met George Steevens, then making a name for himself as correspondent of the *Daily Mail*. She was certainly twenty years older than he. They fell in love and married. They were very happy. She never quite got over the blow of his death at Ladysmith.

When I first knew her she was an old woman, with bright eyes, a wrinkled face and large, clear-cut features; she was the first woman I ever knew to cut her hair short; it was thick and grey and curled naturally. I do not think she could ever have been pretty, but in old age she was far from plain. She never wore anything but black or white and she had her dresses made, regardless of fashion, in such a way as to secure her comfort and ease of movement. Her bearing was gallant and she walked, in low-heeled, square-toed boots, with a masculine stride. Her hats were fantastic. The somewhat unusual appearance she presented expressed very well the independence of her character. She was frank and plain of speech. She had no patience with affectation and never hesitated to speak her mind. If she did not like you she made no bones about

---

Preface to *What a Life!* by Doris Arthur-Jones. Jarrolds, 1932.

letting you know it. She was a good talker. Her vitality was remarkable. She had a singular charm and a very ready sympathy. She was generous, kind and hospitable. Her hospitality, indeed, was wildly extravagant and she was always up to her neck in debt. But this had little effect on her manner of living and none on her spirits. She could never have kept the wolf from the door but for the constant generosity of Lord Northcliffe. I do not expect ever to meet anyone quite like her.

At the time of which I write Mrs Steevens lived at Merton Abbey. This was the house that Nelson had inhabited with Lady Hamilton and it was here that he had bidden farewell to the stout, but alluring Emma when he was about to start on the cruise that ended at Trafalgar. It was impossible to look without emotion upon the brick wall along which, as though it were his quarter-deck, he used to pace waiting for his orders to sail. Mrs Steevens took an immense interest in her fellow-creatures and nothing pleased her more than to surround herself with her friends. The house was filled at week-ends, and since it was so near London that people could come by hansom, on Sundays a great stream of visitors came to luncheon or to tea. They were not the same sort of people as she had known in her youth, they were actors, writers, painters, and their hangers-on, and because her heart was warm and her discrimination none too great, they were often a queer lot. I had a notion that in private (after all she was born at a time when the classes were not so mixed as now) she looked upon us all as riff-raff and saw little to choose between us.

It was on one of these Sunday afternoons that I first met the author of these memoirs. It was just after the runaway marriage which is related in these pages. She was brought down by her father, with her husband, so that he should be introduced to Mrs Steevens, who had a great affection for Henry Arthur Jones and for his wife. Strangely enough I recollect Henry Arthur Jones talking to me of the marriage. I do not think he took the young things' rashness as seriously as he pretended. The indignation he showed was a tribute he paid to his sense of decorum. Like many of us who are concerned with writing he found a certain satisfaction in behaving as a person in his situation might be expected to behave, and he was half-humorously conscious that he was play-acting when for a little while he assumed the rôle of the outraged Victorian parent. Doris Thorne was bright-eyed and vivacious, excited by her adventure and pleased with the interest she aroused as a bride of sixteen; her husband was a trifle shy and sought to cover his embarrassment with a somewhat sardonic facetiousness. I remember only that he was tall and very thin and had enormous black eyes.

All this is a long time ago, Mrs Steevens has been dead for many years, on the pleasant grounds of Merton Abbey stand sordid little houses, and now Doris Thorne, a middle-aged woman with a married daughter, has written an account of what has befallen her since then. It is a very ordinary life she has led, but I have found it interesting to read of, and perhaps the reader of this preface will have patience with me while I tell him why. Celebrated actors give us their reminiscences, statesmen and soldiers describe for our edification the great events in which they have been concerned, the leaders of society write their memoirs, reminding us of past scandals or recalling past glories, writers, often still in their twenties, tell us of their early struggles. These are famous people and it seems natural enough that posterity should not be deprived of the opportunity of knowing what they can tell us of themselves. But Doris Thorne can advance no such claim. Her father was a dramatist distinguished in his day, but the drama is the most ephemeral of the arts, and though his name will be honourably remembered in the history of the English drama during the last years of the nineteenth century, it is unlikely that his plays will ever again hold the stage. Her husband was for many years a judge in Cyprus; afterwards he held a legal position in Egypt. The situation he occupied was respectable, but hardly eminent. This, however, is what gives interest to the work I am inviting the reader to peruse. Authors and actors, great ladies, statesmen and field-marshals are exceptional folk, and oddly enough they are all very much alike; it is the ordinary persons who are interesting. They are up against the circumstances we know ourselves. We suffer from the same troubles as they and are beset by the same embarrassments. It is not given to all of us to lead an army to destruction or to receive the Shah of Persia, but we all know what it is to have the dinner go wrong when we are giving a party and to have ordered a suit of clothes that we can't bear when we get it home. They say that everyone can write one book. Everyone does, but it is generally a novel, and a novel is not so easy as all that to write. How much better it would be if, like Doris Thorne, he wrote a plain and unvarnished account of his own life! It would be valuable material for the novelist and a mine for the historian.

It is true that Doris Thorne, as the daughter of a distinguished playwright and the companion of his last years, has met a great many famous men. She has had the unfortunate hobby of collecting autographs and seems to have gone out of her way to meet people who might write in her album. The collector of autographs is a harmless nuisance; but I have little patience with the persons who make a fuss about gratifying his desires. If you can give anyone pleasure by doing so small a thing as writing your name it is churlish not to, and those who make a favour of it, or refuse outright, exhibit an unpardonable vanity. But it is another matter when you are asked to do more. It is all very well for painters and musicians, they can write a few bars of music or make a little drawing. But the author has to think of something apposite and on the spur of the moment few of us can. We turn the pages of the album and we are paralysed by the inanity of what others have written. The jokes look flat and the moral saws inane. Arnold Bennett, practical and wise, had two little aphorisms that he used alternatively or together. The reader will find them quoted in this volume. The portions of this book that Doris Thorne has devoted to the people she has thus come into contact with are to me the least interesting. The fact is that celebrities are a very dull lot. They live much in the public eye and they insensibly adopt a façade. They are apt to offer the world an appearance which they subconsciously feel is expected from them. It requires a good deal of penetration to get through it. In some cases indeed it has absorbed them so that the appearance ends by being all there is. Should this album of Mrs Thorne's survive a hundred years and then fall into the hands of a curious person, I wonder how many of all these distinguished names will mean anything to him. But if any of them excite his curiosity and he hunts up this book in the dusty shelves of the British Museum to see what the author had to say of so and so, I am afraid he will be disappointed. It might have been interesting to see how they struck a woman's acute and observant eye. One would have liked to know what they looked like and what they wore.

They are dummies, amiable and polite, who sit next to her at dinner and then write in her album.

I think that Doris Thorne has not been much interested, for their own sakes, in the people she has met in life, but only for hers. Evidently a woman of character and of great vitality, she has been concerned with others only as far as they affected her. From the standpoint of the autobiographer this is just as it should be. For such a book the writer's character is all important and it is nothing if it is not egotistic. I can only wish that she had been franker and more explicit. When you write about yourself discretion is out of place. I wish she had told in full how this boy and girl marriage that began to romantically gradually went wrong. One has to read between the lines. One has to guess from a hint here and a casual word there. William Thorne remains an enigmatic figure. I should have liked much more about him. He seems to have been a man of engaging traits, of a flamboyant taste, fantastic and irresponsible, and with a sardonic humour. In this narrative his figure is the most significant and the most original. He makes the generals and the ambassadors even more colourless than in all probability they were. I do not know whether Doris Thorne would look upon this life she has described as happy or unhappy. One of the few compensations of growing old is that you can sum up the course of other people's lives. On the whole I should say that fate is on the side of leniency; things come righter in the end than often we have any right to expect, and few of us, mercifully, have to suffer for our faults, follies and errors as much as we might. It is plain that she has always had high spirits. A natural gaiety has enabled her to withstand many vicissitudes. To my mind the most curious thing about her is her lack of adaptability. She has measured everything by English standards, and if the circumstances were not such as she had been used to in England she found them ridiculous or unpleasant. But not only is she insular, she is a cockney. She has never been happy out of London. Once her husband was offered a post in Zanzibar. One would have thought she would have jumped at it. A new life, new surroundings; the magic of that distant, unknown island. Not at all. It was exile from London, London with its first nights, with supper at the Savoy, London with its lunches at the Berkeley; and the only compensation of Cyprus, to which she eventually went, was that it was within a few days' journey of home. You would never guess from her pages that this island has a history than which none is more fantastic, and that its ruined churches, built by the French barons who there founded a precarious kingdom, are incredibly romantic, while from its prehistoric graves the excavators bring forth archaic statues of the most delicate beauty. To her it was a land of exile, where servants did not know their work and English vegetables were hard to grow. She has but one un-English trait and that is her charming devotion to her family. She hankers after the company of her father and mother and her sisters; and because of her affection for them Morocco has no thrills for her and Egypt no romance. But the British Empire would never have reached its great extent if the English (who after all made it) had not on the whole found their relations very boring.

THE TERRORIST:
BORIS SAVINKOV

I suppose it was something in the air. No one in the ship could sleep. One went to bed tired, but no sooner had one laid one's head on the pillow then all one's senses grew alert and one was wide awake. This was not the case only with a few bad sleepers, but with the passengers in general, and as night followed night, knowing there would be no rest for us in our rooms, we stayed up later and later.

One evening, having played bridge till our eyes ached and our brains were dizzy, we sat in the smoking-room, half a dozen of us, weary but unwilling to face a sleepless bed. We drank and smoked. We talked of one thing and another and presently one of those present threw out a question.

'Who is the most extraordinary man you've ever met?' he asked.

It grew evident in a little while that he had done so not out of curiosity, but out of the harmless vanity which leads people to take credit to themselves because they have rubbed shoulders with the great ones of the earth. The man who spoke had been in some small capacity at the Peace Conference (this conversation took place a good many years ago), and his own answer to the question he had put was Clemenceau. But in our fatigue the topic was as good as another to discuss and various replies were given.

One answered Vivekananda, the Indian Swami, another said J.D. Rockefeller, a third mentioned Verlaine. These were all famous names. I sat silent, for no one spoke to me, and within myself considered whether really the most extraordinary men were to be found among those who have made a splash in the world; I had a notion that perhaps they were to be found rather among the obscure, living secret lives in a great and populous city, solitary on some island in the South Seas or engaged in mysterious occupations far away on the borders of Tibet; for to achieve celebrity you must mix with men, or at least you must have contact with them, and the idiosyncrasies, native or acquired, which make a man remarkable must be to some extent mitigated. He must at least be measureable by the common yard-measure that makes measurement possible.

Redbook, October 1943.

But I noticed that no one had said what he meant by extraordinary. Had it any reference to goodness? Had it to do with force of character or was it the sense of power that is manifest in certain men, which had led the speaker to claim for one or other of the persons mentioned that he was the most extraordinary man whom he had ever met? Or was it just strangeness?

But it was past two o'clock and, dog-tired, I went to bed.

I could not sleep and after tossing from side to side for an hour I got up, slipped a coat over my pyjamas, some cigarettes and a box of matches into my pocket, and went on deck. I found a chair in a sheltered spot and lay down. The night was warm. There was no moon, but the stars were bright, and the sea was calm. I began idly to think of the conversation in the smoking-room; and then suddenly I remembered Boris Savinkov.

I suppose few remember his name now, but is a name that might well have been as familiar to us all as that of Lenin, and if it had, Lenin's would have remained obscure. Boris Savinkov might easily have become a man of tremendous authority in Russia; I do not know whether he failed owing to some defect in his character or because the circumstances of the time were such that no man could have altered the course of events. There is no more sometimes than the trembling of a leaf between success and failure.

It was in 1917 and in the city then called Petrograd that I first met Boris Savinkov. I had been sent there on business with the nature of which I need not trouble the reader, and discovering very quickly that he was one of the persons who might best help me to transact it, I took the steps necessary to get in touch with him. I cannot remember if at that time he was still acting Minister of War in the Kerensky government or if he had already resigned. During that confused period ministers were appointed and dismissed with rapidity.

I was curious to make the acquaintance of a man whom I knew to have been the boldest and most determined of the terrorists during the last years of the Czarist regime. It was he who carried out the assassination of Plehve, and also that of the Grand Duke Sergius. I had read the two novels, written under a pen name, in which he had thrillingly described his life as a revolutionary. He was finally arrested and sentenced to death. While awaiting his execution he was imprisoned at Sevastopol; and there, it was told me, such was the magic of his persuasive speech, he had induced his jailers to join the revolutionary ranks and contrive his escape.

We arranged to meet in a private room at the Bear, which was then the fashionable restaurant in Petrograd; and since Russians are exceedingly unpunctual I expected to have to wait some time for him; but when I arrived he was already there. When I opened the door, he turned round. He had been looking through a chink in the drawn curtains at the street below.

I took him to be between forty and fifty. He was of medium height, slightly built and baldish; his features were insignificant, his face pale, and his eyes small and somewhat close-set. They were hard and I guessed that at times they could be cruel. He was neatly dressed; he wore a stand-up collar, a smart tie with a pin in it, a frock-coat and patent-leather boots. He had the prosperous, respectable look of the manager of a bank. There was nothing violent in his appearance. He gave me the impression of a cultivated man, somewhat commonplace in a rather distinguished way; and if he had been a bank manager I should have guessed that he collected first editions. He was quiet, reserved and modest. It was not till he began to talk that I saw anything remarkable in him.

He spoke in excellent French, idiomatic and correct except for an occasional error in gender; he spoke slowly, as though he were thinking over what he said, but it was clear that he possessed an admirable power of choosing the exact words to express his ideas. His voice was soft and pleasant; his enunciation extremely clear. I had never heard such a captivating talker. He was grave when the subject demanded gravity, humorous when there was occasion for humour, and there was so much reasonableness in what he said that it was impossible not to be affected; he was wonderfully persuasive.

The deliberation of his speech, the impressive restraint of his manner, suggested a determined will which made his ruthlessness comprehensible. I have never come across anyone who filled me with a greater sense of confidence.

After that I saw Boris Savinkov a good deal. On one occasion I suggested that it must have required immense courage to plan and commit those two dreadful assassinations. He shrugged his shoulders.

'Not at all, believe me,' he answered. 'It is a business like another. One gets accustomed to it.'

After the murder of the Grand Duke, he lived for two years in Russia under an English passport, wandering from hotel to hotel, for he never dared to stay in any one place so long that people might notice him and wonder what he did. He was at last run to earth in one of these hotels.

I asked whether he was not frightened.

'No,' he said. 'After all, I knew that sooner or later I was bound to be caught, and when I was, strangely enough, I only felt relief. You must remember that I had been leading a terribly strenuous life, hounded from pillar to post, on the alert morning, noon and night, and I was tired out. I think my first thought was: "Now I shall be able to rest."'

'But you knew it meant death?'

'Of course.'

They took him into the dining-room of the hotel while the official statement of his arrest was being made out. The officer in charge of the soldiers who had arrested him asked him if there was anything he wanted. He asked for soda water and a cigarette. Soda water was brought to him and the officer took a cigarette and contemptuously flung it at him across the table. Then Savinkov lost his temper. Though he had had nothing to smoke for three days, and was craving tobacco, he took the cigarette and threw it in the officer's face. He laughed a little when he told me the words he had used:

'You forget, sir, that I am no less a gentleman than you.'

They bore out my contention that in moments of great emotion men express themselves in terms of melodrama. That is why the best writers are often so untrue to life.

Since he was, on the occasion of this conversation, in an easy mood, I asked him to tell me about his escape from the prison at Sevastopol. To my regret, he did not confirm the picturesque story I had heard. The lieutenant in charge of the guard at the prison was already a revolutionary and he was prevailed upon by others to effect the escape. It was done very simply. He went boldly to the cell, ordered Savinkov to be taken out, and telling the prisoner to follow, marched out. The sentries, seeing an officer pass, made no comment and presently the pair of them found themselves in the street.

'It must have been an exciting moment,' I said.

'Not really,' he answered. 'You see, we'd arranged that if we were stopped he should shoot me before he shot himself.'

They went down to the harbour and got into the open boat that had been prepared for them and set sail. They encountered fearful storms and were more than once in danger of foundering, but in four days reached the Rumanian coast and safety. From there Savinkov went to France and lived in Paris and on the Riviera till the revolution allowed him to return to Russia.

He had returned with high hopes. At the time I knew him, his great energies were directed to keeping the Russian armies in the field till the Allies had won complete victory. His firm conviction was that only in such a victory could Russia achieve the greatness which was her due. But he had no confidence in Kerensky, who was then at the head of affairs. He described him as a man of words, not of acts, a man, tired out and neurotic, of small education and limited imagination. How could such a one remain in power? Savinkov hated the Bolsheviks. When he spoke of them, though his voice remained soft, his eyes grew steely. The last words he ever said to me were these:

'Between me and Lenin it's war to the death. One of these days, perhaps next week, he will put me with my back to the wall and shoot me, or I shall put him with his back to another wall and shoot him. One thing I can tell you is that I shall never run away.'

But the Bolsheviks came to power and Savinkov disappeared. I cannot believe that this man who had so often risked death, who had lain under the shadow of the gallows, was seized with panic. He had a nerve of iron. I am more inclined to suppose that thinking, like many others, that the Bolshevik success was but a flash in the pan, and knowing that at the moment nothing could be effected, he went into hiding till the fitting opportunity to strike presented itself. For all his passion there was a certain coldness in his temperament: he was not a man to allow his emotions to interfere with his judgment. He had that great gift, the capacity to wait till the moment was ripe.

The moment never came. I saw him no more. All I know is that eventually he saw fit to leave Russia and once more he trod the bitter path of exile. Time passed. I cannot tell if at last he despaired of a change of government or if he hankered so violently for his native country that he felt any sacrifice was worthwhile that would enable him to return to it. He went back. When he crossed the frontier he was arrested; later it was said he had committed suicide.

Yes. I think Boris Savinkov the most extraordinary man I have ever met. And as I lay there in my deck chair looking out at the starry night, I suddenly saw him standing beside me, in his frock-coat and his patent-leather boots, and I saw the look in his small, cruel eyes which were set too close together. I must have fallen into a light doze and, my thoughts thus occupied, have dreamed a dream so vivid that for an instant I took it for reality. I do not know exactly when he died, but it would have been an odd coincidence if it had been on the very day that I thus seemed to see him standing by my side.

SPANISH JOURNEY

Negotiations are now being conducted which will enable British subjects to travel in Spain on similar conditions to those which have for some time obtained for travel in some other countries in Europe.

Spain is a delightful country to visit. I do not wish to speak here of its great cities. Everyone has heard tell of Madrid with its Prado, which contains a collection of pictures, in certain respects richer than any in the world; and of the Escorial, the grim, magnificent pile which Philip II built to fulfil a vow and where he died.

I do not wish to speak of Toledo with its artistic treasures, of Cordova with its great mosque, nor of Seville with its Giralda and its Cathedral, the interior of which, with its towering columns, has a sombre majesty which is awe-inspiring; nor even of the unique beauty of the Alhambra at Granada and the exquisite, romantic charm of the garden of the Generalife. These are cities of world-wide renown and the guide-books will tell you all about them.

There are others not to have seen which is to have missed a valuable experience. Santiago de Compostela, Salamanca, Burgos, Valladolid, Avila, Segovia, Tarragona – each by the beauty of its situation, by its architectural riches or its romantic associations, has something to enchant the eye and uplift the spirit. Moreover, all these places have adequate and sometimes luxurious hotels; and it cannot be denied that you get more enjoyment out of visiting a famous town if you are well housed and well fed.

My object in writing this article is to call your attention to other places which the guide-books at most only mention. They can be reached by train or bus by those who are not pressed for time and do not object to some friendly crowding; but they are best visited by car. The main roads are good. Sometimes you come to a patch which is under repair, or needs it, and then you must drive carefully; but even the side roads are not so bad but that if you are prepared to drive with prudence you will reach your destination without mishap.

The country is beautiful and varied; it is a land of smiling plains and mountain ranges. It offers you rugged grandeur. It offers you vast stretches of open country. And if you go in the spring you will see such a profusion of wild

Continental Daily Mail, 11 August 1948.

flowers as you have never seen before, flowers whose names, alas! I cannot tell you, blue, white, red, yellow, sometimes growing together in motley luxuriance, sometimes in great patches of one colour as though each variety had staked out its own claim and would admit no intruders. Then you will have a carpet of bright yellow flowers and next to it a lake of vivid blue ones.

In the mountainous districts you will pass through miles and miles of a shrub with sticky green leaves which bears a white flower like a wild rose; and the hillside is snowy with them. In the plains you will pass through little villages, the houses gleaming white with whitewash, for they are sprayed once a year, and in every balcony you will see growing geraniums, carnations and lilies, the sort of lilies we grow in England under glass, and roses. I think it would be hard to find a Spaniard who does not love flowers.

In a number of small towns and villages, and in two or three of the great cities, the State has established *paradors*, which are inns in which the traveller can be sure of finding all the comfort he can ask for, nicely furnished rooms, very clean, modern bathrooms and excellent food. They put to shame the hotels in the university towns and cathedral cities of England.

With good sense the authorities have taken for this purpose fine old houses of the seventeenth and eighteenth centuries and have arranged them with taste. They give you the opportunity of visiting places which hitherto the tourist has hardly ventured to stay at. Your board and lodging are provided at a fixed and reasonable inclusive price. I have stayed at several and I should like to describe the *parador* at Oropesa. I meant only to stop off for lunch, but found it so charming that I stayed on.

On the crest of a steep hill stands a ruined castle, formerly a stronghold, and from its towers you see far and wide; but when the country was pacified and there was no longer need of a fortress to withstand assault a grandee of Spain built himself in front of it a huge stone house. It is in part of this that the *parador* has been placed.

Between the castle and the palace is a great yard in which boys play football. On two sides are tiers of stone benches and here once a year, on the 9th of September, the feast day of the village, there is a bull-fight. On the third side, opening on to a pillared gallery, are the quarters of the Civil Guard. You enter the house through a vast hall in which there are some good bits of old furniture, and going through a door come to the modernised apartments of the inn.

From the windows of your room you see the kestrel hawks in graceful flight and in the distance the snow-capped mountains. A little way away there is a disused church, neo-classical in style, and on the top of the belfries storks build their nests. They stand for hours ruminating and then, moved by some impulse, on a sudden sail lumbering away.

Oropesa would be a good place in which to spend a lazy holiday. There is nothing to do there, but to admire the view and watch the village life. It can hardly have changed since the grandee built his palace two or three hundred years ago.

On the day I arrived, walking along, I saw outside a door a great piece of wood so strangely fashioned that I couldn't think what it was. A man was standing by, so I asked him. He was an oldish man with a lined face and the work-worn hands of the tiller of the soil.

'It's a plough,' he said, 'the same as the Romans used when they were here and it'll last out any of the ploughs they make now. My father used it before me and my son will use it after me. You see, the earth likes it better than one of these newfangled iron ploughs, it knows the wood and feels well disposed towards it.'

In the plaza shaded by acacias and in one or two streets leading out of it the houses are of two storeys, neatly faced and painted grey, and they have glass in the windows. These are the houses of the prosperous citizens, the doctor, the lawyer, the merchant; but in the other streets the houses are low, roofed with tiles mellowed by age, and they have no glass in the windows, but only shutters.

Some of them have little patios gay with flowers, geraniums, golden rod and banksia roses, and you will hear a pleasant chatter of women's voices as you pass. Now and again the owner of a white house has given it a touch of colour by painting a blue frieze under the roof and a broad band of blue round the door.

The streets are narrow and unpaved and they wander up and down the hill according to the lie of the land. Innumerable children play in the streets, little black pigs race to some spot only to find they didn't want to go there, goats, wearing their chronic air of disatisfaction, rout peevishly in the garbage, chickens scurry busily around looking for something to peck at.

A peasant, bringing his produce to sell in the village, passes along with his donkey, its pannier laden with lettuces, leeks, onions and what not; the donkey steps daintily, with a soft tread, as though picking his way over earth for which he felt a faint disdain. Women sit in the street, on low chairs, in little groups, making lace or mending their men's underwear; and sometimes a youth sits with them lazily plucking the strings of a guitar.

Girls pass with great stone jars which they are going to fill with water from the well, and at the well-head by the church they linger to gossip as the girls did in Goethe's *Faust* when poor Gretchen came along to fill her jar and they mocked her because she had loved not wisely.

At the corner there is a woman with a cart and a donkey who has brought crockery to sell. It is displayed on the ground, rough, garishly-coloured pottery; and people bring their rags, old skirts, torn coats, fragments of shawl: a boy weighs them, makes a price and they take away in exchange a bowl or a plate.

I wish I had room to tell you of other villages and little-known towns, Ronda with it dramatic ravine, Ecija with its charming plaza, Arcos the unbelievably picturesque, Ubeda where the *parador* is in an ancient mansion in a vast square of fine churches and noble buildings.

As a foreigner in places where foreigners do not often go you will find yourself an object of curiosity. But it is a friendly curiosity. For the Spanish are surely the most polite people in the world. Go into a shop to ask your way and the owner is quite likely to leave his customers and come out into the street to point out the direction in which you must go.

Casual strangers will often walk half a mile out of their way to be sure that you don't lose yours; and once when I stopped a workman in overalls to ask him how to get to some place, after telling me, he begged my pardon because he had an appointment and could not take me there himself.

Spaniards like to talk and you will get much more out of a journey to their country if you will take the trouble to acquire at least a smattering of the language. It is not a difficult one to learn and it will enable you to get into closer touch with a courteous and affable people.

NELSON DOUBLEDAY

I do not wish to speak of the publisher, which others can do with greater effect than I, but of the man. With his great height he was in youth of a striking beauty, in middle age of an imposing and handsome presence, and even at the end, though worn by sickness, with death in his face and the awareness of death in his eyes, he bore a look of distinction. He was a shy man and never much at his ease in mixed company. Though generous, hospitable and courteous to all and sundry, for he was a well-bred man, outside the circle of his immediate family he cared for few people, but when for one reason or another he happened upon someone who was congenial to him he gave his friendship wholeheartedly. He had a great power of affection and a need for affection. It was touching to see the thoughtful tact with which this great big man sought for ways in which he could give pleasure to his friend, the little attentions of which he was so lavish, the unremitting kindness with which he used him and the trouble he took, never too great, to add to his happiness and well-being. For thirty years Nelson Doubleday gave me his constant and affectionate friendship. The recollection of it is a treasure that can never be taken away from me.

From *Nelson Doubleday 1889–1949*. Privately printed, 1950.

EDDIE MARSH

1

Sir Edward Marsh is a social creature. He has enjoyed the company of his fellow men, and seeing them with the indulgence of his generous nature he has found in them all something to like and in a great many something to admire. Being, it is obvious, entirely devoid of envy, he has been able to appreciate their gifts without reservation. He has encouraged the young and by his praise given them a self-confidence which, more often than is generally supposed, they greatly lack. The conceit which the young display, often to the irritation of their elders, is very frequently no more than a mask to conceal their instinctive dissatisfaction with themselves. With his buoyant enthusiasm Edward Marsh has given hope to many a poet and painter who was inclined to distrust his powers; his own vehement belief in the value of the arts has reassured them that in pursuing them they were engaged in a noble task; and his sympathetic interest in their work, the trouble that he was prepared to take, first by advice and suggestion to enable them to improve their productions and then by persistence to attract public attention to them, have for a generation and more made it possible for many to make the most of gifts which otherwise would have been allowed to remain sterile. It is true that now the Georgian Poets, whom he may be said almost with justice to have created, have proved for the most part to be no great shakes, it is true that the painters whom he bought and ingeniously advertised, have scarcely fulfilled their promise; but it is possible for no one to create genius. He has given them a chance which but for him they would not have had, and he has fostered in a large section of the public an honest interest in art which has prepared it to be receptive to the appearance of a new manifestation should the coming years produce it. In the arts many are called, but few are chosen; their path is always difficult, but the difficulties are not insuperable if there is abroad a general spirit of sympathy and a willingness to welcome innovation. If there is in England now such a spirit and such a willingness it is due to the untiring efforts of Edward Marsh. This is a considerable achievement.

'Proof-reading as an Avocation', *Publishers' Weekly*, 14 October 1939.

But Edward Marsh has been a civil servant and his life has brought him into contact with persons of social and political importance. His kindliness, his sense of decorum and his loyalty have led him to paint them in his book[1] in flattering colours. A less amiable person (such as I am myself) might have treated some of them with less indulgence. He might have found a good deal of silliness in some of these meretriciously shining creatures, a good deal of self-seeking in some of these patriotic statesmen and in some of these strong men lamentable weaknesses. But Edward Marsh's enthusiasm for the great and good with whom he has come in contact is happily offset by the keenness of his humour. He not only can say apt, clever and amusing things himself, but (and this is not so common among wits) he has an intense appreciation of them when said by others. Seldom has a book been so full of good stories.

But it is not my business to write a criticism of it. In one place Edward Marsh mentions his activities as a proof-reader and it is in this respect that I wish to speak of him. I have known him, I suppose, for thirty years; I have met him at innumerable parties, some in my own house, I have chatted with him during the intervals at I don't know how many first nights; but it is only somewhat recently that I discovered he was in the habit of reading proofs for some of his friends. I was not a little surprised; for it is dull enough to read one's own proofs. I should have thought it intolerable to read somebody else's. I was told, however, that he not only enjoyed it, but did it with great competence. To read one's proofs is very necessary, but it is something the author himself generally does very badly; he knows what he wants to say and because a phrase is clear to him, he thinks it must be equally clear to the reader; he has in his mind the word he intended to use and if by a slip of his pen or a printer's error another word has been put in its place he is very likely to miss it; he is careless or lazy, so that he has not verified a date or a reference; and often he is ignorant. English grammar is extremely difficult and an author frequently puts things, maybe with misgiving, in a certain way because he simply has not known how to put them any better. The most celebrated writers are often guilty of astounding laxities. Dickens of course is notorious for his bad grammar and even so careful a writer as Henry James can make mistakes. Though for long I had taken great pains to write well I was well aware that I did not write as well as I wanted to, and I welcomed the opportunity that presented itself of getting so good a scholar as Edward Marsh to go over my book when I had done my best with it and take note of where I had gone astray; but for a long time I did not like to propose it to him. He is a highbrow, and he has always mixed with highbrows, and I was humiliatingly conscious that they did not look upon me as fit to belong to their august body; I was afraid he would not think it worth his while to waste pains over work that was so popular. When at last, however, I plucked up the courage to ask Edward Marsh whether he would read the proofs of a book called *Don Fernando* which I had recently written, I was embarrassed by the cordiality with which he acceded to my request. He spoke as though I was positively doing him a favour. I was more embarrassed still when some time later he returned my proofs with the notes he had made, for I saw that he had

[1] *A Number of People*, Harper Bros., 1939.

put at least a solid week's work into the tedious task. Here were not the few casual corrections I had expected, but an imposing series of remarks on punctuation, grammar, style and fact. He had gone through my book with a fine comb. I was humiliated to discover that with all my care I had been very careless; but I accepted gratefully all his emendations, corrected the blunders, and had the satisfaction when the book was at last published of having *The Times* observe that it was beautifully written. I must add that if Edward Marsh in his relations with people somewhat overflows with the milk of human kindness, he makes up for it when he corrects proofs; for then his comments are by turn scornful, pained, acid and vituperative. No obscurity escapes his stricture, no redundance his satire, and no clumsiness his obloquy. I think few authors could suffer this ordeal and remain persuaded that they wrote tolerably well. Since then Edward Marsh has examined with the same ruthlessness several of my books and I believe myself to have learned a great deal as a result. I am hoping to live long enough to write a book in which he will not even find a misplaced comma to cavil at. But I will admit that when he was good enough to send me his memoirs to read I cherished the hope that here was the opportunity to get something of my own back. Everyone knows that it is harder to produce than to criticize, though from reading the works of certain critics you would not suppose so, and I looked forward to finding in this book at least a few errors which I proposed with all possible gentleness, in sorrow rather than in anger, to point out. Well I thought I found one, a little matter of a double relative, which if I had written it, I was convinced would have excited my mentor's animadversion. I wrote and told him so, but he took a very high hand and replied that he was perfectly right and he couldn't imagine what I saw amiss. I still think *I* was right, but I *know* that he couldn't possibly be wrong. So that was that.

2

Other friends of Eddie Marsh can speak of him more intimately than I can, for though I knew him a very long time I don't think I can claim to have been more than a close acquaintance of his. I first met him at luncheon with the Churchills. At that time the present Prime Minister was at the War Office and Eddie Marsh, then a Civil Servant, was acting as his secretary. It was quite a small party, we weren't more than six, and I can remember nothing of the conversation. I have an impression that Eddie and I, content to listen to our host, spoke little. I don't remember meeting Eddie again till after the war was over. Then he came sometimes to dine or lunch with me at a house I had in London. I must also have run across him now and then at the parties I went to. I think people used to laugh at him in those days, not maliciously, but with good nature, for the extravagance of his enthusiasms. One was inclined to shrug one's shoulders at his spluttering admiration for actors, artists, and poets whom with the best will in the world one could not regard as heaven-

From *Eddie Marsh: Sketches for a Composite Literary Portrait*. Lund Humphries, 1953.

sent. Time has shown that he overestimated and overpraised persons in whom he took an interest. But it made him happy to think over-well of them, and I don't know that it did any harm.

My close connection with Eddie came about by, for me, a happy chance. I was chatting with him one evening at a party and he mentioned that he had been correcting the proofs of a book that Winston Churchill was about to publish. I asked him how he could undertake to do anything so tiresome, for it is boring enough to correct one's own proofs, to correct someone else's, I should have thought, was deadly. To my surprise he told me that there were few things he enjoyed more. He found the task interesting, restful, and (strangely enough) great fun. I don't know how it came about that we then arranged that he should correct a book of mine that I had recently written: I don't believe I should have had the nerve to ask him to do this and I think he must have himself hinted that he would be willing to do so. Anyhow, shortly after this I sent him a book, he corrected the proofs, and then until just before his death he corrected those of everything I wrote.

I cannot tell the reader of these lines how great is the debt I owe Eddie and how sorely, on this account as on others now, I regret his death. When it became a regular thing that he should do me this particular service I suggested that it would be only reasonable if we came to some business arrangement, for I could not see why I should profit by his knowledge and his experience, why he should put quite a lot of work into a job, and get nothing for it. But he would not hear of anything of the kind and persisted in saying that what he did for me was pure pleasure. If in the last twenty years or so I have learnt to write better English the credit is largely owing to Eddie. English is not an easy language to write well and its grammar abounds with difficulties. Hardly anyone has succeeded in writing it without making an occasional mistake. The best we authors can hope is that we shall not make too many or too obvious ones. In the heat of composition an author is very apt to make grammatical slips and then when he comes to correct his proofs he reads what he intended to write rather than what he has actually written. It was a comfort to know that Eddie would notice the blunder. But there are inadvertences of fact which the author is fortunate if he can always avoid. For instance, in *Tom Jones* Fielding made Partridge see Garrick play Hamlet in London on a day in 1745, when in point of fact Garrick was in Dublin and did not return to London till six months later. Eddie would never have passed such an error, nor in the same great novel would he have allowed a respectable woman to have two children seven years apart when she had been married only five years.

Though I welcomed Eddie's corrections, my type-setters groaned when they heard that my book, after I had myself done my best with the proofs, was to be subjected to Eddie's meticulous scrutiny. The reason for this was that he had a mania for commas and the insertion in the proofs of hundreds of them naturally gave a lot of extra work. Anyone who cares to look at an eighteenth-century book, at one written a hundred years ago, and one written recently, will see how greatly punctuations has, since Burke's time for instance, changed. Now less and less use is made of commas. Indeed the tendency is, I think, to omit them unless they are absolutely necessary to make the sense clear. There has been thereby perhaps a certain loss of elegance. Eddie was, however, deliberately old-fashioned in this matter and he peppered my pages with commas. Though in the end I accepted Eddie's emendations, even sometimes when I thought them slightly pedantic, it was not on occasion without argument. It was hard to get him to allow that it was well to follow common usage. Whenever I wrote *lunch*, he changed it to *luncheon*. I protested that the word was obsolete and there was no reason why a modern author should use it. It was natural to say, I urged, 'Will you come and have lunch with me', and so why shouldn't you use it in a book. 'But it isn't natural to me', Eddie cried in his shrill voice, 'I won't come and have lunch with you. I will, however, if I am disengaged be pleased to come and have luncheon with you.' Though he made a long and stubborn fight against the word *intrigue* in the sense of puzzle or perplex, which Fowler declared has no merit except that of unfamiliarity to the English reader, he eventually capitulated. The sense that Fowler so strongly condemned has been generally accepted and indeed it does signify something that cannot be so well said by the use of any other word.

Eddie Marsh was an indefatigable *raconteur*. That is a gift that is dying out now that most people are more eager to put in a quip of their own than to listen to someone else tell an amusing anecdote. I who would always rather listen than talk look upon this as unfortunate. Eddie was genial, *serviable*, and though his means were small, lavish. He had a rare generosity of spirit.

THE
AGA KHAN

I have known the Aga Khan for many years. He has been a kind and helpful friend. The introductions he gave me when I spent a winter in India enabled me to profit by the rich experience of my sojourn in that wonderful country as otherwise I could never have done, so that when he paid me the compliment of asking me to write a preface to his autobiography I was glad to be given the opportunity to do him this small, and really unnecessary, service. For the book speaks for itself. It was not till I had read it that it was borne upon me how difficult a task I was undertaking. The Aga Khan has led a full life. He has been a great traveller and there are few parts of the world that he has not visited either for pleasure or because his political and religious interests made it necessary. He has been a great theatregoer; he has loved the opera and the ballet. He is an assiduous reader. He has been occupied in affairs in which the fate of nations was involved. He has bred horses and raced them. He has been on terms of close friendship with kings and princes of the blood royal, maharajahs, viceroys, field-marshals, actors and actresses, trainers, golf professionals, society beauties and society entertainers. He has founded a university. As head of a widely diffused sect, the Ismailis, he has throughout his life sedulously endeavoured to further the welfare, spiritual and material, of his countless followers. Towards the end of this autobiography he remarks that he has never once been bored. That alone is enough to mark the Aga Khan out as a remarkable man.

I must tell the reader at once that I am incompetent to deal with some of his multifarious activities. I know nothing of racing. I am so little interested in it that one day when I was lunching with the Aga Khan just before Tulyar won the Derby we talked only of India and I never thought of asking him whether his horse had a chance of winning. I know no more of politics than does the ordinary newspaper reader. For long years the Aga Khan was intimately concerned with them. His advice was constantly sought, and it was generally sound. He believed in moderation: 'Of one fact,' he writes, 'my years in public life have convinced me; that the value of a compromise is that it can

---

Foreword to *Memoirs of the Aga Khan*. Heinemann, 1954.

supply a bridge across a difficult period, and later having employed that bridge it is often possible to bring into effect the full-scale measures of reform which, originally, would have been rejected out of hand.' He knew well the statesmen on whose decisions during the last fifty years great events depended. It is seldom he passes a harsh judgment on them. He pays generous tribute to their integrity, intelligence, patriotism, wide knowledge and experience. It seems strange that with these valuable qualities they should have landed us all in the sorry mess in which we now find ourselves.

The Aga Khan is a charitable man, and it goes against his grain to speak ill of others. The only occasion in this book of his on which he betrays bitterness is when he animadverts on the behaviour of our countrymen in their dealings with the inhabitants of the countries in which in one way and another they held a predominant position, in Egypt and India and in the treaty ports of China. During the eighties relations between British and Indians were in general easy, amiable and without strain, and had they continued to be as they were then, 'I greatly doubt,' he writes, 'whether political bitterness would have developed to the extent it did, and possibly something far less total than the severance of the Republic of India from the Imperial connection would have been feasible.' It is a disquieting thought. He goes on as follows:

> What happened to the Englishman has been to me all my life a source of wonder and astonishment. Suddenly it seemed that his prestige as a member of an imperial, governing race would be lost if he accepted those of a different colour as fundamentally his equals. The colour bar was no longer thought of as a physical difference, but far more dangerously – in the end disastrously – as an intellectual and spiritual difference. . . . The pernicious theory spread that all Asiatics were a second-class race, and 'white men' possessed some intrinsic and unchallengeable superiority.

According to the Aga Khan the root-cause of the attitude adopted by the ruling class was fear and a lack of self-confidence. Another was the presence in increasing numbers of British wives with no knowledge or interest in the customs and outlook of Indians. They were no less narrow and provincial when, forty years after the time of which the Aga Khan writes, I myself went to India. These women, who for the most part came from modest homes in the country and since taxation was already high had at the most a maid of all work to do the household chores, found themselves in spacious quarters, with a number of servants to do their bidding. It went to their heads. I remember having tea one day with the wife of a not very important official. In England she might have been a manicurist or a stenographer. She asked me about my travels and when I told her that I had spent most of my time in the Indian States, she said: 'You know, we don't have anything more to do with Indians than we can help. One has to keep them at arm's length.'

The rest of the company agreed with her.

The clubs were barred to Indians till by the influence of Lord Willingdon some were persuaded to admit them, but so far as I could see it made little difference since even in them white and coloured kept conspicuously apart.

When I was in Hyderabad the Crown Prince asked me to lunch. I had spent some time in Bombay and was then on my way to Calcutta.

'I suppose you were made an honorary member of the Club when you were in Bombay,' he said, and when I told him I was, he added: 'And I suppose you'll be made an honorary member of the Club at Calcutta?'

'I hope so,' I answered.

'Do you know the difference between the Club at Bombay and the Club at Calcutta?' he asked me. I shook my head. 'In one they don't allow either dogs or Indians; in the other they do allow dogs.'

I couldn't for the life of me think what to say to that.

But it was not only in India that these unhappy conditions prevailed. In the foreign concessions in China there was the same arrogant and hidebound colonialism and the general attitude towards the Chinese was little short of outrageous. 'All the best hotels refused entry to Chinese, except in wings specially set aside for them. It was the same in restaurants. From European clubs they were totally excluded. Even in shops a Chinese customer would have to stand aside and wait to be served when a European or an American came in after him and demanded attention.' Lord Cromer was the British Resident when the Aga Khan went to Egypt. He found the British were not merely in political control of the country, but assumed a social superiority which the Egyptians appeared humbly to accept. 'There was no common ground of social intercourse. Therefore inevitably behind the façade of humility there developed a sullen and brooding, almost personal, resentment which later on needlessly, bitterly, poisoned the clash of Egyptian nationalism with Britain's interests as the occupying power.' Now that the foreign concessions in China exist no more, now that the last British soldiers are leaving Egypt, now that, as the Aga Khan puts it, British rule in India has dissolved and passed away like early morning mist before strong sunlight, the British have left behind them a legacy of hatred. We too may ask ourselves what happened to Englishmen that caused them so to act as to arouse an antagonism which was bound in the end to have such untoward consequences. I am not satisfied with the explanation which the Aga Khan gives. I think it is to be sought rather in that hackneyed, but consistently disregarded aphorism of Lord Acton's: Power corrupts and absolute power corrupts absolutely.

It is no good crying over spilt milk, so the determinists tell us, and if I have dwelt on this subject it is with intention. In the world of today the Americans occupy the position which the British so long, and for all their failings not ingloriously, held. Perhaps it would be to their advantage to profit by our example and avoid making the errors that have cost us so dear. A brown man can fire a sten gun and shoot as straight as a white man; a yellow man can drop an atom bomb as efficiently. What does this mean but that the colour bar is now a crass absurdity? The British wanted to be loved and were convinced that they were; the Americans want to be loved too, but are uneasily, distressingly, conscious that they are not. They find it hard to understand. With their boundless generosity they have poured money into the countries which two disastrous wars have reduced to poverty, and it is natural that they should wish to see it spent as they think fit and not always as the recipients would like to spend it. It is true enough that the man who pays the piper calls the tune, but if it is a tune the company finds it hard to dance to, perhaps he is well-advised to do his best so to modify it that they may find it easy. Doubtless it is more blessed to give than to receive, but it is also more hazardous, for you put the recipient of your bounty under an obligation and that is a condition that only the very magnanimous can accept with good will. Gratitude is not a virtue that comes easily to the human race. I do not think it can be denied that the British conferred great benefits on the peoples over which they ruled; but they humiliated them and so earned their hatred. The Americans would do well to remember it.

But enough of that. The Aga Khan is descended from the Prophet Mohammed through his daughter Fatima and is descended also from the Fatimite Caliphs of Egypt. He is justifiably proud of his illustrious ancestry. His grandfather, also known as Aga Khan, by inheritance spiritual head of the Ismailis, was a Persian nobleman, son-in-law of the powerful monarch, Fateh Hali Shah and hereditary chieftain of Kerman. Smarting under the insult that had been put upon him, he took up arms against a later Shah, Mohammed by name, was worsted and forced to make his escape, attended by a few horsemen, through the deserts of Baluchistan to Sind. There he raised a troop of light horse and after various vicissitudes eventually reached Bombay with his two hundred horsemen, his relations, clients and supporters. He acquired a vast estate upon which he built palaces, innumerable smaller houses for his dependants and outbuildings, gardens and fountains. He lived in feudal state and never had less than a hundred horses in his stables. He died when the author of this book was a child and was succeeded by his son who, however, only survived him a short time; upon which the Aga Khan whom we know, at the age of eight inherited his titles, wealth and responsibilities, spiritual and temporal. His education was conducted to prepare him for the sacred charge to which he was born. He was taught English, French, Arabic and Persian. Religious instruction was imparted to him by a renowned teacher of Islamic lore. No holidays were allowed him. The only relief from work was on Saturdays and feast days when he received his followers who came to offer gifts and do him homage.

The Aga Khan, raised to such eminence at so early an age, was fortunate in that his mother was a highly cultivated woman. She was deeply versed in Persian and Arabic poetry, as were several of her ladies in waiting, and at meal times at her table 'our conversation was of literature, of poetry; or perhaps one of the elderly ladies who travelled to and from Teheran a great deal would talk about her experiences at the Court of the Shah'. The Begum was a mystic and habitually spent long hours in prayer for spiritual enlightenment and union with God. 'I have, in something like ecstasy,' he writes, 'heard her read perhaps some verses by Roumi or Hafiz, with their exquisite analogies between man's beatific vision of the Divine and the temporal beauty and colours of flowers, the music and magic of the night, and the transient splendours of the Persian dawn.' The Aga Khan is a deeply religious man. One of the most interesting chapters in this book is that in which after telling of his personal beliefs, he gives a concise exposition of Islam as it is understood and practised today. It is there for the reader to read and I will say no more about it than that it is sympathetic and persuasive. It may be that it will occur to him that the duties of man as he may learn them from the verses of the Koran and the Traditions of the Prophet are not very different from those he may learn from the Sermon on the Mount. But man is an imperfect creature, at the mercy of his passions, and it should surprise no one that too often these duties are no more practised by Muslim than by Christian.

The general public knows the Aga Khan chiefly as a racing man and it is not unlikely that the reader of the book, remembering the pages in which he narrates his experiences as a breeder of bloodstock and the happy winner of many classical events, will be a trifle taken aback by this moving, thoughtful and sincere chapter. There is no reason why he should be. The chase was the main occupation of the Iranian nobles from whom he is descended. It is part of the tradition he inherited and the environment in which he was brought up. His grandfather, his father, had hounds, hawks and horses, the swiftest and finest money could buy or they could breed. On the death of his father only twenty or thirty of the ninety racehorses he had possessed were kept and they, through the Aga Khan's minority, were raced under his colours all over Western India. Racing is in his blood. But first and foremost he is the spiritual head of a sect of Islam which counts its adherents by the million. He has a secure belief in the faith which was the faith of his great ancestors and he is ever mindful of the sacred charge, with the great responsibilities it entails, which is his by right of birth. We are none of us all of a piece. The Aga Khan says somewhere that we are all composed of diverse and conflicting elements: of few men could this be more truly said than of himself. But he is fortunate in that the elements in him only superficially conflict; they are resolved by the strength and consistency of his character.

ON HIMSELF

ON
THE APPROACH
OF
MIDDLE AGE

It is like any other of the necessary trials of life, such as marriage or death; you think of it vaguely as something that must be endured, but you seldom give it serious consideration till you are face to face with it. A man will hardly wait to learn swimming till he is thrown into the sea, but he will take no thought for his conduct in a crisis which is as dangerous and, unlike the other, by no prudence to be avoided.

Before he knows where he is, he finds himself floundering in the perilous forties. He is now that baldish, stout person whom twenty years before he jeered at when he saw him dancing, a little out of breath, with girls who might be his daughters. He is now the gentleman in the Rolls Royce, smoking a long cigar, whom he used to outdrive at golf by thirty yards and who wilted not a little towards the end of the second round. Yesterday, he was a young man, and today he drinks lithia water.

Because, as a lad, I had seen much of the world and travelled a good deal, because I was somewhat widely read and my mind was occupied with matters beyond my age, I seemed always older than my contemporaries; but it was not until the outbreak of the Great War that I had an inkling of the horrid truth. I learned then, to my consternation, that I was a middle-aged man. I consoled myself by reflecting that I could be thus described only militarily, so to speak; but not so very long after, I had an experience which put the matter beyond doubt. I had been lunching at a restaurant with a woman whom I had known a long time, and her niece. This was a girl of seventeen, pretty, with blue eyes and very pleasing dimples. I found it vastly agreeable to look at her, and I did my best to amuse her. She rewarded my sallies with rippling laughter. Well, after luncheon we took a taxi to go to a matinée. My old friend got in, and then her niece. But the girl sat down on the tip-up seat, leaving the empty place at the back beside her aunt for me.

For a moment I stood rooted to the pavement. Amid the clatter of street cars and the screams of klaxons I heard the ominous tolling of a bell. It was the knell of my dead youth. In the gesture of this maiden, I discerned the civility of youth (as opposed to the rights of sex) to a gentleman no longer young. I realized that she looked upon me with the respect due to age. Respect: it is a chilling thing for a girl to give to a man. The boat had given a sudden lurch, and there was I, all unprepared, struggling for my life in an unknown sea.

It is not a very pleasant thing to recognize that for the young you are no longer an equal. You belong to a different generation. For them your race is run. They can look up to you; they can admire you; but you are apart from them: for boys you are no longer a competitor, for girls you are no longer marriageable. It is only the widow of a certain age who still casts an inquisitive eye on you. You may just as well marry and have done with it. I wonder if the little jests with which I sought to enliven that tragic drive from the restaurant to the theatre sounded as forced to my guests as they did to myself.

I think I have always been more conscious of my age than most men. It is generally supposed that the young live in the present, but I know that I lived only in the future. I was ever looking forward, generally to something I proposed to do in some place other than that in which I found myself; and no sooner was I there, doing what I had so much wanted, than it became of small account, for my fancy raced forward and I busied myself with what next year would bring. I never enjoyed the daffodils of today, because I was always thinking of the roses of tomorrow. Sometimes I think that it is the unimaginative who get the most out of life, for to them alone the fleeting moment is all in all.

My youth passed me unnoticed, and I was always burdened with the sense that I was growing old. To me, nothing is more wonderful than the consciousness of youth which in these days the young have. They are deeply aware that it is lovely and fugitive. They know, as we of a past day did not, that it is precious, and that they must make the most of it. I was young in an elderly world. Then people shrugged their shoulders at youth; it was an indisposition which time would cure, and the young were impatient to grow older. For the middle-aged held the reins with a tight hand. You were a promising young man at forty. A bald head was the first proof of merit. The old thought they knew better than the young; and the young, rebelliously perhaps, were ready to agree with them. Now the old have been taught that they do not know better; they only know different.

But middle age has its compensations. One is that, on the whole, you feel no need to do what you do not like. You are no longer ashamed of yourself. You are reconciled to being what you are, and you do not much mind what people think of you. They can take you or leave you. You do not want to impose upon them with false pretences. Youth is bound hand and foot with the shackles of public opinion.

I was never of great physical strength, and even as a lad long walks tired me; but I went on them because I would not confess my weakness. I do not mind now, and so I save myself much weariness. I hated cold water, but for many years I took cold baths and bathed in cold seas because I wanted to be like everybody else. I used to dive from heights that made me nervous, because I was afraid of seeming afraid. I was mortified because I played games less well than my companions. When I did not know a thing, I was ashamed to confess my ignorance; and it was not until quite late in life that I discovered how easy it is to say: I don't know. I am prepared now to admit cheerfully that I never can tell where I and J come in the alphabet. I find that my neighbours do not expect me to walk five and twenty miles, or to play a scratch game of golf, or to dive from a hateful board thirty feet from the water. That is all to the good, and makes life much less unpleasant; but I should no longer care if they did. It is discreet even in middle age to treat the opinion of your fellows with a show of politeness, but in your heart you can cock a snook at them.

When I left school (gathering my passion for freedom into a compact symbol), I said to myself: henceforward, I can get up when I like and go to bed when I like. That, of course, was an illusion; and I soon found that the trammelled life of civilized man only permits a modified independence. When you have an aim, you must sacrifice something of freedom to achieve it. But by the time you have reached middle age, you have discovered just how much freedom it is worthwhile to sacrifice in order to achieve the aim you have in view.

Though I find the young in the mass charming, I do not find them good company. I can bear it with fortitude when they show me that the society of persons of their own age is more grateful to them than mine. For they take themselves with a seriousness which is only unintentionally diverting. Humour is rooted in disillusion, and golden illusions press them around about. It is middle age that laughs, since it is difficult to laugh at the world until you have first learned to laugh at yourself.

So here are at least two good things that middle age gives you: the inestimable boon of freedom, and the precious gift of laughter. What makes youth unhappy is its desire to be like everybody else: what makes middle age tolerable is its reconciliation with oneself.

But frankness well becomes the man who is no longer young: I would sooner be a fool of twenty-five than a philosopher of fifty.

SELF-PORTRAIT

I had just finished an autobiography[1] which, I reckoned, was of about the same length as an ordinary novel when the author of this drawing asked me to write an autobiography in two hundred and fifty words to accompany it. If it were possible in three or four sentences to put what I had taken three hundred pages to tell, it would mean that the book to which I had given so much pains was worthless. I will not make the attempt. I do not believe it would succeed. I will content myself with telling what I have tried to do in a life which now, in the ordinary course of nature, must be drawing towards its end. I have tried to remember that life is there, not to be written about, but to be lived. I have tried to have every experience that was possible to me within the limitations that Nature imposed upon me, and I have looked upon the practice of literature, not as my sole aim, though my chief one, but as an activity that must be combined in due proportion with the other activities proper to a human being. I have tried to make my life a completed and rounded thing. I have sought freedom, material and spiritual, and now, on the threshold of old age, I am not disinclined to think that I have at last achieved it.

From *Portraits and Self-Portraits* by G. Schreiber. Houghton, Mifflin, 1936.
[1] *The Summing Up* (1938).

SIXTY-FIVE

The profession of authorship is on the whole a healthy one and authors are apt to live on long after they have given the world whatever of significance they had to offer. There are few whose reputations would not now stand higher if a release from the turmoil of living, a release merciful to their readers, had prevented them from continuing to write when their vitality was impaired and their originality exhausted. For many years I wrote plays, but, having reached a certain age, I decided to write no more; when I announced my determination (which attracted more attention than I could have expected) a number of persons expressed a doubt whether I should be able to adhere to it. I was convinced I should but what I was not so sure of was whether or no I should regret making such a determination. The theatre is attended with a great deal of publicity, and the habit of notoriety is as insidious as the habit of smoking cigarettes; you have no notion that it has a hold on you till you seek to break it; and I could not be certain that I should not feel the want of it. I need have had no qualms. It has not troubled me to enjoy no longer the publicity which accompanies the projects and movements of the popular dramatist; indeed, so far as I can tell, the only difference to my life that ceasing to write for the stage has made is that whereas at one time when I applied for seats on a first night I was allotted them in the second or third row of the stalls, now I am relegated to the eleventh or twelfth where I find myself seated among the leading ladies of a generation ago and the mothers and wives of members of the cast. It has the slight inconvenience (if the play has merit) that actors today speak so indistinctly that I often cannot hear them, but I cope with this by the simple expedient of not going to first nights. I have never regretted my decision and I have never had the desire to write another play.

I am a person more inclined to look forward than to look back. I have settled with myself what books (not many) I propose to write in the future and have made my plans so that I may finish them while I can reasonably expect with the aid of common sense and the care of good doctors still to possess the powers, such as they are, which I have inherited from nature and developed by application. Then the pattern will be complete.

In *W. Somerset Maugham: Novelist Essayist Dramatist, A Pamphlet about his Work, together with a Bibliography, an Appreciation by Richard Aldington and a New Note on Writing by Mr Maugham.* Doubleday, Doran, 1939.

But we dwell in a world of hazard. A mishap in an aeroplane, a skiddy road, an anopheles mosquito, a pneumococcus may easily upset our best-laid schemes. These are the common chances that beset existence and it is well to ignore them except now and then when we may consider what a marvel it is that with all these dangers encompassing us we are alive at all. The times we live in, however, are stormy and none can tell what may ensue. Modern war spares no one and should we find ourselves engaged in such a desperate conflict as what has been called, perhaps alas, too magniloquently, the Great War, it may be that poison gas or a bomb will put a speedy end to all our activity, and the risk of this we must face with what philosophy we may; but even should no such accident befall us it is unlikely, in the event of war, that we men of letters will have either the heart or the inclination to pursue our peaceful avocation. If the struggle is as devastating and as prolonged as the prophets of evil suggest it will be no time to write novels or stories. Then these books of mine will remain unwritten. At my time of life I can hardly hope to live on into an age when the things of the spirit once more may seem to have a certain value; I can hardly expect an age, which must surely be occupied with questions to which I can give no answers, to take any further interest in me; I can hardly suppose that I, who have dealt with the world I knew, can continue to invent stories about a world which will be strange to me.

And so, with the possibility before me that my work is completed, I amuse myself from time to time by casting my eye over it as a whole in an attempt to form an unbiased judgment upon it. I do not want to say again what I have already said in *The Summing Up* and such of my readers as have read that will know what have been my ambitions and what my aims. I have been a teller of tales. This has resulted in my finding myself somewhat alone in my generation. Though I am not less concerned than another with the disorder of the world, the injustice of social conditions, the confusion of politics, I have not thought the novel the best medium for uttering my views on these subjects; unlike many of my more distinguished contemporaries I have felt no inclination to preach or to prophesy; I have taken an absorbing interest in human nature and it has seemed to me that I could best communicate my observations on it by telling tales. It is said that General Booth, the founder of the Salvation Army, asked why the devil should have the best tunes; I have thought it unreasonable that the authors of detective novels should have the best stories. But if it satisfies an author to tell stories he must bear it with becoming resignation if he enjoys neither the power not the prestige of the preacher and the prophet. I think the desire of novelists to assume these rôles has occasioned them not seldom to lose sight of the fact that the novel is first of all a work of art. It is this as definitely as a symphony or a painting. And if it is not, it fails, whatever didactic qualities it may possess, to be a good novel.

To produce a work of art has always been my purpose; it is not for me to say whether I have now and then achieved it. Just as happiness, they tell us, is attained not by aiming at it directly, but is a result that may accompany and reward efforts that seem to conduce to other ends, so I do not suppose anyone can create a work of art by setting out to do so; so far as the writer of fiction is concerned he develops to the best of his ability the subject that for the time engages his attention and it is a happy accident if when he has got all he could out of it he has fashioned a work of art. As I look back now on the work I have produced during the last forty years I am amazed at the extent to which what one would have said was pure chance has been responsible for what is best in it. Sometimes I look at a casual acquaintance and think how truly wonderful it is that, rising from the primeval slime as did his remotest ancestor, the innumerable generations since then who were his forbears passing through every imaginable vicissitude, each member avoiding by miracle the destruction that might have severed the line, he should stand here and now in front of me. A story is an infinitely smaller thing than a man; but still almost as many seeming accidents must occur to bring it into being. Of course the author must have certain gifts by nature and if he wants to make the most of them he must cultivate them with industry and determination; but chance, or what looks strangely like it, must take a hand; he must be in the mood to receive the spark when it flies, he must be here and not there at a certain instant of time, circumstances which none could have foreseen must combine to open a stranger's heart or to bring to a face the fleeting expression which betrays a pregnant secret. The sudden fall of a stock, the change of a sailing date, a block in the traffic, even a shower of rain may so alter the plans of people that they are thrown into fortuitous contact with the author and give him occasion for a story which but for these accidents, for which neither he nor they were in any way responsible, he could never have thought of. One of the most unfortunate experiences of my life would never have taken place if someone had not had a cold in the head so that I was asked to take his place as a fourth at bridge: my best known story would never have been written if there had not been an outbreak of chicken-pox on a South Sea island.

But if I have contented myself with telling tales I have tried for my own satisfaction to present them to the reader in the best shape I could. I have paid more attention to the technique of narrative than most English novelists have done. I have attempted various methods, as the story I had to tell suggested, for in order to get the best out of a story it has to be told in the way that best suits it, and no one is more conscious than I that sometimes I have used a method that was indifferent. My early study of the French novelists taught me the value of construction, and I have always sought to build up a story, however slight, on solid lines so that it might have, if possible, the same sort of architectural merit as a Georgian house. I have given pains to learning to write as I wished to write. People often speak of style as though it were something that you had by nature (if you were lucky) or acquired by labour, and once in possession of it used systematically. That may be very well for the historian or the essayist; I do not believe it does for the novelist. The novelist must adopt, if he can, a different style for every different novel he writes; and even within the limits of a single novel his style must vary according to whether he is writing dialogue, reporting events or describing an environment. There are authors who think to get a uniform impression by using the same style throughout, for conversations, for their own reflections and for the narration of incidents; and I suppose the most eminent example of this is Henry James; but to my mind the result is highly artificial. The design may be as elegant as that of a Persian carpet, but life has escaped from its meshes. Of course no one can get quite away from himself and in general an author's style will follow certain lines, for after all it is a reflection of his own personality. I have aimed at writing in such a way as to express with brevity and clearness what I wanted to say and to allow nothing in my language to come between the reader and my meaning. But I know that there are other ways of writing. I admire those who can clothe their thoughts in rich textures and using words like pieces of a jigsaw puzzle can form them into patterns of a varied and multi-coloured loveliness. But even if I had had gifts in that direction I do not know that they would have helped me in writing the particular sort of stories I had it in me to write. I have given a great deal of thought to the art of writing. I have never ceased my effort to attain the simplicity, lucidity and euphony which were the qualities I aimed at; but now when I survey my achievement it is with a smile of misgiving; for I am well aware that the greatest novelists the world has ever known, Balzac, Dickens, Tolstoy and Dostoyevsky, wrote in a very slovenly fashion. I can only conclude that if you have vitality, invention, originality and the gift of creating living persons it does not really matter a row of pins how you write. All the same it is better to write well.

ON
PLAYING BRIDGE

1

I am not at all the proper person to write an introduction to this book, for I am an indifferent bridge player and my chief asset as a partner is that I have never thought myself anything else. I do not engage in post-mortems, for I think the players who habitually do so make a bore of the most entertaining game that the art of man has devised; the fact is that if you cannot see a mistake when you have made it no argument will convince you of your error and so the carping critic may just as well hold his peace and deal the next hand. When my partner blames me for having played the wrong card, I accept his reproof with humility, and when he has let me down fourteen hundred by grossly overcalling, I bid him cheerfully not to give it another thought. Of such, you will say, is the kingdom of heaven, and I modestly agree.

Charles Goren asked me to write a short piece to present his new book to the public and I accepted with alacrity; I thought it a great compliment that he paid me. I felt as proud as a lieutenant might feel if he were bidden by his admiral to lead the flagship into battle. But having a practical side to an otherwise idealistic nature I told him that I thought I had better let him know at once what my terms where. He blanched, but agreed to them. They were that he should dine and play bridge with me. Of course I knew I should lose my money, but I was convinced that the fun it would be must make whatever it cost well worth it. I have played only half a dozen times with the life masters and it is rash to generalize on such a slight experience, but it has seemed to me that they are easier to play with than players of the second or third class, for you know that they have a good reason for doing what they do, and when they speak they mean what they say. The chief difficulty the indifferent player playing with indifferent players has to contend with is that they will trust their hunches rather than their common sense and allow their wishes to influence their judgment. I was glad to be given the opportunity to write this

Introduction to *Standard Book of Bidding* by C.H. Goren. Doubleday, Doran, 1944.

introduction also because it will have enabled me to disembarrass my conscience of a sense of guilt.

Charles Goren is an amiable man, and I have aroused in the breasts of those with whom I habitually play bridge a cordial dislike of him. It came about by accident. I had been reading and re-reading my author's *Better Bridge for Better Players* and I was playing a contract which I had little hope of making. A suit was led of which I had the ace and king in my hand with the jack in dummy, and as I put up the jack I murmured: 'Charles Goren does not recommend the lead from the queen'. The jack held, and this innocent remark so disorganized the defence that I made my contract and won the rubber. Since then, when the occasion has presented itself, I have used Charles Goren's precepts as useful weapons in the war of nerves, and the effect has been highly satisfactory, but I am bound to admit that with my friends he has become a highly unpopular character. It is in vain that I ask them mildly: 'But why don't you read his book?' They reply with an indignant snort.

. . . I hope I have profited by reading the book I now present to you. On a first reading, which is all I have so far been able to give it, I felt that I could never hope to remember all the rules it gives and that to try to do so would only confuse me, but as I thought it over, it occurred to me that very few of them, not more than half a dozen, perhaps, were obligatory – rules which must be followed as you follow those of any game; all the rest depended on common sense, and if you had common sense and were prepared to abide by it you need not clutter your brain with any great number of precepts. The moral I have gathered from reading Charles Goren's book is that if you have a cool head, the ability to put two and two together and get the right answer, and tell the exact truth about your hand when you bid, you will be a useful partner at the bridge table and a formidable opponent.

2

. . . But having finished my [introduction], I found that I had various things to say about bridge which I had not had occasion to say. I am going to say them now.

The first thing I want to do is remonstrate with the people who don't play bridge. They are apt to be hoity-toity with those of us who do and tell us they can't understand how presumably intelligent persons can waste their time on such an idle pastime. That is stuff and nonsense. Everyone has a certain amount of leisure and everyone needs distraction, and when you come to inquire of these supercilious folk how they prefer to occupy their leisure and in what they seek their distraction, the chances are that they will say in conversation. The conversationalist needs an audience, and it is true that the bridge table robs him of it. No wonder he is bitter. But the fact is that few people can talk entertainingly for three or four hours at a time. It needs gifts that few of us possess, and even the most brilliant talker grows tedious if he

'How I Like to Play Bridge', *Good Housekeeping*, December 1944.

goes on too long; and when, as he is apt to do, he monopolizes the conversation, he is intolerable. I dare say it profits the soul more to read great literature than to play bridge, but not many of us are prepared to spend our leisure in that improving pursuit. When we can't get a game of bridge, we are more likely to take up a detective story. I have read hundreds of them myself, but I cannot put my hand on my heart and say that I am conscious of receiving more spiritual benefit from reading the latest whodunit than from playing half a dozen hard-fought rubbers.

No, let the carping carp, they don't know what they miss. If I had my way, I would have children taught bridge as a matter of course, just as they are taught dancing. In the end it will be more useful to them, for you cannot with seemliness continue to dance when you are bald and potbellied; nor, for the matter of that, can you with satisfaction to yourself or pleasure to your partners continue to play tennis or golf when you are past middle age; but you can play bridge as long as you can sit up at a table and tell one card from another. In fact, when all else fails – sport, love, ambition – bridge remains a solace and an entertainment.

But though I think everybody should learn bridge, I do not think everybody should play it. Not lessons, books, or practice will make players of those who have no card sense. These unfortunate creatures must look upon it as a defect of nature, like tone deafness or colour blindness, and resign themselves to solitaire, crossword puzzles, or what not.

Bridge is the most entertaining and intelligent card game the wit of man has so far devised, and I deplore the fact that so many people go out of their way to make it a bore. There are the people who, after a hand has been played, will tell you all the thirteen cards they held. Well, you'd seen them played, so you know; but even if you didn't, why should they suppose you care? Then there are the people who during the deal or when you're sorting your cards start to tell you about Aunt Annie's operation or the trouble they're having with decorators in their new apartment. There is no stopping them.

'One Heart,' you say.

They take no notice.

'My dear, I've had three cooks in the last two weeks and not one of them could boil an egg.'

'One Heart,' you repeat.

'Well, I'll tell you what happened to me,' says your partner. 'I got a couple. They drove up in their car, looked at the house, and didn't even come in. They just drove away, and I was expecting eight people to lunch on Sunday.'

'One Heart,' you say.

'You know that Betty's got a new beau?' the player on your right puts in.

'Oh, you mean Harry,' replies the player on your left. 'I've known that for months. She always has liked heels.'

Just to get a little attention, you have a mind to say, 'Seven No Trumps,' but of course it might be expensive and your partner wouldn't be sympathetic, so you meekly repeat, 'One Heart'. . . .

From time to time I have read books on bridge, profiting by them as much as it was in my sinful nature to do, and I have been surprised that they lay no more stress than they do on the advantage it is to you to find out as quickly as you can something of the nature of the persons you are playing with. I had a friend once who held the opinion that you could tell the character of people by the way they played. I think he was generalizing on the single instance of himself. He played a bold, generous, and dashing game, and he liked to think of himself as a dashing, generous, and bold fellow. He was a picture dealer and by the proper exercise of the qualities on which he prided himself succeeded for many years in selling many second-rate old masters to the rich at fantastic prices. Well, I don't know whether there was much truth in this notion, but I'm pretty sure it is a distinct help if you can guess the peculiarities of your partners and opponents with accuracy. There is the diffident player who consistently undercalls, the aggressive player who as consistently overcalls; there is the cautious player who follows the rule when it is obvious that the rule doesn't apply; there is the sly player who thinks you are such a fool he can fox you every time. All these you can size up pretty quickly and deal with according to their idiosyncrasies. But there is one player whom I have never learned how to cope with and that is the player who never stops to consider that you also hold thirteen cards; he will ignore your bids, he will pay no attention to your warnings, come hell or high water he will take command of the hand, and when he has been doubled and gone down several tricks, he'll ascribe it to nothing but bad luck. You are fortunate if he doesn't smile blandly and say, 'Well, I think it was worth it, partner.' I am still looking for the book that will show me how to deal with him. Shooting is too quick and too painless, and besides, there might not be another fourth available.

As I look now at what I have written, it seems to me that the essentials for playing a good game of bridge are to be truthful, clearheaded, and considerate, prudent but not averse to taking a risk, and not to cry over spilt milk. And incidentally those are perhaps also the essentials for playing the more important game of life.

LOOKING BACK
ON
EIGHTY YEARS

An eightieth birthday is, of course, nothing at all remarkable. People live very much longer today than they lived in the past and one constantly hears of persons who are in their nineties and still in possession of all their faculties. The only excuse I can make for talking to you today is that one is eighty only once in one's lifetime.

In my long life I have seen many changes in our habits and customs and our general outlook and it has occurred to me that you might be interested if I told you of some of them. Memories are short, and even those who were in their prime half a century ago can recall only with an effort how different the world was then. The young, of course, never knew it and they accept present conditions as though they had existed from time immemorial.

The world I entered when at the age of eighteen I became a medical student was a world that knew nothing of 'planes, motor-cars, movies, radio, or telephones. When I was still at school a lecturer came to Canterbury to show us boys a new and very inadequate machine which haltingly reproduced the human voice. It was the first gramophone. The world I entered was a world that inadequately warmed itself with coal fires, lit itself by gas and paraffin lamps, and looked upon a bathroom as a luxury out of the reach of all but the very wealthy. The well-to-do – carriage folk they were known as – drove in broughams and landaus, lesser folk in hansoms and four-wheelers, popularly known as growlers, and lesser folk still in buses drawn by stout horses. German bands and organ grinders wandered about the streets of London and had to be bribed to move on. On Sundays the muffin man made his rounds ringing his melancholy bell and people came out of their doors to buy muffins and crumpets for afternoon tea.

It was a very cheap world. When I entered St. Thomas's Hospital I took a couple of furnished rooms in Vincent Square for which I paid 18s. a week. My landlady provided me with a solid breakfast before I went to the hospital and

Home Service broadcast, *Listener*, 28 January 1954.

high tea when I came back at half-past six, and the two meals cost me about 12s. a week. For 4d. I lunched at St. Thomas's on a scone and butter and a glass of milk. I was able to live very comfortably, pay my fees, buy my necessary instruments, clothe myself, and have a good deal of fun on £14 a month. And of course I could always on a pinch pawn my microscope for £3.

I had enough money over to go to the theatre at least once a week. The pit, to which I went, was not the orderly thing it is now. There were no queues. The crowd collected in a serried mass at the doors, and when they were opened there was a fierce struggle, with a lot of pushing and elbowing and shouting, to get a good place. But that was part of the fun. I saw Henry Irving and Ellen Terry. I saw Mrs Patrick Campbell in *The Second Mrs Tanqueray* and George Alexander in *The Importance of Being Earnest*. But my greatest pleasure was to go to the Tivoli of a Saturday afternoon. The music hall, now alas, obsolete, was at the height of its glory. Dear Marie Lloyd, Bessie Bellwood, Vesta Tilley, Albert Chevalier, Dan Leno were at the top of their form. Each of them, alone on the stage, was able to hold an audience entranced for twenty minutes at a time. They were indeed marvellously gifted. The only comedian I have seen in recent years who could be compared with them was the greatly lamented Sid Field.

Travelling was cheap, too, in those days. When I was twenty I went to Italy by myself for the six weeks of the Easter vacation. I went to Pisa and spent a wonderful month in Florence, where I got a nice room and my board in the house of a widow lady (of mature age) for 3s. a day; then I went to Venice and Milan and so back to London. The trip, including railway fares, had cost me £20 and given me several hundred pounds' worth of pleasure.

I spent five years at St. Thomas's Hospital. I was an unsatisfactory medical student, for my heart was not in it. I wanted, I had always wanted, to be a writer, and in the evenings, after my high tea, I wrote and read. Presently I wrote a novel, called *Liza of Lambeth*, sent it to a publisher, and it was accepted. It appeared during my last year at the hospital and had something of a success. It was of course an accident, but naturally I did not know that. I felt I could afford to chuck medicine and make writing my profession; so, three days after passing the final examinations which gave me my medical qualifications, I set out for Spain to learn Spanish and write another book. Looking back now, after all these years, and knowing as I do the terrible difficulties of making a living by writing, the small chance there is of being successful, I realise that I was taking a fearful risk. It never even occurred to me. I abandoned the medical profession with relief, but I do not regret the five years I spent at the hospital – far from it. They taught me pretty well all I know about human nature, for in a hospital you see it in the raw. People in pain, people in fear of death, do not try to hide anything from their doctor, and if they do he can generally guess what they are hiding.

I began this talk not intending that it should have an autobiographical element, but I do not seem to have been able to avoid it. The next ten years were very hard. I did not follow up my first success with another. I wrote several novels, only one of which had any merit, and I wrote a number of plays which managers more or less promptly returned to me. During those ten years I earned an average of £100 a year. Then I had a bit of luck. The lessee and manager of the Court Theatre, Sloane Square, put on a play that failed; the next play he had arranged to put on was not ready and he was at his wits' end. He read a play of mine, called *Lady Frederick*, and though he did not much like it, thought it might just run for the six weeks till the play he had in mind to follow it with could be produced. It ran for fifteen months. Within a short while I had four plays running in London at the same time. Nothing of the kind had ever happened before, and the papers made a great to-do about it. If I may say it without immodesty, I was the talk of the town. One of the students at St. Thomas's Hospital asked the eminent surgeon with whom I had worked as a 'dresser' whether he remembered me. 'Yes, I remember him quite well,' he said. 'Very sad. Very sad. One of our failures, I'm afraid.'

From his standpoint, I suppose it was. A good many other people looked upon my success as unmerited and for all I know they were right. Anyhow it raised me from poverty to affluence and brought me many new friends. To go to the theatre I no longer scrambled with the crowd to fight my way into the pit. I went in the stalls.

Now I come back to my original intention which was to tell you about the changes that have come about in the last fifty years or so. As a popular dramatist, much in the public eye, people asked me to dinners and some of the dinners were very grand indeed. The men wore tails and white ties; the ladies rich gowns with long trains. Of course they wore their hair long, piled up on their heads, and much of it was false. As the guests assembled in the drawing-room the men were told which lady they were to take down to dinner and when this was announced you offered her your arm. The host went first with the dowager of highest rank and the rest followed down the stairs in a solemn procession which ended with the hostess, her hand on the arm of a duke or an ambassador. The amount of food provided at a party of this kind was prodigious and I do not expect you to believe what I am going to tell you. It is true, nevertheless. There was a choice of thick soup and clear soup to start with, then fish; after that came a white *entrée* and a brown *entrée*, then a roast. After that a sorbet was handed round. This was a water ice and its object was to give you your second wind; then came such game as was in season, followed by a choice of sweets, a savoury and fruit. Sherry was served with the soup, and a variety of wines, including champagne, accompanied the courses that followed.

We who are used to the modest dinner of our own day cannot but marvel at the amount people habitually then ate. And eat it they did. Of course they suffered for it. They grew monstrously fat. At the end of the season they went to German watering places to put their livers in order and get their weight down. I knew one man who went to Carlsbad every year with two sets of clothes, one set that he travelled out with and the other set that he put on, having lost a good twenty pounds, at the end of his cure.

After you had been to dinner somewhere it was polite to pay a call on your hostess within a week. If she was not at home, which you fervently prayed she would not be, you left two cards, one for her, one for her husband; but if she was, you, in a frock coat and pepper-and-salt trousers, patent leather button boots with grey cloth uppers, holding your top hat in your hand, were shown upstairs to the drawing-room. You made such conversation as you could for ten minutes, and then, picking up your hat, which you had laid on the floor beside you, took your leave. When the front door was closed behind you, you heaved a great sigh of relief.

All through the season balls were given and if you were on the proper list you might receive two or three invitations for the same night. They were not at all the casual affairs which I am told balls now are. The men wore tails and a white waistcoat, a high collar and white gloves. The girls had a card on which you wrote your name for whatever dances you could get. They were accompanied by chaperones, mothers or aunts, who sat about chatting with one another till four or five in the morning, but with a watchful eye on their charges to see that they did not compromise themselves by dancing too often with the same young man. There were no such dances as are danced now. We danced the polka and the lancers; we waltzed demurely round the room, and it was considered the height of bad form to reverse.

Then there were the week-end parties. By the time of which I am now speaking I had bought myself a little house in Mayfair, still purely a residential district, and had acquired a cook, a housemaid, and a butler. In many grand houses twenty people, or more, would be asked for a week-end, and since the household staff could not cope with so many, one's hostess would write and ask one to bring a valet and the women were asked to bring a maid. I had no valet, so I took my butler. Now in those days the guests' servants were placed for their meals in the servants' hall according to the precedence of their masters and mistresses. I as an author had no precedence, and one day after we had been going to these parties for some months my butler came to me and said: 'Look here, sir, I'm just about fed up with always being put right at the bottom of the table at all these houses we go to. Couldn't you be made an M.P. or something?' I regretfully told him I could not and he must put up with the humiliation as best he could. Of course at these parties everyone dressed for dinner, as elaborately as at a London dinner party, but when the women retired for the night, the men repaired to their rooms to change their tails for dinner jackets, then recently introduced, and then went to the smoking-room to talk, drink, and above all smoke, which they had not been allowed to do in the drawing-room.

Life was very pleasant in those days – for some. The poor lived in squalid, verminous slums, worked long hours for a pittance, and in their old age had little to look forward to but the workhouse. The fear of unemployment was always on their minds.

The first world war, as far as I remember, made little difference in people's lives. During the 'twenties the rich seemed no less rich; the poor no better off. It was the second world war, with its ruinous cost and the heavy taxation it entailed, which has brought about the momentous changes that affect us all. The rich are rich no longer. The great houses in which they lavishly entertained are turned into schools and institutions, or are left to go to rack and ruin, and their owners are content to live in the porter's lodge or in a London flat. The great houses in Mayfair are now offices, and that once select district is a fashionable shopping centre.

It is to the great credit of those who have lost so much that in general they accept the change in their circumstances not only with fortitude but with good will. The poor, no longer so very poor, are better housed and better clothed, they have radios, gramophones, and television sets. They have at last obtained the chance to live decent lives and can look forward to their future without misgiving. We should all be heartily thankful for that. It is true that as a nation we are sadly impoverished, but in compensation as individuals we are freer. We have rid ourselves of many stupid prejudices. Relations between the sexes are more unconstrained. We are less formal in our dress and far more comfortable. We are less class-conscious. We are less prudish. We are less arrogant. In fact, I think we are nicer people than we were when I was young, and for all the hardships we have had to undergo, the scarcities, the restrictions, the regimentations, I think we, the great mass of the people, are better off than ever before. The outstanding characteristic of the English people is good humour, and that, however adverse circumstances are, we seem able to maintain. It is a great strength.

ON
HIS NINETIETH BIRTHDAY

My memory leaves much to be desired these days and I find that, as I walk the meagre tightrope which separates me from death, such memories as I have of my 90 years are so dim as to fill me with regret for the past.

Perhaps the most vivid memory left to me is the one which has tortured me for more than 80 years – that of the death of my mother. I was eight when she died and even today the pain of her passing is as keen as when it happened in our home in Paris.

Other memories there are but most are so dim that I find it easier to forget than to remember. Neither do I think of the future, for at 90 there is only emptiness before me.

I walk with death, hand in hand, and death's hand is warmer than my own. Each night as I bid goodnight to Alan Searle, who has been on a 40-year journey through life with me, I beg him to pray that I shall sleep on. I don't wish to live longer.

I have had such a full life – but I face what will come calmly. I still do not fear death; in fact, I look forward to death with no apprehension for I do not believe in a hereafter and so, if I have sinned in men's eyes and have not been punished, I have no fear of punitive treatment when I cease to remain on this planet.

I do not know whether God exists or not. None of the arguments that has been adduced to prove His existence carries conviction, and belief must rest, as Epicurus put it long ago, on immediate apprehension. That immediate apprehension I have never had.

Death is inevitable and it does not much matter how one meets it. I do not think one can be blamed if one hopes that one will not be aware of its imminence and be fortunate enough to undergo it without pain.

Not long ago I had a very serious illness – in fact, I have many bad days now – and one morning I was so weak that I felt I had only to grow a little weaker to die. I said to myself that, if dying was as easy as that, I was all for it. It irked me a trifle that I should not be able to finish a book I was then engaged in

Sunday Express, 26 January 1964, Maugham talking to Ewan MacNaughton.

writing, but then I thought it did not matter because in any case it would have been forgotten in a year or two.

I have always lived so much in the future that now, though the future is so short, I cannot get out of the habit, and my mind looks forward with a certain complacency to the completion within an indefinite time of the pattern that I have tried to make.

There are moments when I have so palpitating an eagerness for death that I could fly to it as to the arms of a lover. It gives me the same passionate thrill as years ago was given me by life. I am drunk with the thought of it. It seems to me to offer me the final and absolute freedom. I shall be sorry to part from my friends. I cannot be indifferent to the welfare of some whom I have guided and protected, but it is well that after depending on me so long they should enjoy their liberty whithersoever it leads them.

One of the infirmities of old age – and I am now very, very old – is the preoccupation with it, just as, in the past, I was so preoccupied with life.

I still walk every afternoon in my garden with Alan, my dachshund George, and the two oldest Pekingese in Europe, Ching, 15, and Li, 14.

The dogs and I make a very old picture these days. We walk very slowly now as we seek out the gardener working on something we may never see completed.

I have done too much in my four score and ten years, too much for any man and now I am sick of this way of life. The weariness and sadness of old age make it intolerable. I have been a hedonist always and now there are so few pleasures left to me. There isn't the pleasure even of work to fill my days. I can still eat a good meal and I enjoy my drink still. Every morning I have a stiff whisky at 11. But deafness is overtaking me and my stammer is still persistent. My eyesight is no longer what it was and this, above all, perhaps, upsets me most. For it makes reading very hard. I am re-reading *Moby Dick* with difficulty. The other day I found a copy of *Madame Bovary* on a shelf and I took it down to read it again because it has been a favourite of mine for so many years.

I have, of course, given my library away – there are others now who have more need of it than I. That action didn't please my late brother, the last time he was here.

Some books I kept, as I thought to end my days reading as the pleasure took me. It is most irritating that my eyesight should fail and cause me considerable trouble to read at all.

I have been asked on occasion whether I should be willing to live my life over again. On the whole it has been a pretty good one, perhaps better than that of most people, but I can see no point in repeating it. It would be as idle as to read a detective story that you have read before. But supposing there were such a thing as reincarnation, belief in which is held by three-quarters of the human race, and one could choose whether or no to enter upon a new life on earth, I have in the past sometimes thought I would be willing to try the experiment on the chance that I might enjoy experiences which circumstances and my own idiosyncrasies, spiritual and corporal, have prevented me from enjoying and learn the many things that I have not had the time or the opportunity to learn.

But now I should refuse. I have had enough. There are indeed days when

I feel that I have done everything too often, known too many people, read too many books, seen too many pictures, statues, churches and fine houses, and listened to too much music. I neither believe in immortality nor desire it. I should like to die quietly and painlessly, and I am content to be assured that with my last breath my soul, with its aspirations and its weaknesses, will dissolve into nothingness.

A decade ago I looked forward in retirement to some years of travel. I have had these years. I have visited parts to which I went 30 and 50 years ago. And, of course, I revisited Heidelberg where, in my youth, I studied.

It was during that early visit that I met an Englishman with whom I struck up a friendship from which I was to learn much about literature. It was also to put me on the path that took me to so many parts of the world in search of Life, from which I drew so much to become a teller of tales. What pleased me most recently was to be made an Honorary Senator of the University of Heidelberg. It suited the vanity of an old man.

Journeys tire me now but I shall not stop my travelling. I will go to Marrakesh, a town in a part of the world to which my father was much attracted. It was from there that he saw the Moorish sign to ward off evil which adorns the gate to my drive and is on all the covers of my books.

There are times when I look round this old house – it is an anachronism in these modern times and very expensive to run – which I bought nearly 40 years ago and think the time has come to shut it up and wander. I have wandered all my life and it would be no bad thing to die while making a sentimental journey to the one place on earth where, for me, there is beauty still and a contentment that I have found nowhere else.

I refer to Angkor Wat, in Cambodia. I have one desire left, which is to return to that lost village in the jungle in the Far East. When last I visited it, a year or so ago, I intended to stay but a day or two. Instead, I lingered there three weeks.

To make the journey there now would probably kill me, but I would have no regrets in dying in such beauty.

This house now belongs to the past – as I do. I have no feelings for it or the other material signs of wealth. I do not think I have such an attachment to my various possessions as to regret their loss for long. My books have now sold over 80,000,000 copies, but the money I have received from them has been like a sixth sense without which I could not have enjoyed the other five. I am glad that I will not be poor when I die. For to be old and poor is bad; to be dependent on charity for a roof over one's head and for bread to eat is not to be borne.

I spent many years buying pictures that I liked. I bought Impressionists and Moderns, and now that I have them no more I do not miss them. Some say my house is naked without my pictures. If it is I don't notice the fact. I have even rid myself of the glass door panel which Gauguin painted in Tahiti and which I bought while on a visit there. It is now privately owned in America.

All I have left of my pictures are theatrical ones. They do not belong to me now, for some time ago I gave them to the Victoria and Albert Museum which kindly lent them back until my death.

I have not [cared] and still do not care if people agree with me. Of course

265

I think I am right, otherwise I should not think as I do, and they are wrong, but it does not offend me that they should be wrong.

To myself I have always been the most important person in the world . . . but from the standpoint of common sense, I am of no consequence whatever. It would have made small difference to the universe if I had never existed.

Somewhat early, but at what age I cannot remember, I made up my mind that, having but one life, I should like to get the most I could out of it. I wanted to make a pattern of my life, in which writing would be an essential element, but which would include all the other activities proper to man, and which death would in the end round off in complete fulfilment.

That complete fulfilment has been reached in my case. Having held a certain place in the world for a long time I am content that others should soon occupy it. After all, the point of a pattern is that it should be completed. When nothing can be added without spoiling the design the artist leaves it.

It was suggested to me recently that I should make the journey to Switzerland to visit Dr Niehans to whose clinic I have been before. But I see no point in prolonging my life at my age as there is no longer the will to live.

I have no wish to write further. My head is empty now of thoughts, plots, and the makings of a story. I have long since written the words that were inside me and put aside my pen.

And so, when my obituary notice at last appears in *The Times* and they say: 'What! I thought he died years ago', my ghost will gently chuckle.

APPENDICES

APPENDIX I

Great Modern Reading
W. Somerset Maugham's Introduction
to
Modern English and American Literature
(1943)
(*see page 87*)

CONTENTS

Eudora Welty	PETRIFIED MAN
Andy Logan	THE VISIT
William Saroyan	THE DARING YOUNG MAN ON THE FLYING TRAPEZE
Anonymous	AN AIRMAN'S LETTER TO HIS MOTHER
	THREE WAR LETTERS FROM BRITAIN
Muriel Rukeyser	BOY WITH HIS HAIR CUT SHORT
Stephen Spender	THE EXPRESS
Stephen Spender	IN RAILWAY HALLS
Stephen Spender	WHAT I EXPECTED
Louis MacNeice	BIRMINGHAM
Cecil Day Lewis	TEMPT ME NO MORE
W.H. Auden	LOOK, STRANGER, AT THIS ISLAND NOW
W.H. Auden	A SHILLING LIFE WILL GIVE YOU ALL THE FACTS
W.H. Auden	AS I WALKED OUT ONE EVENING
James Agee	NO DOUBT LEFT. ENOUGH DECEIVING
John Steinbeck	THE GIFT
T.O. Beachcroft	THE ERNE FROM THE COAST
Elizabeth Bowen	MARIA
Erskine Caldwell	THE PEOPLE *vs.* ABE LATHAN, COLORED
Katharine Brush	NIGHT CLUB
H.E. Bates	THE LILY
John Collier	MARY
H.A. Manhood	BROTHERHOOD
Alva Johnston	LET FREEDOM RING
John Dos Passos	ART AND ISADORA

Frances Cornford	TO A FAT LADY SEEN FROM THE TRAIN
Dorothy Parker	UNFORTUNATE COINCIDENCE
Dorothy Parker	GODSPEED
Dorothy Parker	SOCIAL NOTE
Dorothy Parker	INDIAN SUMMER
Dorothy Parker	FAUTE DE MIEUX
Dorothy Parker	HEALED
Ogden Nash	KINDLY UNHITCH THAT STAR, BUDDY
E.E. Cummings	IF YOU CAN'T EAT YOU GOT TO
E.E. Cummings	THE NOSTER WAS A SHIP OF SWANK
Marianne Moore	THE FISH
John Betjeman	IN WESTMINSTER ABBEY
Hilaire Belloc	ON HIS BOOKS
Hilaire Belloc	ON NORMAN, A GUEST
Hilaire Belloc	ON LADY POLTAGRUE
Hilaire Belloc	EPITAPH ON THE POLITICIAN
Hilaire Belloc	ANOTHER ON THE SAME
Hilaire Belloc	FATIGUE
Hilaire Belloc	ON A DEAD HOSTESS
Roy Campbell	ON SOME SOUTH AFRICAN NOVELISTS
F. Scott Fitzgerald	BABYLON REVISITED
Ernest Hemingway	THE SHORT HAPPY LIFE OF FRANCIS MACOMBER
William Faulkner	A ROSE FOR EMILY
William March	BILL'S EYES
Osbert Sitwell	DEFEAT
Michael Arlen	LEGEND OF THE CROOKED CORONET
D.H. Lawrence	LETTER TO T.D.D.
D.H. Lawrence	LETTER TO LADY OTTOLINE MORRELL
Walter Hines Page	LETTER TO HERBERT S. HOUSTON
Oliver Wendell Holmes	LETTERS TO MR. WU
John Jay Chapman	LETTER TO MRS. WINTHROP CHANLER
John Jay Chapman	LETTER TO WILLIAM JAMES
John Jay Chapman	LETTER TO HIS WIFE
John Jay Chapman	LETTER TO MRS. WINTHROP CHANLER
John Jay Chapman	LETTER TO S.S. DRURY
Lawrence Binyon	FOR THE FALLEN
Siegfried Sassoon	EVERYONE SANG
Wilfred Owen	FROM MY DIARY
Wilfred Owen	GREATER LOVE
Wilfrid Gibson	BREAKFAST
Rupert Brooke	THE SOLDIER
Alan Seeger	I HAVE A RENDEZVOUS WITH DEATH
Charles Hamilton Sorley	THE SONG OF THE UNGIRT RUNNERS
A.E. Housman	EPITAPH ON AN ARMY OF MERCENARIES
Anthony Berkeley	THE AVENGING CHANCE
Carter Dickson	THE CRIME IN NOBODY'S ROOM
Dashiell Hammett	A MAN CALLED SPADE

T.S. Eliot	ASH-WEDNESDAY
T.S. Eliot	THE HOLLOW MEN
T.S. Eliot	MR. ELIOT'S SUNDAY MORNING SERVICE
Aldous Huxley	COMFORT
Virginia Woolf	MARY WOLLSTONECRAFT
E.M. Forster	WHAT I BELIEVE
Gertrude Stein	HOW WRITING IS WRITTEN
Stephen Vincent Benét	THE DEVIL AND DANIEL WEBSTER
Katherine Anne Porter	FLOWERING JUDAS
James Thurber	THE GREATEST MAN IN THE WORLD
Konrad Bercovici	'THERE'S MONEY IN POETRY'
Gertrude Atherton	THE FOGHORN
Carl Sandburg	CHICAGO
William Henry Davies	LEISURE
Edna St. Vincent Millay	WHAT LIPS MY LIPS HAVE KISSED
Lawrence Binyon	O WORLD, BE NOBLER
John Crowe Ransom	BLUE GIRLS
Wallace Stevens	SUNDAY MORNING
Robinson Jeffers	SHINE, PERISHING REPUBLIC
Robinson Jeffers	PROMISE OF PEACE
Charlotte Mew	THE CALL
Charlotte Mew	IN THE FIELDS
Lytton Strachey	DR. ARNOLD
Gamaliel Bradford	PHINEAS TAYLOR BARNUM
Rudyard Kipling	AT THE END OF THE PASSAGE
Edith Wharton	ROMAN FEVER
Sherwood Anderson	I'M A FOOL
Ring Lardner	THE GOLDEN HONEYMOON
H.H. Munro ('Saki')	THE MATCH-MAKER
Katherine Mansfield	REVELATIONS
Henry James	THE BEAST IN THE JUNGLE
Vachel Lindsay	THE GHOSTS OF THE BUFFALOES
Edgar Lee Masters	BENJAMIN PANTIER
Edgar Lee Masters	MRS. BENJAMIN PANTIER
James Weldon Johnson	SAINT PETER RELATES AN INCIDENT OF THE RESURRECTION DAY
Edward Arlington Robinson	MINIVER CHEEVY
Edward Arlington Robinson	RICHARD CORY
Robert Frost	ONCE BY THE PACIFIC
Robert Frost	THE PASTURE
Robert Frost	THE ROAD NOT TAKEN
Elinor Wylie	PURITAN SONNET
Max Beerbohm	SEEING PEOPLE OFF
Logan Pearsall Smith	AFTERTHOUGHTS
George Santayana	CLASSIC LIBERTY
Winston Churchill	DUNKIRK

Walter de la Mare	THE LISTENERS
Walter de la Mare	AN EPITAPH
Rudyard Kipling	MANDALAY
A.E. Housman	A SHROPSHIRE LAD, XXII
A.E. Housman	LAST POEMS, XI
A.E. Housman	LAST POEMS, XXVI
A.E. Housman	MORE POEMS, XII
A.E. Housman	MORE POEMS, XXXVI
Thomas Hardy	IN TIME OF 'THE BREAKING OF NATIONS'
Thomas Hardy	THE DARKLING THRUSH
Thomas Hardy	IN TENEBRIS
Robert Bridges	NIGHTINGALES
William Butler Yeats	WHEN YOU ARE OLD
William Butler Yeats	THE WILD SWANS AT COOLE
William Butler Yeats	SAILING TO BYZANTIUM
Francis Thompson	'IN NO STRANGE LAND'

APPENDIX II

Reading List
Accompanying
'Reading and Writing and You'
(1943)
(*see page 202*)

Here are a few books that have nothing to do with the war and no connection with today. They are definitely and unashamedly escape literature.

NON-FICTION

1. DIARY OF FANNY BURNEY
2. Boswell's TOUR IN THE HEBRIDES
3. MEMOIRS OF THE COURT OF GEORGE II by John Hervey
4. MEMOIRS OF GREVILLE
5. THE AUTOBIOGRAPHY OF BENJAMIN FRANKLIN
6. DIARY OF THE FRENCH REVOLUTION by Gouverneur Morris

FICTION

1. BARCHESTER TOWERS by Anthony Trollope
2. THE HEIR OF REDCLYFFE by Charlotte M. Yonge
3. OLD CREOLE DAYS by C.W. Cable
4. A BELEAGURED CITY by Mrs Oliphant
5. THE BOSTONIANS by Henry James
6. THE WOMAN IN WHITE by Wilkie Collins
7. THE RISE OF SILAS LAPHORN by W.D. Howells
8. THE HOUSE OF MIRTH by Edith Wharton

APPENDIX III

List of Contents

in

Chronological Order of Publication